Seeking Common Ground

Recent Titles in
Contributions in Women's Studies

SEEKING COMMON GROUND

Multidisciplinary Studies of Immigrant Women in the United States

Edited by
DONNA GABACCIA

Westport, Connecticut
London

Library of Congress Cataloging-in-Publication Data

Seeking common ground : multidisciplinary studies of immigrant
  women in the United States / edited by Donna Gabaccia.
      p. cm.
  Includes bibliographical references and index.
  ISBN 0–275–94387–9 (pbk. : alk. paper)
    1. Women immigrants—United States. 2. United States—Emigration
and immigration. I. Gabaccia, Donna R.
  HQ1421.S45 1992
  305.42—dc20   92–14378

British Library Cataloging in Publication Data is available.

A hardcover edition of *Seeking Common Ground* is available from the Greenwood Press
imprint of Greenwood Publishing Group, Inc. (Contributions in Women's Studies; 129;
ISBN 0–313–27483–5).

Library of Congress Catalog Card Number: 92–14378
ISBN: 0–275–94387–9

First published in 1992

Praeger Publishers, 88 Post Road West, Westport, CT 06881
An imprint of Greenwood Publishing Group, Inc.

Printed in the United States of America

The paper used in this book complies with the
Permanent Paper Standard issued by the National
Information Standards Organization (Z39.48–1984).

10 9 8 7 6 5 4 3 2 1

Copyright Acknowledgment

The author and publisher gratefully wish to acknowledge permission to
reprint the following:

Interview with Lucy Acosta, conducted by Mario Garcia, October 28, 1982,
courtesy of the Institute of Oral History at the University of Texas at El Paso.

Every reasonable effort has been made to trace the owners of copyright
materials in this book, but in some instances this has proven impossible. The
author and publisher will be glad to receive information leading to more
complete acknowledgments in subsequent printings of the book and in the
meantime extend their apologies for any omissions.

Contents

Figures and Tables

FIGURES

TABLES

Acknowledgments

This volume of essays on immigrant women originated in a number of interdisciplinary sessions organized for the meetings of the Social Science History Association, the American Historical Association, the American Studies Association, the Organization of American Historians, and the Berkshire Conference on Women's History in 1989 and 1990 and for the Labor Migration Project's final conference, "Women in the Migration Process," in Bremen, West Germany, in 1990. My conversations with colleagues at these meetings both inspired me to begin this project and allowed me to bring it to completion. Some of the participants in these sessions have made contributions to *Seeking Common Ground*; others provided useful advice, sound criticism, or merely their own thoughts about central topics at various points in the complex process of organizing a multi-author volume. I especially thank Caroline Brettell, Kathleen Conzen, Hasia Diner, Nancy Foner, Marilyn Halter, Christiane Harzig, Deirdre Mageean, Ewa Morawska, Silvia Pedraza, Yolanda Prieto, Vicki Ruiz, Maxine Seller, Rita Simon, Sydney Weinberg, and Suzanne Sinke for helping to convince me that conference sessions can be as intellectually challenging and personally satisfying as they are professionally necessary.

Mercy College and its Faculty Development Committee helped nurture this project by twice reducing my teaching responsibilities—once during the planning of the volume and once closer to its completion. I much appreciated this relief.

Finally, I offer my thanks to Thomas and Tamino Kozak. As always, too, they know why.

Introduction

Donna Gabaccia

The title for this book on immigrant women points toward both an interpretation of immigrant life and an agenda for scholarly study. Although immigrant men and women often view their lives in America through the lens of ethnic particularism—recalling, for example, neighborhoods and even entire lives peopled only by those of their own background—we know that the common ground of American life inevitably brought immigrants of many cultures into contact with each other and with the native-born. In workplaces, schools, neighborhoods, marketplaces, public institutions, and even homes and families, women of many backgrounds shared common experiences. Thus, while most of the chapters in this volume focus on the women of one particular background, the goal of the anthology is to raise questions for comparison and synthesis. Studies of German women immigrants in the 1870s may shed light on or raise questions about the lives of Cuban women in the 1980s.

Parallel to ethnic particularism in the study of immigration is the disciplinary particularism of the scholars studying women. It is surprising—and too little known, even among scholars—how many disciplines have developed specialized literatures on female immigrants.[1] To a certain degree, cross-disciplinary communication on immigrant women is limited precisely because so many disciplines are interested in the topic.[2] In scholarly terms, then, the topic of immigrant women itself could be a common ground on which scholars from many fields meet. A second goal of this volume is to encourage that interdisciplinary communication.

Obviously, both immigrants and scholars have had good reasons for ignoring the common ground they share with others. That they do so also reveals much that is significant about the subjective experience of being an immigrant or, alternatively, a professional historian or sociologist. I do not intend to question the importance or the validity of either type of subjectivity. Still, the overall purpose of this anthology is to encourage readers to consider alternatives to ethnic and disciplinary particularism. Its purpose is to highlight and to encourage thought about common ground in the study of immigrant women—and in both the senses introduced above. In doing so, *Seeking Common Ground* aims to suggest alternative modes of interpretation and research that can enrich our understanding of each.

Toward this end, *Seeking Common Ground* includes two very different types of chapters. Part I opens with the viewpoints of a historian (Sydney Stahl Weinberg), a sociologist (Rita J. Simon), and two anthropologists (Caroline B. Brettell and Patricia A. deBerjeois). Their essays summarize how research on immigrant women has developed in their three home disciplines—disciplines which in recent years have generated the largest literatures on the topic.

Read together, these chapters suggest why historians, sociologists, and anthropologists have not always perceived themselves as participants in a common interdisciplinary project focused on understanding the lives of the foreign and female. Each chapter provides an excellent introduction to and an example of the distinctive language, categories, methods, and approaches of its author's discipline. Read together, however, the three chapters also identify important points of intersection and communication. Concepts like generation, double or triple oppression, assimilation/acculturation, and gender are widely used in all three fields. The chapters of Part I thus provide both a critique of past practice and the foundations for a common undertaking.

Parts II and III of *Seeking Common Ground* build on these introductory discussions with a series of empirical and interpretive chapters on immigrant women of many backgrounds, past and present, through the long sweep of the history of the United States as a nation of immigrants. In selecting these contributions (which are published here for the first time), my goal was to achieve methodological, ethnic, and regional balance. Chapters in these sections examine the lives of immigrant women in the East, Midwest, Southwest and far West.[3] There are essays on the women of the so-called old and new migrations of the nineteenth century (from northwestern Europe and from Asia, Mexico, and southeastern Europe, respectively) and also on today's migrations from Asia, the Caribbean, and Latin America.

The chapters in Parts II and III both exemplify the methodologies discussed in Part I and point to new approaches. In both sections, the reader will see historians, sociologists, demographers; scholars from the interdisciplinary fields of women's studies, American studies, and ethnic studies; and scholars from praxis-oriented fields like social work exploring the lives of immigrant women through the distinctive lenses of their own disciplinary and professional concerns.

In addition, these chapters offer readers the opportunity to observe common themes in the study of immigrant women. Some of these themes—women in the migration process and the formation of ethnic communities, the relationship between wage-earning work and domesticity, uniquely female aspects of adjustment to urban and industrial life in the United States, the existence of autonomous female culture or consciousness, the gendered dimensions of ethnogenesis—reach across both disciplinary boundaries and the histories and experiences of women of a surprisingly diverse range of backgrounds.

The chapters in Parts II and III do not, of course, exhaust the methodological possibilities for the study of immigrant women. There is, for example, no chapter by a literary scholar. (Fortunately, Betty Bergland's discussion of immigrant women's autobiographies introduces sources and issues related to postmodernist research in literature.) Similarly, the particular immigrant groups and themes represented in this volume are by no means exhaustive or completely representative—nor were they meant to be.

Seeking Common Ground demonstrates the diversity of those who are foreign and female and the unique methodological insights of each discipline, while simultaneously urging readers to consider comparative and interdisciplinary approaches. Although no single chapter in *Seeking Common Ground* promises a synthesis of immigrant women's experience in the United States, and only two (Katharine M. Donato's analysis of sex ratios in a variety of immigrant streams and Alice Chai's look at Japanese, Korean, and Okinawan women in Hawai'i) fully illustrate the rewards of comparison, all identify themes that should make the next decade of research on immigrant women one of interdisciplinary explorations, synthesis, and comparison. The result should be a richer understanding of both ethnic life in the United States and American women's diversity.

INTEGRATION AND GHETTOES IN THE STUDY OF IMMIGRANT WOMEN

To understand why scholars so rarely found common ground in the study of immigrant women, it is helpful to understand how the interests of immigration/ethnic studies and women's studies scholars have diverged over the past two decades. Each of these fields could logically claim immigrant women as a central focus, yet neither ultimately did so. Instead, as a group of Afro-American women early pointed out, in most research, "All the blacks are men; all the women are white."[4] Those who belonged in both categories disappeared from view, as they "fell between the cracks" separating distinct new scholarly discourses.

Despite their shared origins in the political struggles of the 1960s, ethnic and women's studies' diverging concerns are quite striking. In the wake of the U.S. ethnic revival of the 1960s and 1970s and the rise of immigration levels after 1965, the study of ethnicity in the United States has generally focused on the rich and unique characteristics and histories of particular immigrant and ethnic groups. Older views of inevitable assimilation and the diminishing influence of ethnicity were discarded and replaced with a new respect for the persistence of cultural diversity and a pluralistic understanding of American society. Family economies, family ties, and ethnic communities were often seen as the source of ethnic persistence and solidarity, which in turn were viewed as healthy oppositional strategies for coping with discrimination and marginality. Needless to say, scholars in ethnic and immigration studies assumed that men and women shared these ethnic cultures, were shaped positively by them, and benefited from their oppositional character.[5] In history, male and female differences were often ignored (although, as Sydney Weinberg argues in her essay on immigration history, only men's lives were actually studied). Or—as was initially true in sociology and anthropology, according to Brettell and deBerjeois—the separate study of women migrants was dismissed as reductionist.

During these same years, scholars in women's studies traced the implications of sisterhood through scholarly studies that focused on the unique dimensions of female experience. Much work focused on the origins and implications of a distinctive female consciousness, culture, or value system. If ethnic studies ignored male and female differences, women's studies initially slighted differences among women. In sharp contrast to ethnic studies, too, women's studies scholars increasingly defined the family as the locus of female oppression, not the starting place for cross-gender solidarity.[6] Overall, ethnicity was not an important variable in women's studies; to the extent that feminist scholars recognized differences among women, they focused on class (with immigrant women usually described as working class) and race (defined in characteristically U.S. fashion by skin color).[7] More recently, women's studies has become concerned with the multicultural diversity of women's experiences; culture, however, is still usually conflated with "racial ethnic" or "minority" culture; foreign birth or nationality, language, and religion are less frequently considered, and immigrant women in multicultural studies are labelled culturally as either Euro-Americans, Hispanics, or Asian-Americans.[8]

Outside the interdisciplinary fields of ethnic studies and women's studies, the fragmenting impact of diverging methods and assumptions could be equally pronounced. The introductory chapters in this volume demonstrate that those who study immigrant women had two alternatives but that choices were made differently in history, sociology, and anthropology. Immigrant women could be studied with the aim of integrating their experiences and stories into general gendered accounts of immigrant and ethnic life in the United States. And, in this case, research findings were normally related to the themes of immigration and ethnic studies. Alternatively, researchers could focus explicitly on immigrant women, interpreting their research findings in light of the themes of women's studies.

Historian Sydney Stahl Weinberg makes the strongest case for a gendered history that integrates the histories of men and women into a unified account of immigrant life, although she also demonstrates and explains why integration scarcely occurred in the historical studies of the 1970s and 1980s. It might be noted, too, that since 1980, many historical studies of immigrant women (including one by Weinberg) have instead followed the early example of women's studies: the numbers of volumes exploring immigrant women separately from men now exceed the volumes that successfully integrate women into general accounts.[9] This is the approach taken as well by most of the contributors to this volume; only Yolanda Prieto's study of Cuban women and work in New Jersey examines gender issues by interviewing both men and women.

Rita Simon's description of the reception of research on immigrant women in sociology suggests a very different, and less problematic, pattern.[10] Not only does Simon show that sociologists studying immigrant women now ask the same questions that are asked about men, but she strongly emphasizes the enthusiasm with which sociologists have welcomed research on immigrant women, even apparently—as in the case of the widely read volume she edited together with Brettell[11]—when women are explored separately from men.

Caroline Brettell and Patricia deBerjeois outline a third possibility, reminding us of the significant influence anthropologists exercised on developing feminist theory, mainly through Rosaldo and Lamphere's influential early anthology.[12] The division of domestic from public worlds and the hypothesis that this division was not only universal but a source of women's universal "otherness" was central to anthropological (and, according to Weinberg, eventually to historical) studies of immigrant women; it also provided one of the central early debates in women's studies, and separate critiques of the Rosaldo/Lamphere thesis developed in both anthropology and history. Lamphere's subsequent research on immigrant women, focusing on the connections between these two spheres, has helped maintain close ties between anthropologists and women's studies scholars.[13] Still, as Weinberg found, the result is that studies of immigrant women are regarded as a separate subfield as much in anthropology as they are in history. Integration has proved elusive in both history and anthropology.

TOWARD COMMON GROUND: HISTORY, SOCIOLOGY, AND ANTHROPOLOGY

As the three introductory chapters also suggest, the study of immigration by historians shared common roots with both sociology and anthropology. Still, Weinberg's, Brettell and deBerjeois's, and Simon's summaries of recent developments in their three fields suggest that historians and anthropologists will more easily find common ground in the study of immigrant women in the decade ahead, as their research agendas make cultural and interpretive turns largely (although not completely) abjured by sociologists.

Historians, anthropologists, and sociologists have turned to the study of immigrant women out of overlapping motives. Simon argues convincingly that sociologists become interested in migration during periods when mobility is either increasing or becoming a matter of intense policy debate; like the early Chicago school of sociology that developed during the mass migrations of the early twentieth century, sociological studies today are often problem oriented and policy driven—responses to the rapid increase of immigration into the United States since the 1960s. (That the same can sometimes be true in anthropology is seen in Brettell and deBerjeois's discussion of medical anthropological studies in recent years. In this volume, an essay on postpartum depression by Young I. Song represents the pragmatic concerns of much sociological and anthropological research.)

In similar fashion, anthropologists first took notice of migration when urbanization and international wage earning became part of life in the third-world societies that have traditionally been anthropologists' focus. These developments reminded anthropologists that processes associated with migration were common to first and third worlds alike, that the two worlds were often linked in migrants' lives, and that anthropologists could thus as easily study culture and cultural change in their own urban or Western backyards as in third-world locations.

Because contemporary migration is not a phenomenon limited to the United States, or even the developed world, both sociological and anthropological studies of immigrant women often exhibit concern with international and comparative developments rare in historical studies, which until recently viewed migration as a subtopic of U.S. history. Their interests are understandable when one recalls that many contemporary migrations are female dominated. The immigration historians described by Weinberg still have much to learn from the international and comparative findings of their colleagues.

Unlike sociologists and anthropologists, historians' interests in immigrant women can be traced directly either to the period of new ethnicity (when the persistence of ethnicity was rediscovered and glorified in the-

ories of cultural pluralism) or to the reemergence of the feminist movement in the United States. Ironically, perhaps, immigration historians'
concern with ethnicity and community caused them to draw intensively
on the research, approaches, and concepts of sociology's early Chicago
school, which was not particularly interested in gender differences. And,
since sociologists (according to Simon) had almost completely abandoned
the methods of their Chicago predecessors, this diminished the likelihood that sociologists and historians would find a common language for
discussing immigration studies. Perhaps this is why Weinberg, the historian—rather than Simon, the sociologist—refers to developments in
historical sociology, the sociological subfield that has remained closest to
the discipline's origins in the Chicago school.

What is shared by anthropologists and historians interested in immigrant women, and what distinguishes them from many of their sociology
colleagues, is their concern with culture, strategy, and process, with subjectivity, and with the diversity of lived experience (or with what women's
studies scholars once called women's voices). Simon's chapter reveals
very different concerns. She barely mentions culture, except to note that
it has no long-term impact on fertility. Simon emphasizes sociologists'
concerns with economic issues and the structures of immigrant opportunity in the United States. Subjectivity is not without interest to sociologists, as Simon's comments on the educational expectations of
immigrant mothers and daughters suggest, but it is interesting more as
an element in predicting future behavior or addressing societywide problems than as a separate or female world of interest in and of itself. Thus
history and anthropology share a concern for what Alice Chai, in the
introduction to her chapter on Asian picture brides, calls a holistic approach, often pursued through careful case studies of particular groups
of women in particular settings. Sociologists, by contrast, more frequently
work with samples, aggregated or nationwide data about specific dimensions of women immigrants' lives; in this anthology, Katharine M.
Donato's essay on immigrant sex ratios provides a good illustration of
this approach. Here, the concern is with describing objective structures
that shape human behavior, with theory building, and with prediction.

The chapters in Parts II and III of *Seeking Common Ground* provide
some tentative examples of the interdisciplinary possibilities suggested
in Simon's, Weinberg's, and Brettell and deBerjeois's chapters. Scholars
are no longer strictly tied to source materials, methods, concepts, or time
periods traditionally associated with their home disciplines. Sociologists
like Deirdre Mageean and anthropologists like Alice Chai tackle the
nineteenth century, while historians like Vicki Ruiz consider the recent
past. Analysis of statistical sources or literary texts or oral histories—all
well represented in this volume—are no longer the exclusive properties
of one discipline or another. Heavily influenced by anthropological

methodology and thought, sociologist Yolanda Prieto provides us, in her chapter on Cuban women, with an excellent example of how a concern with subjectivity and process in the lives of immigrant women is reaching even into the structural/economic and analytical traditions of sociology, providing a basis for truly cross-disciplinary common ground. Betty Bergland's chapter on immigrant women's autobiographies should further encourage future scholars to ponder critically the problems of exploring experience in the sources that women themselves generated; drawing on theoretical work in several disciplines, Bergland emphasizes how ideologies embedded in language shaped the very stories that women were able or likely to tell about their own lives. Her work hints at a different interdisciplinary approach for research on immigrant women within the arena of cultural studies.

WOMEN AND MIGRATION

Thematically, too, the essays in *Seeking Common Ground* should introduce the reader to important issues shared across the disciplines and across studies of immigrant women of widely diverse backgrounds. Long an important subfield within sociology, the study of migration is of growing interest to historians as well. Several chapters in this anthology shed light on old contrasting stereotypes of female migrants as either passive family-oriented followers of men or active initiators in migratory experiments. All demonstrate how difficult and ultimately unprofitable it is to separate family, material, and labor concerns in analyzing women's migrations.

Suzanne Sinke's chapter on the international marriage market and the migration of German women explores the parallels and connections of this market with the better-understood international market for male laborers in the late nineteenth and early twentieth centuries. Excepting only the Irish case, men heavily outnumbered women in most nineteenth-century migrations, and Sinke's essay explores the social meaning of this imbalance. While single women immigrants have often been viewed as labor migrants, she reminds us that many young German women saw the United States as a place to marry as well as to work. Indeed, coming to the United States with hopes of marriage could reflect female initiative; Sinke describes ways in which some women increased their marital choices and their control over their own familial destinies through migration. Young German women often quickly left work as domestic servants in order to marry, but Sinke's discussion shows how material calculations and assessments of men's and women's ability and willingness to labor within farm families influenced decision making far more than individualized notions of romantic love. Throughout, Sinke's portrayal of German women and men's concern with marriage might be compared to Hasia Diner's and Janet Nolan's descriptions of labor and marriage in the female-dominated migrations from Ireland during the same period.[14]

The Asian picture brides studied by Alice Chai also came to Hawai'i to marry, and since many of their marriages were arranged by their parents prior to departure, they appear initially to confirm stereotypes of passive female migrants—following in men's footsteps, and at their behest. But the subsequent lives of the picture brides show little evidence of passivity. Chai graphically describes the relationship between marriage, hard physical labor, and economic opportunity. She highlights Korean, Okinawan, and Japanese women's economic and social initiatives, which were as often pursued in cooperation with other women as within male-dominated families. Like Deirdre Mageean in her study of Irish nuns in this volume, Chai suggests further that religious faith and spiritual values, learned from female forebears, sustained Asian picture brides through hardships associated with male dominance, class prejudice, and racism.

Using very different sources from Sinke and Chai, Katharine Donato offers an explanation for women's numerical dominance among immigrants arriving in the United States during the past two and a half decades. (As several authors note, female majorities developed among U.S. immigrants around 1930; the United States today attracts proportionately more female migrants than do most other immigrant-receiving nations.) Donato shows how U.S. immigration law preferences (for skilled workers) and for close relatives of naturalized citizens encourage different kinds of female majorities in each case. She emphasizes the characteristics of women's lives in the homeland countries as critical influences on migrations for family formation, reunification, and wage earning. This interaction of immigration law and homeland structures could easily be pursued in studies of earlier male-dominated migrations, a topic that few historians have as yet addressed.[15]

Earlier studies have described women constructing and maintaining the social relationships between migrants and potential migrants and helping to create migration chains of cooperating world travelers.[16] Clearly, too, migration to the United States changes the kinship and community networks in which immigrants live, with profound implications for women's lives.[17] Although her chapter does not focus explicitly on the migration process, Young I. Song's study of depression reminds us of one of its possible consequences—social isolation. Without the support of mothers and elderly women relatives, many Asian women suffer disproportionately from depression following childbirth. Other studies of depression among immigrant women of many backgrounds have also pointed to the presence or absence of a female support network as a key variable.[18] Future studies of women as builders of social networks during migration should help shed light both on cases of women's social isolation and on their work as creators of ethnic communities upon settlement in the United States.

WOMEN IN IMMIGRANT FAMILIES AND COMMUNITIES

Many chapters in this volume cite the early work of Michelle Rosaldo and Louise Lamphere; obviously it has enjoyed special significance in the studies of immigrant women's lives. Although the two anthropologists posited the separation of the domestic from the public as a cross-cultural universal and a source of women's oppression, few studies of immigrant women have found either the definition of the two arenas or the boundary separating them to have been culturally unvarying or socially immutable. Few scholars would argue, for example, that the move to the United States introduced change only in the public world or that women in their domestic lives remained protected from change as a result.[19] Instead, changes in the public world, which inevitably accompany migration, are usually seen as the cause of transformation of women's domestic lives.

Probably no topic has intrigued more sociologists and historians of immigrant women's lives than the impact of wage earning on women's domestic roles and responsibilities—a fact noted by Brettell and de-Berjeois in their review chapter. In *Seeking Common Ground* the theme is explored in a chapter on Cuban women in New Jersey by Yolanda Prieto. Much of Prieto's earlier work sought to explain the high rates of wage earning among Cuban women in the United States—despite their inexperience with wage earning in Cuba and intense cultural opposition to women leaving the domestic world in order to work. In her follow-up study in this volume, Prieto notes how wage earning among Cuban women immigrants has encouraged more positive attitudes toward wage earning in the Cuban community; she also explores how wage earning encouraged new domestic patterns in the first and second generations. Cuban women now report more intrinsic enjoyment of wage earning, and both men and women accept the desirability of women working outside the home. Still, Cuban men more than women seem reluctant to abandon women's continued and special responsibility for domesticity—even though significant behavioral changes are reported in home life, too.

No chapter in this volume focuses exclusively on the domestic world of immigrant women, but most contributors assume that the domestic world of immigrants of many backgrounds remains one largely dominated by patriarchal values that work to women's disadvantage. (See my earlier comments on differences between immigration and women's studies views of family life.) Perhaps the most striking example is to be found in Young I. Song's analysis of postpartum depression. Song shows that Asian immigrant women who gave birth to daughters were most likely to suffer from depression. She traces their suffering both to a strong cultural preference for boys and to cultural validation of a woman as mother only after she gives birth to a son.

Other chapters, however, suggest alternative readings of power within immigrant families. In her study of chaperonage and Mexican-American dating and leisure habits, Vicki Ruiz introduces the concept of familial oligarchy. Immigrant parents—mothers as well as fathers—sought to maintain control over the lives of children generally, both as wage earners and as social beings. In Ruiz's analytical schema, familial oligarchy shaped an inevitable cultural conflict with American individualism; her chapter describes Mexican-American teenagers creatively negotiating this complex arena.

Still, as Ruiz documents in her study, control over daughters often became a particularly difficult issue in immigrant families because Latin attitudes toward female sexuality differed significantly from American ones. Ruiz's chapter complements Prieto's in exploring how new public experiences—at school, movie theater, or workplace—brought Latin attitudes toward female virginity and sexual shame under scrutiny by both older and younger members of immigrant families. Both Ruiz and Prieto suggest that wage earning and the power of American popular culture gave immigrant girls new tools in generational negotiations with their mothers and fathers. Ruiz argues explicitly that girls' resistance to chaperonage represented a first important step toward their sexual liberation.

As Deirdre Mageean's chapter reminds us, too, many immigrant women stepped out of their domestic world into immigrant or ethnic community activism. In understanding women's community activism, scholars will need to tackle an analytical problem posed by their dependence on concepts like domestic and public. Where exactly does the ethnic or church-centered immigrant community fit into this analytical scheme? Were such communities informal extensions of the domestic world, thus ones into which women could easily move and mingle with men? Certainly many Progressive Era observers of immigrant community believed this to be the case. Or were immigrant communities instead the first in a series of public spaces from which immigrant women were largely excluded? That is the impression left by John Bodnar's description of immigrant communities.[20]

The nuns Mageean describes were unsung community activists and pioneers in the development of ethnic and religious community services. Their dedication to the improvement of women's lives through improving female education and providing services of use to women and children is now well documented. The meaning of these choices, however, awaits further study. Whether women's responsibilities tied them to the limitations of a sex-segregated world or opened up new areas of autonomy in a separate, female world is not a settled matter. In the case of the Asian picture brides, Alice Chai shows that sex segregation was not so much an effective way of enforcing female passivity within families as the basis for Asian women's collective strength within their own communities. At the very least, then, the chapters in this volume hint at the coexistence of two linked immigrant communities, one male and one female. This is an important point because many scholars have assumed that a separate woman's culture characterized mainly middle-class or Anglo-American cultures in the nineteenth century. Here we see at least hints of its existence in working-class and immigrant worlds.

WOMEN AND AMERICAN ETHNICITY

Might not the creation of an ethnic women's culture in the United States also be viewed as one response to American examples and new experiences—part, that is, of immigrant adaptation to life in their new home? While early historical studies of immigration to the United States emphasized either the obliteration or triumphant persistence of immigrant cultures in the United States, most recent studies instead aim to trace the invention of American ethnicity. Betty Bergland, in her chapter on immigrant autobiographies, offers an alternative to earlier work by literary scholars on this invention by focusing on the construction of identity rather than ethnicity. Along with other chapters in *Seeking Common Ground*, she thus poses in new ways some of the gendered dimensions of the process inelegantly called "ethnogenesis" or the "construction of ethnicity."

Suzanne Sinke's discussion of the international marriage market contributes to analysis of this process by introducing the useful term "social reproduction," a concept that Sinke sees as linked to but much broader than biological reproduction of the species. Social reproduction, as defined by Sinke, would easily include the creation of ethnic identity, ethnic culture, and ethnic group. Reproduction in this sense begins with the socialization of infants, particularly with the work of mothering. Language acquisition, personal identity, food habits, religious faith, personality structures—indeed, everything that might be termed early childhood development in both its psychological and social dimensions— are thus integral, and largely unstudied, elements in the invention of American ethnicities. Women's role should become as obvious in social reproduction as it is in the biological creation of each new generation, and the topic deserves further study.

Betty Bergland's analysis of three immigrant women's autobiographies suggests differing intersections between ethnicity and gender in the invention of American identity. Like many male writers of autobiographies, Russian-Jewish Mary Antin ended her own life's account while she was still an adolescent, suggesting that full adulthood in this country was limited to the American-born, regardless of sex. Women autobiographers who told of their own adulthood, by contrast, did so as conscious critics of the United States—here, Bergland uses works by the well-known anarchist Emma Goldman and the less-known socialist and community activist Hilda Polachek as examples.

Vicki Ruiz, in her study of Mexican-American chaperonage, is more interested in generational dimensions of culture change. Teenaged girls who asserted their control over wages, clothing, hairstyles, and dating took a step toward sexual liberation by stepping away from the cultural values of their parents—a source of some familial stress, as Ruiz notes. Rather than portray the rebellions of teenaged girls as Americanization, however, Ruiz describes their choices as "cultural coalescence." She argues that second-generation Mexican-Americans used American materials and possibilities to create a new amalgam, a Mexican-American culture. Individuals created a range of Mexican-American options as they experimented and negotiated this contested cultural terrain. An obvious question remains: were there special incentives that made women—whether as daughters or mothers—particularly eager or reluctant cultural innovators? A gendered analysis of cultural innovation is as badly needed as a gendered analysis of social reproduction.

Hinted at but nowhere systematically addressed in the chapters in this volume is the interaction of foreign-born with native-born women in the creation of ethnic definitions of womanhood and individual identity. Betty Bergland argues that the immigrant Hilda Polacheck's autobiographical account of her own life was a representation of life linked to native-born social settlement workers' discourses on marriage, motherhood, and community activism. In Suzanne Sinke's chapter, by contrast, we are reminded of the negative views immigrant men often held of American women as lazy and spoiled. What emerges strikingly from these chapters is the segregation of native-born from foreign-born across immigrant groups and time periods. The question of whether this is a result of perception or of structural isolation deserves further attention.

NEW IMMIGRANTS AND OLD

Many general studies of the most recent wave of immigration into the United States emphasize the vast differences between today's immigrants and those of the past. "The newcomers are different," writes one pair of collaborators, "reflecting in their motives and origins the forces that have forged a new world order in the second half of this century. And the America that receives them is not the same society that processed the 'huddled masses' through Ellis Island."[21]

The chapters of *Seeking Common Ground* were chosen to illustrate similarities rather than differences in immigrant women's lives. Still, even in these chapters, some differences are obvious. Rita J. Simon notes that immigrant women today are overrepresented both in professional fields and in some of the least-skilled jobs in the U.S. hierarchy. Katharine M. Donato refers to migrations of professional women workers, especially of health care workers, from some countries of the world.[22] And Yolanda Prieto emphasizes the middle-class backgrounds of many Cubans to explain the high commitment of women to wage-earning work in the United States; many other refugee groups share with the early Cubans the experience of downward mobility after arrival in the United States. Class differences among immigrant women, then, seem particularly strong today, and must be taken into account in studies of contemporary immigrant women's lives. By contrast, the vast majority of immigrant women in the nineteenth and early twentieth centuries were of humble background, having worked in agriculture, domestic service, and small-scale industry before migration.

Today, too, women seem much more likely to travel alone or even as the first in their families, pioneers finding work in the United States, than to follow in men's footsteps. Donato suggests that this too may be traced to strong U.S. demand for female labor and the peculiarities of its occupational preference system.

When scholars write about the vast differences between immigrants of past and present, however, they usually are referring to racial differences. Before the 1920s almost 95 percent of immigrant men and women originated in Europe. Today most originate in the third world. In the past, the racial identity of southern and eastern European migrants was regularly debated; most scholars agree that discriminatory quotas aimed at them built on the precedent of Asian exclusion and on racial assumptions about the inferiority of both. The notion that southern and northern Europeans represented distinctive races slowly died over the course of the twentieth century. But given this country's persisting awareness of skin color, it is logical to assume that the experiences of today's immigrants will differ significantly from those of the past and that some of those differences will be the product of American racism.

Exploring the significance of race for immigrant women and men will be possible only through comparative studies. The challenge for future comparativists will be careful choice of appropriate categories for comparison. In sociology, the field that has generated the most comparative work, minority categories—black, Hispanic, Asian-American, Native American, non-Hispanic white—have generally been preferred, but the categories are of little help in analyzing immigrants since they make no distinction by nativity or generation. Nor are they particularly helpful in identifying the independent influence of race, since Hispanic is a cultural not a racial category.

Of the chapters in this volume, those by Alice Chai and Vicki Ruiz provide some useful guidance for those pondering further study of race and ethnicity in immigrant women's lives. Ruiz points out in a footnote that popular minority categories like Hispanic or Chicana had little relevance to the women she interviewed; they called themselves either Mexicanas or Mexican-Americans, depending on their place of birth and generation. Chai's essay carefully balances comparisons among Japanese, Korean, and Okinawan picture brides with generalizations about some experiences they shared as Asian women in Hawai'i. Sensitivity to race *and* nativity, to ethnic differences within minority categories (Yolanda Prieto's comments on black and white Cubans, for example), and to ways women and men name their own identities should ease the complex task of sorting out the impact of foreign birth, racial difference, and generation in future comparative studies.

NOTES

1. Gabaccia, *Immigrant Women in the United States.*
2. Gabaccia, "Immigrant Women."
3. A careful reader may perceive a slight preponderance of chapters on and by New Yorkers. I made conscious efforts to reach beyond it, but my professional network—like those of many scholars—is still, in part, geographically based.
4. Gloria T. Hull et al., *All the Women Are White, All the Blacks Are Men, but Some of Us Are Brave: Black Women's Studies* (Old Westbury, N.Y.: Feminist Press, 1982).
5. Gabaccia, "Immigrant Women."
6. Heidi Hartmann, "The Family as the Locus of Gender, Class and Political Struggle: The Example of Housework," *Signs* 6 (1981):366–394.
7. Hewitt, "Beyond the Search for Sisterhood."
8. DuBois and Ruiz, *Unequal Sisters.*
9. Diner, *Erin's Daughters*; Baum, Hyman, and Michel, *The Jewish Woman in America*; Weinberg, *The World of Our Mothers*; Yung, *Chinese Women of America*; Mora and Del Castillo, *Mexican Women in the United States*; Caroli, Harney, and Tomasi, *The Italian Immigrant Woman in North America*; Mirandé and Enriquez, *La Chicana*; Ross and Wargelin Brown, *Women who Dared*; Melville, ed., *Twice a Minority.*
10. For a contrasting view, see Judith Stacey and Barrie Thorne, "The Missing Feminist Revolution in Sociology," *Social Problems* 32 (1985): 301–315.
11. Simon and Brettell, *International Migration.*
12. Michelle Zimbalist Rosaldo and Louise Lamphere, eds., *Women, Culture and Society* (Stanford, Calif.: Stanford University Press, 1974).
13. Lamphere, *From Working Daughters to Working Mothers.*
14. Nolan, *Ourselves Alone*; Diner, *Erin's Daughters.*

15. For a preliminary report, see Gabaccia, Chapter 2, *From the Other Side* (forthcoming, Indiana University Press).

16. Smith, "Networks and Migration Resettlement."

17. See Gabaccia, "Kinship, Culture and Migration: A Sicilian Example," *Journal of American Ethnic History* 3 (1984): 39–53.

18. See, for example, Vega et al., "Migration and Mental Health."

19. This argument is advanced, for example, in Constance Cronin, *The Sting of Change* (Chicago: University of Chicago Press, 1970).

20. John Bodnar, *The Transplanted, A History of Immigrants in Urban America* (Bloomington: Indiana University Press, 1985), ch. 4–5.

21. Alejandro Portes and Rubén G. Rumbaut, *Immigrant America, a Portrait* (Berkeley: University of California Press, 1990), p. xviii.

22. See also Donato and Tyree, "Family Reunification."

Part I

The Study of Immigrant Women in History, Sociology, and Anthropology

1

The Treatment of Women in Immigration History: A Call for Change

Sydney Stahl Weinberg

The study of immigration history has been distorted and impoverished by the omission of women's roles in the transition to life in the United States. This chapter traces how changes in immigration history in recent years have affected the treatment of women in books about ethnic groups that settled in the United States by the mid-1990s. It considers studies of immigrant groups generally, rather than those dealing specifically with women, in the hope that creating a new framework for understanding women's lives might lead to a more balanced picture of immigrant society than now prevails.[1] Ten years ago, Carl Degler observed that the women's movement had made it clear that women could no longer be ignored in American history,[2] and this is as true in immigration and ethnicity as in other areas of social history. Yet one must question how they have been included, and whether the field as a whole reflects the approaches to the study of women's experiences that have been pioneered by feminist scholars in history and anthropology. Perhaps most important, we must ask what difference increased attention to women might make in our image of immigrant culture as a whole.

In a review of a book about a woman's life as a political prisoner in a Russian prison camp, Francine du Plessix Grey suggested why it is essential to consider the experiences of women as well as those of men to achieve a true understanding of how a society operates.[3] Although all the women in the "small zone," as the prison was called, were political prisoners, their manner of coping differed vastly from that of the men whose Gulag memoirs have shaped our perceptions of Soviet prison camps. In the scant "leisure" of the camps, men fantasized about escape, solved chess problems, and talked incessantly of politics. The women, on the other hand, although they were also intellectuals, concentrated on bringing ceremony into their otherwise drab and spartan lives. They spent weeks preparing for one another's birthdays and managed to create gifts—an embroidered skirt out of an old sheet, or a cake with oil and flour obtained with difficulty. They observed religious rituals and decorated their midsummer dinner table with wildflowers. Faced with a similar situation, women and men reacted in strikingly different ways.

The lives of Russian prisoners explain what feminist scholars meant when they wrote, fifteen years ago, that "the writing of women into history necessarily involves redefining and enlarging traditional notions of historical significance, to encompass personal, subjective experience as well as public and political activities. . . . Such a methodology implies not only a new history of women, but also a new history." [4] History written with men's lives assumed to be the norm and women's experiences subsumed under those of men, narrowly categorized, or omitted altogether, presents a distorted image not simply of women's history, but of history in general, and this is the status of much of immigration history today.

When Oscar Handlin wrote his pathbreaking history of immigration *The Uprooted*, in 1951, and even when a new edition was published in 1973, the immigrant was assumed to be male, and the role of women was treated in a few pages.[5] As with most histories of the period, the history of men was considered gender neutral, making it unnecessary to deal with women in any area apart from a brief passage about families. In fact, among the earliest major nineteenth-century immigrants, the Irish, the majority were female, but women's experiences or approaches to their lives were not treated at all.[6] This was the predominant view among immigration historians until the mid-1970s (despite the fact that since the 1930s, more women than men have emigrated to the United States).[7]

The original reason for the omission of women in historical studies of immigration is not hard to understand. All societies have recognized differences between gender roles and have treated male activities as more significant than female ones.[8] Historians have explored the so-called public sphere dominated by men, and until fairly recently, only elite groups within that sphere, while women were confined to the domestic realm of home and family, which was not the subject of historical investigation. Only when women left the home to enter the labor force, take part in strikes, join organizations, or work to secure suffrage did their activities even become part of the public record and accessible to traditional historical methodology. It was the male role in that public world—the realm of work, organizational activities, church, and politics—that was assumed by Handlin and many who came after to be the model for understanding how a culture worked.

History had to become more interdisciplinary before it could expand beyond this compartmentalized conception and begin to integrate women. Over fifty years ago, anthropologists began examining the societal roles of women in their studies of cultures, and more recently, feminist anthropologists have taken this subject further in identifying some of the problems involved with evaluating the contribution of women.[9] For example, in a pioneering collection of articles edited by Michelle Rosaldo and Louise Lamphere in the early 1970s, Jane Collier wrote of the family not as a unified whole, as historians were only beginning to do, but as a political arena in which women attempted to achieve specific goals, sometimes by manipulating other household members.[10]

Since then, feminist anthropologists have written a number of studies of immigrant and ethnic women, focusing mainly upon work and family, in which they have portrayed women not only as males perceived them, but as they viewed themselves.[11] They have shown that women in many societies, while barred from men's activities, created their own forms of satisfaction and power within the limitations of their position. For example, Lamphere followed Collier's lead by integrating public and private aspects of women's lives to explain changes in women's patterns of paid labor. In *From Working Daughters to Working Mothers*, her study of immigrant women in a New England industrial community, Lamphere analyzes women's strategies in their marriages to deal with variation and change in work behavior over time. She thus raises the issue of the ways that women's workplace activities reflect their conception of their role.[12]

Other anthropologists have emphasized the importance of "networking" for ethnic women. For example, in *Transforming the Past: Tradition and Kinship among Japanese Americans*, Sylvia Yanagisako has explored the idea of women-centered kin networks in her work on first- and second-generation Japanese-American women.[13] Yanagisako showed the interaction of historical and attitudinal changes that helped explain how women in particular created new cultural forms and symbols after emigrating to California—changes that their own children erroneously assumed to have been cultural importations from Japan. In a study of black families in the Chicago area, *Family and Kin*, Carol Stack demonstrated how poor women devised schemes for self-help by creating extensive networks of kin and friends that traded and exchanged goods, services, resources, and child care.[14] This cooperative support system enabled otherwise impoverished women to create a sense of community and sometimes to improve their lives materially. More recently, in *Women's Work and Chicano Families*, Patricia Zavella wrote of the kin and work-related friendship networks among Chicana cannery workers in the Santa Clara Valley, networks that were central to their social lives.[15]

In *The Varieties of Ethnic Experience*, Micaela Di Leonardo has also focused upon the way women create extended families by examining what she calls the "kinship work" of women within an Italian community in California. Apart from work in the home and the labor market, Di Leonardo adds this third category—which describes how women bring extended families together for holiday celebrations, take charge of ritual observances like birthdays, decide upon visits, the giving of presents, and so forth. By exploring this work of kinship, Di Leonardo shows us women establishing bonds that reach beyond nuclear families. Her ethnic households are not isolated units linked only through such formal devices as organizations or churches, but are units connected as well through kinship ties that women maintain.[16] This domestic domain explored by Yanagisako, Stack, and Di Leonardo, among others, represents a significant aspect of the creation and maintenance of ethnic communities, albeit one unexamined by historians of immigration. Furthermore, the connections between workplace and home—or between public and private spheres—emphasized by such anthropologists as Zavella and Lamphere are generally not considered in immigration history.

The insights of these anthropologists, however, have not been applied universally, even within their own discipline. As Marilyn Strathorn observed, most anthropologists view feminist scholarship as simply the study of women or gender—one among many possible specialties—rather than an approach that should affect the study of society as a whole.[17] And what is true among anthropologists, who are so much more aware of nuances in different societies, is doubly true of historians, despite the fact that immigration history itself has changed greatly during the past fifteen years.

Although disciplinary boundaries tend to inhibit the transmission of methodology and information, in the past decade or so, practitioners of what might be called ethnic studies have begun to learn from one another's techniques. As a result, some earlier conflicts have faded. The struggle between historians who emphasized class as the major determinant of an immigrant's successful acculturation and those who believed culture was more important has mostly blended into what might be called a contextual school of thinking.[18] Olivier Zunz, for example, has encouraged historians to consider the possibility that culture and class may impact differently upon an immigrant population depending upon external societal forces like industrialization.[19] Historical sociologists like Ewa Morawska have merged the quantifying techniques of demographers and sociologists with a historical context to give us a rich picture of Eastern European immigrants in Johnstown, Pennsylvania. According to Morawska, historical sociologists try to "account for the relationships between people's actions and the social environment as it evolves in their everyday lives."[20] The world view of immigrants is thus molded by their prior existence in their native land, the conditions where they settled in this country, and the networks and ambience of the immigrant organizations they created.

In similar fashion, historians like John Bodnar have borrowed from sociologists to show the interaction of the immigrant family with the demands made by America's industrial system.[21] Like Zunz, Bodnar and other historians or historical sociologists like Josef Barton and Tamara K. Hareven have learned from anthropologists that ethnicity is not simply "cultural baggage" carried from the country of immigration, but frequently owes as much to the circumstances of settlement.[22] Immigrants thus become a dynamic force, not simply acquiescing in the demands of an industrial society, but shaping their immediate circumstances to fit their needs as much as they were able. This perception also owes much to the insights of E. P. Thompson, who, in his classic *The Making of the English Working Class*, emphasized the ability of workers to "make" themselves into a class.[23]

This shift in emphasis has enabled historians to view women as something more than a footnote to history—women in families. These scholars were greatly affected by the explosion of family history, which until the late 1960s, remained the preserve of anthropologists and sociologists. However, with the enormous growth of social history, which sought to connect everyday experiences with major historical transformations,[24] historians too began to take an interest in families as important agents of social change.[25] Until that time, as Ellen Ross observed, historians simply did not take into account "the overwhelming power of family feeling and ties,"[26] and underestimated their effect upon society. What gave the most impetus to the inclusion of families in history was the concept of the family economy explored by Joan W. Scott and Louise Tilly,[27] which connected the workings of the family with the external world of developing capitalism.

Thus, social historians came to agree upon the importance of the family economy and kin networks in mediating the effect of industrial society upon the individual. Ordinary people were no longer simply acted upon by forces beyond their control, but actors able to affect their own lives and create new cultures.[28] Working-class households in the late nineteenth century were now seen as part of a larger economic picture where resources were combined to cope with the requirements of the capitalist system.[29] Zunz has tried to demonstrate that early in the twentieth century, the immigrant family changed from the type of unit that relied on income pooling to benefit the family as a whole to a support structure for individual achievements.[30] Both this interpretation and Zunz's corollary rest on the conception that the late-nineteenth-century family was an organic whole whose members shared benefits and aspirations.

However, this perspective, emphasizing the unity of the immigrant family, does not address the different effects of family policies on wives, on sons, on daughters. Age, gender, and generation mattered. For despite the interests of the family in acting as a unit to deal with the capitalist economy, decisions did not necessarily affect all members of the household equally, and tensions or conflict could arise over decisions that seemed to require more sacrifice from some members than others. Sons might be sent to school longer than daughters, who went out to work; children of both sexes might be removed from school so that a wife would not have to find wage work. In a contribution to *Labour and Love*, Lynn Jamieson discusses how sons kept their income and paid mothers room and board, while daughters were expected to give their entire paychecks and receive a small allowance in return.[31] Sons were permitted more individual expression than daughters, and the benefits of the family economy often were distributed unevenly. Hareven and Langenbach, for example, recorded the resentment of young women and wives in New England mill towns denied the possibility of education.[32] My own work on Jewish families has highlighted the sacrifices made by older immigrant children that benefited their younger siblings.[33]

It was not historians of the family, but women's historians who began to investigate the family as something more complex than a working unit. Until the past decade, even feminist scholars seldom studied women in the family except as members of organized groups or as part of an entity with mutual concerns.[34] But in recent years, practitioners of women's history have demonstrated that women within families often held attitudes and engaged in activities that differentiate them from men.[35] Like Jane Collier's path-breaking article in the early 1970s, they have shown that family decisions were not necessarily made in the best interests of all members.[36] One of the purposes of social history, Zunz suggests, is to expose "the conflicts hidden behind the rhetoric of harmony,"[37] and this is as important for the family as it is for other aspects of society. Laborers' confrontation with the industrial order in the workplace also affected relationships within the home.

This less harmonious aspect of family life, however, has been neglected in most social history: women usually have been subsumed under "family" with little consideration of their distinctive roles within or outside the home.[38] As Joan Scott has observed, much of social history compartmentalizes life, relegating sex and gender to the institution of the family rather than viewing them as basic aspects of social organization creating hierarchies of difference in society.[39] Family generally has been treated as a whole, with little distinction made among its parts. Conflicts among its members, or different attitudes toward, for example, the treatment of children, have seldom been considered. This view tends to obscure the context in which family patterns functioned and changed by denying the importance to society of relationships between family members and the influence they have on one another.

Immigration history has incorporated many of these attitudes of social history, and despite the research that has been done on women, the issues emphasized by Handlin and other early writers remain the focus of immigration historians generally. Handlin's image of a male immigrant coming alone, disoriented, passive, and lacking a familial support group, has given way to an interpretation stressing the mediating effects of kin and family as well as the strengths and adaptability of immigrant groups. But the source material of immigrant history has not changed enough to enable historians to see beyond the categories of discourse that were shaped earlier.

In *The Transplanted*, for example, Bodnar, while challenging Handlin's thesis on the disruptive nature of the immigrant experience, does not differ from him significantly in his treatment of women. Although historians of women have demonstrated that in the late nineteenth century a separate female culture existed among the middle classes,[40] Bodnar assumes that women of the working classes always shared common values and interests with their men. The similarity of his chapter structure to that of Handlin also suggests that Bodnar generally explored the experiences of male immigrants and assumed they were those of women as well.[41] The focus in most chapters is largely on men in relationship to such subjects as wage earning, the church, social mobility, and home ownership. This is a continuation of a similar approach in an earlier book, *Lives of Their Own*, which Bodnar wrote with Michael Weber and Roger Simon.[42] Apart from a brief mention here and there, women are discussed only twice: as part of families and as workers.

Even when historians borrow methodology from sociologists and include women in their statistics, they often fail to ask questions of their materials that might place gender roles in a more meaningful context. For example, Jon Gjerde, in *From Peasants to Farmers*,[43] includes women in his analysis of Norwegian immigrants: he discusses courtship, fertility, the changing nature of women's farm work, their use of English, and activities in societies such as the Ladies Aid. We learn about changes created by a new sexual division of farm labor: men gained more power since Norwegian women's traditional work—caring for animals, housekeeping, the kitchen gardens—was now nonpaying, while men's farm work earned money.[44] But we are not told how these changes altered perceptions of women's roles and status, either by men or by the women themselves.[45]

In Gary Mormino and George Pozzetta's prize-winning study of Italians and their Latin neighbors in *The Immigrant World of Ybor City*,[46] the authors create a fascinating and colorful montage showing the growth of an unusual multicultural community consisting of Spaniards, Cubans, and Italians. Yet once again, the role of women is slighted. Although over 70 percent of the Italian immigrants were married, fewer than one-quarter of the authors' interviews were with women, and many of the issues that would have engaged women do not seem to have been addressed. For example, Mormino and Pozzetta devote a chapter to the difficulties of life in Ybor City in its first days of settlement, but we do not learn how women coped and made homes in what must have seemed an inhospitable environment.

Throughout the book, the authors, perhaps inadvertently, raise questions about the lives of women that they do not follow up. A fine section on Italian women working in the tobacco factories (men generally left the factories for other employment) mentions in passing the fact that they often made more money than their husbands. But Mormino and Pozzetta leave unexplored how this unusual reversal of traditional roles affected family life. We do not learn whether, since many women worked, they developed networks of kin or neighbors to care for children. There are five pages on the effects of sports on immigrant (male) culture, but nothing on neighborhood or women's relationships. We read that the first settlers valued their children's work above education, especially for girls. Then, as the Italians prospered, they wanted more education for their children, but it is unclear whether this meant girls as well as boys.[47] What hints we get about women's roles—for example, chaperoning daughters in the 1920s, cooking foods tied in with ethnic identity, grandmothers teaching their grandchildren Italian—speaks to the function of women as upholders and symbols of cultural values. Women also seem to have had a different attitude toward the church than their husbands, but again, these issues are hinted at rather than explored.

In *For Bread with Butter*, Morawska also documents significant changes in the lives of Eastern European women immigrants without analyzing what this might have meant in terms of women's role or status. For example, we read of the value women's labors brought to the family by taking in boarders, canning, sewing, and performing other types of home work, but it remains unclear what effect this activity had in altering family relations. Similarly, Morawska discusses the subordinate position of women in Eastern Europe without subsequently explaining how or why it seems to have altered in this country. The only indication of changing attitudes is mention of the fact that second-generation women were absorbed into leadership positions of Slavic and Magyar women's societies during the interwar period, whereas these positions in male societies were dominated by first-generation men. Although the majority of organizations in the 1920s and 1930s were founded by women, there is no speculation about what this may have meant in terms of women's status, particularly among other women (it is pointed out that women leaders were often married to male leaders), apart from the comment that possibly "the positions in women's societies were not considered a source of power in the immigrant community." [48] Left unexamined is what this suggests about the relationships between first-generation women and their daughters, what women thought of their own authority, their attitudes toward acculturation, changes in women's status between the old country and here, and perhaps even significant differences between the attitudes of first-generation men and women.

The books examined in this chapter are not unique in the treatment of gender: many other examples of male-biased distortion can be seen in recent histories of Irish, Jewish, Polish, and Asian immigrant groups. [49] Although the very different experience of Irish women immigrants was amply documented in 1983 in Hasia Diner's *Erin's Daughters in America*, Jewish women's lives have been explored in several books, and a number of monographs have considered the lives of Asian immigrant women, [50] general histories of these groups seldom incorporate the perceptions of this scholarship.

The picture we get of women's lives from most studies is limited indeed. It is entirely appropriate to consider immigrant women as workers and as part of families, since the vast majority in fact worked and married. [51] But most immigration histories limit coverage of women to these two categories, rigidly conceived. They do not extend their area of research to (1) the connections between work and home life, the domestic and public spheres; (2) women-centered activities performed in the context of household or neighborhood; and (3) women's perceptions of their world—the satisfactions it could offer and the way they could achieve authority within their realm.

Thus, we do not learn about the texture of women's lives: how did they see themselves, socialize their children, participate in neighborhood life, maintain kinship relationships, establish sex-linked ties, and create their own sense of values within home and neighborhood? [52] If immigrant men operated small businesses, we do not learn what role their wives played in these enterprises or how this demanding form of labor affected family relations. [53] When women crusaded for causes as varied as temperance or urban sewage disposal, their activities are seldom incorporated into political studies of immigration history. [54] "Women's history" is too often viewed by historians of immigration as a particular specialty, while "history" remains mainly the story of men: immigrant women remain in a ghetto of their own.

This "ghettoization" of women is even less justifiable in immigration studies than in other branches of history, where men held recognized power and women appeared to hold none. Most immigrants came to the United States powerless, and had to create their own forms of authority and satisfaction within the limited sphere that was under their control in an urban, industrial society. Both men and women had to adjust to a life in this country that made different demands upon them than those they were accustomed to before emigrating. Only men's forms of coping, however, have been considered by most historians of immigration.[55] All the books examined in this chapter demonstrate how male immigrants derived dignity and fulfillment from their position within their ethnic milieu, but they fail to view women in the same context. Men's religious organizations and priests are discussed, but there is little if nothing about nuns and women's associations or auxiliaries. Subjects of male interest, like politics and sports, are considered, but not neighborhood and kin networks, which were largely in women's bailiwick. Thus historians, probably without being aware of it, assumed traditional forms of patriarchal dominance and values and shaped their research to conform with those assumptions. As DuBois and Kelly have observed, we remain faced with "the tenacity of the presumption that male experience and points of view are universal and exhaustive." There is more than a grain of truth in their assertion that "archaic interpretive frameworks act like old rusty gates to keep out all that we now know about women's history."[56]

Historians of immigration need not follow the pattern set by anthropologists and consider women's history simply an additional field for investigation—an appendage of the real thing. It would be unfortunate if women's experiences remained the subjects of isolated monographs without being incorporated into the analytic framework of immigration research, as scholars in the field have recently warned.[57] The challenge is to enlarge the framework we use to include gender and thus correct assumptions that prevent a meaningful inclusion of women's roles in immigration history.

How might women's roles be more adequately included? First, by eliminating the artificial division between work and home that has prevented us from understanding the interrelationship between public and private places. For example, in Lenore Davidoff and Catherine Hall's *Family Fortunes: Men and Women of the English Middle Class*, the domestic sphere is seen as a central point of investigation for writing about the history of *men* as well as women.[58] Most historians have assumed that men's affairs are carried out outside a familial context, that men's only need was to make a living in industrialized society. Davidoff and Hall demonstrate, however, how "autonomous" entrepreneurs were dependent on financing from their kin networks and their wives' dowries and on family participation in the enterprise and how men's career choices were influenced by family considerations. They contend that many men were as much motivated by domestic values as by those of the marketplace, and that these values, in turn, helped shape economic development. Their work shows the shortcomings in the assumption that one can understand a culture by exploring only the public lives and discourse of men.[59]

Second, we can learn more about women's lives by creating new, more flexible categories to consider their perceptions of work, family life, neighborhood, and kinship. In a critique of *The Transplanted*, Donna Gabaccia suggests one way to accomplish this objective.[60] We cannot understand how the family functioned, she argues, without investigating women's lives within the home and neighborhood and learning, in addition, about budgets, marketplace behavior, and consumption. In addition, we must learn more about such home-centered activities as childbearing, child rearing, and housekeeping, for they are intimately connected to the outside world. Perhaps most important, we must attempt to comprehend how wives perceived their roles in household and community.[61] Some feminist scholars have explored how women used informal forms of influence to sway other women and the men who held recognized authority within the community.[62] Might we not learn more about the actual mechanics of this power with a subtle analysis of the role women played in decision making?

Ample precedent exists for reassessing the role of women in their own milieu. French scholars of the mentalities approach to cultural history, by focusing on the individual, family, and community, have questioned the assumptions of social and economic dominance that have previously attributed to women a marginal position in society. Several of them have explored the lives and culture of village women in such a way as to encourage future historians to consider not only the technical division of chores between the sexes but also the values and symbols that accompany the division. They point out that if women have their own perception of social order, if they perform functions that help the community from birth to death, "they obviously have 'some' power." How, these scholars ask, does the difference between the sexes function? How does each sex "represent and redefine itself and its relationship to the other?"[63] The same questions might profitably be applied to immigration history.

Even if the answers were easily accessible, one might still ask what difference they would make in our understanding of American immigration history generally. A major concern of social historians has been to reconstruct the mind-sets of people in an earlier time.[64] Similarly, a major goal of feminist scholars has been to better understand how women comprehend their world, without making the assumption that women's status changed in tandem with that of men.[65] Joan Scott has challenged the validity of a history that assumes a fixed distinction between men and women, and advises feminist historians to "analyze ways in which politics construct gender and gender constructs politics."[66] However, because most historians of immigration have yet to add gender to the standard analytic concepts of ethnicity and class, they have yet to explore either the role of gender in culture or the mind-set of women in different societies.

An important consequence of ignoring this mind-set may be an inability to understand significant aspects of immigrant society as a whole. In the work of historians, we seldom learn about informal neighborhood and kin networks, created or maintained by women, and the effects they had upon the establishment of immigrant communities. Yet work done mainly by feminist anthropologists has encouraged scholars to reassess the value placed on such aspects of women's lives previously considered private. As noted earlier, in recent years, women's historians have questioned whether private and public can be considered separate spheres at all on the basis that politics is grounded in and in turn shapes social arrangements. The boundaries of separate spheres have often shifted and required constant repair.[67] Applying deconstructionist techniques to immigration history might result in some interesting changes in historical perception of the lives of immigrant communities.[68]

Attention to gender might shed new light on the relation between public and private and thus add a new dimension to the culture of everyday life. Indeed, Davidoff and Hall have demonstrated in *Family Fortunes* that by investigating how the system of gender worked, we can learn more about the lives of men as well. Such an investigation could help explain the economic connections between women, their families, and the market economy through elements other than wage work. For example, what were the informal kin and neighborhood links that enabled Jewish housewives in 1902, with great speed and efficiency, to mount a boycott against Kosher meat dealers who had raised their prices?[69] Or to lead rent strikes in 1904 and 1908? Or to organize on a neighborhood level to fight the influence of Jewish gangsters?[70] These Jewish women's sense of community differed from the male-dominated, institutionally defined entity considered by most historians of immigration. The use of gender once again calls into question the distinction between public and private and points the way toward a broadening of the conception of community.

Historians might also examine women's perceptions of their familial roles to explore elusive differences in acculturation between first- and second-generation immigrants. Writing about the assimilation process may presently be out of favor among social historians—although it is indeed paradoxical, as Zunz suggested, that such scholars downplay the role of ethnicity in American life after stressing the cultural independence of minorities[71]—but few recent studies investigate in depth differences between immigrants and their children. Recently, Pozzetta has also called for scholars of Italian immigration to study the second generation to understand how immigrant culture was passed on, and in what form.[72]

This is obviously a gap in the current writing of immigration history. For example, the books discussed in this chapter assert that immigrant families gradually adjusted during their confrontation with capitalism and American culture, but they tell us little about how this process took place. Nor is there evidence in any of them as to whether the overriding concern for family solidarity was shared by the second generation.[73]

The roles played by mothers might help in explaining the attitudinal differences between the immigrant generation and their children. How might patterns of socialization within the home, for example, have shaped the aspirations of second-generation children? My own research has led me to see immigrant mothers as facilitators in their attempt to mediate when a father wishes to retain many of the old ways and a child wants to be a "real American."[74] For most immigrant groups, research has yet to explore the function of such women in easing intergenerational strife and, perhaps, in determining living patterns and habits of consumption as upward mobility gave a family choice in such matters. These issues may prove an important clue in understanding patterns of acculturation across generations.

By altering the traditional approach to immigrant societies and including gender as an analytical concept, a small but increasing number of historians have shown, without slighting the male role or the political context, the important part immigrant and ethnic women have played in maintaining or adapting the native culture of their group to the demands of the United States.[75] In studies of different immigrant societies, Virginia Yans-McLaughlin, Donna Gabaccia, Sarah Deutsch, S. J. Kleinberg, Judith Smith, and Laura Anker have demonstrated how women's lives and aspirations differed from those of men; how gender, age, and family responsibilities affected behavior within families; and how women bore a primary responsibility for adapting old world traits and thus preserving group culture.[76]

Several of these historians have concentrated on the role of kinship bonds in cementing the family economy. Fifteen years ago, in *Family and Community*, Virginia Yans-McLaughlin demonstrated that the role of women in kin networks was crucial in both the family economy and the maintenance of culture among Italian immigrants in Buffalo.[77] More recently, Judith Smith and Laura Anker, in examinations of Connecticut and Rhode Island immigrant communities, have shown the importance of women in sustaining old kinship ties or creating new ones in neighborhoods—thus organizing support systems for the essential family economy and, over time, redefining responsibilities for families across household lines and giving a new meaning to the word ethnicity.[78]

Another major area of investigation has been differences in the impact of immigration and the process of urbanization on men and women of the same ethnic group. In *From Sicily to Elizabeth Street*, Donna Gabaccia has explained how housing patterns in a Sicilian neighborhood in New York fulfilled male ideals but restricted the lives of wives, whose dissatisfaction led to changes in those patterns.[79] Conversely, in *Jamaica Farewell*, her study of more recent Jamaican migrants in London, Nancy Foner, an anthropologist, has shown how, after emigrating, women gained the freedom to break with traditional patterns, while men suffered a more constricted way of life.[80]

S. J. Kleinberg, in her study of immigrant and ethnic working-class families in Pittsburgh, *The Shadow of the Mills*, also concentrates on the different effects of urbanization and industrialization on men and on women. She explains the interrelationship of men's jobs in steel mills with women's work in the home, which enabled men to labor long hours in the mills. "Pittsburgh's modern industrial economy," she states, "rested as much upon these unpaid services as it did upon the work of the men in the mills.[81] Just as historians of immigration generally describe men's industrial work, Kleinberg explores in detail the many aspects of women's domestic labor, from washing clothing, which required hauling heavy buckets from the hydrant on the street, to caring for children or cooking for boarders. But she goes beyond description to explain how, as industrialism and mandatory schooling removed husbands and children from the home for long periods of the day, women's work became even more confined to the home. Because men and women were leading increasingly separate lives, their disparate needs could create conflict as easily as harmony. Kleinberg's study calls for a fresh look at the differing effects of industrialization on men and women in immigrant families.

In *No Separate Refuge*, a path-breaking study of Mexican-Hispanic society on the southwest frontier, Sarah Deutsch has documented the major role women played in maintaining the culture and structure of the regional community, until the policies of the federal government during the New Deal undermined their position. Deutsch discovered that before the 1930s, when men were often away doing migrant labor, these women were largely responsible for the survival of Hispanic culture in the dominant Anglo milieu of the Southwest. "Through their visiting, their sharing of food, ... childbearing, and most important, their stability, production and earnings as non-migrants, women provided for increasingly mobile villagers not only subsistence, but continuity and networks for community, health, and child care, for old age and emotional support."[82] But this function—as property owners who could perform tasks usually reserved for men as well as communal work and religious services—was alien to missionaries and New Deal agencies, who tried to transform Hispanic women into proper housewives or servants, the positions in which the dominant society envisioned them. It was a change in this stabilizing role of women, Deutsch demonstrates, that was responsible for the erosion of the culture that they maintained in the villages.

By showing this important function women had filled in southwestern Hispanic villages, Deutsch's work implicitly calls for a reevaluation of the role ethnic women play in maintaining or changing the culture of their group. It also, parenthetically, shows us a striking example of the social construction of gender roles, a process of which immigration historians usually seem unaware.

These few examples present a compelling argument for historians to take a fresh look at the effect of women on the process of immigration and acculturation. Although progress has been made by anthropologists and women's historians, it is time for historians of immigration to utilize their methods and perceptions to explore immigrant culture and society. By expanding our conception of what is historically significant to include gender and the roles of women as well as the complex web of relationships within a society, we can add a deeper level of understanding to the ways in which ethnic groups confronted, adapted to, and ultimately helped recreate the life they found in this country.

NOTES

1. Other scholars in immigration studies have written of the marginality of women in immigration history. See, for example, Pedraza, "Women and Migration: The Social Consequences of Gender"; Bergland, "Immigrant History and the Gendered Subject"; Sinke, "A Historiography of Immigrant Women"; Gabaccia, "Immigrant Women"; Seller, "Beyond the Stereotype."

2. Carl Degler, "What the Women's Movement Has Done to American History," in Elizabeth Langland and Walter Gove, ed., *A Feminist Perspective in the Academy: The Difference It Makes* (Chicago: University of Chicago Press, 1983), p. 70.

3. Francine du Plessix Grey, "Sisterhood in the Small Zone," a review of Irina Ratushinskaia, *Grey Is the Color of Hope* (New York: Knopf, 1988), *The New York Times Book Review*, October 30, 1988.

4. Ann D. Gordon, Mari Jo Buhle, and Nancy Shrom Dye, "The Problem of Women's History," in Berenice Carroll, ed., *Liberating Women's History* (Urbana: University of Illinois Press, 1976), p. 89. On this point, see also Joan Kelly, "The Doubled Vision of Feminist Theory," *Feminist Studies* 6, 2 (Summer 1979): 216–227; Jane Flax, "Postmodernism and Gender Relations in Feminist Theory," *SIGNS* 12, 4 (Summer 1987): 621–643.

5. Oscar Handlin, *The Uprooted* (Boston: Little, Brown, 1973), 2nd. ed., ch. 9. Handlin was criticized mainly for his assertion that the immigration experience was widely disruptive and for his generalities. See, for example, Rudolph Vecoli, "Contadini in Chicago: A Critique of *The Uprooted*," *Journal of American History* 41 (December 1964): 404–417.

6. See, for example, Oscar Handlin, *Boston's Immigrants 1790–1865* (Cambridge, Mass.: Harvard University Press, 1941).

7. See Houstoun, Kramer, and Barrett, "Female Predominance of Immigration."

8. Michelle Zimbalist Rosaldo, "Woman, Culture and Society: A Theoretical Overview," in Michelle Zimbalist Rosaldo and Louise Lamphere, eds., *Woman, Culture and Society* (Stanford: Stanford University Press, 1974), pp. 18–19.

9. Rosaldo and Lamphere, *Woman, Culture and Society*, esp. pp. 8–9, 31–32, 99–100. Rosaldo, for example, demonstrated how an emphasis on woman's maternal role led to an opposition between public roles, inhabited by men, and domestic roles inhabited by women, who therefore lack access to the authority, prestige, and cultural value that are the prerogatives of men.

10. Jane Fishburn Collier, "Women in Politics," in Rosaldo and Lamphere, eds., *Woman, Culture and Society*, pp. 89–97. This approach to anthropology owed much to Clifford Geertz, who, in his *Interpretation of Cultures* (New York: Basic Books, 1973), urged anthropologists to observe the symbolic content of behavior.

11. For example, among the most recent, see Di Leonardo, *The Varieties of Ethnic Experience*; Zavella, *Women's Work and Chicano Families*; Lamphere, *From Working Daughters to Working Mothers*.

12. Lamphere, *From Working Daughters to Working Mothers*, pp. 17, 27.

13. Yanagisako, *Transforming the Past*.

14. Carol Stack, *Family and Kin: Strategies for Survival in a Black Community* (New York: Harper and Row, 1975), pp. 9, 28, 32.

15. Zavella, *Women's Work and Chicano Families*.

16. Micaela Di Leonardo, "The Female World of Cards and Holidays: Women, Families, and the Work of Kinship," *SIGNS* 12 (Spring 1987): 440–453. See also Di Leonardo, *The Varieties of Ethnic Experience*.

17. Marilyn Strathorn, "An Awkward Relationship: The Case of Feminism and Anthropology," *SIGNS* 12 (Winter 1987): 176–192. Nonfeminist anthropologists often view women through their own sexual stereotypes or through the eyes of their male informants and continue to write about ethnic groups without incorporating the perspectives of women as they see themselves rather than "what women represent in men's dealings with men." See also Jane M. Atkinson, "Anthropology: Review Essay," *SIGNS* 8 (Winter 1982): 245, 253. These disagreements also reflect differences among anthropologists who try to view a society from the perspective of its inhabitants and those who prefer what they consider a more objective view. Thus, anthropology in general has not absorbed and integrated the perceptions of women's studies, and the feminist view remains almost exclusively the domain of women scholars who study women immigrants.

18. John Higham, "Current Trends in the Study of Ethnicity in the United States," *Journal of American Ethnic History* 2 (Fall 1982): 5–15.

19. Olivier Zunz, *The Changing Face of Inequality: Urbanization, Industrial Development, and Immigrants in Detroit, 1880–1920* (Chicago: University of Chicago Press, 1982); see also Zunz, "American History and the Changing Meaning of Assimilation," *Journal of American Ethnic History* 4 (Spring 1985): 53–72.

20. Morawska, *For Bread with Butter*, p. 6.

21. John Bodnar, *The Transplanted: A History of Immigrants in Urban America* (Bloomington: Indiana University Press, 1985), p. xvii.

22. See Olivier Zunz, *Reliving the Past: The Worlds of Social History* (Chapel Hill: University of North Carolina Press, 1985), p. 85; see also Bodnar, "Immigrants, Kinship, and the Rise of Working-Class Realism in Industrial America," *Journal of Social History* 14 (Fall 1980): 59.

23. E. P. Thompson, *The Making of the English Working Class* (New York: Random House–Vintage, 1966), p. 9.

24. See Zunz, *Reliving the Past*, pp. 5–6. Much of early family history, however, was mostly concerned with demographics—fertility rates, household composition, etc.

25. See Mary Ryan, "The Explosion of Family History," *Reviews in American History* 10 (December 1982): 181–192. Ryan wrote, "Family transitions ... are critical historical junctures, movements rife with the possibility of change even as they link the past to the future," p. 183.

26. Rayna Rapp, Ellen Ross, and Renate Bridenthal, "Examining Family History," *Feminist Studies* 5 (Spring 1979): 181.

27. Joan W. Scott and Louise Tilly, "Women's Work and the Family in Nineteenth-Century Europe," *Comparative Studies in Society and History* 17 (1975): 36–64; *Women, Work and Family* (New York: Holt, Rinehart and Winston, 1978).

28. See Lawrence Levine, "The Unpredictable Past: Reflections on Recent American Historiography," *American Historical Review* 94 (June 1989): 672.

29. See Bodnar, *The Transplanted*; Ellen C. DuBois et al., *Feminist Scholarship: Kindling in the Groves of Academe* (Urbana: University of Illinois Press, 1985), p. 85.

30. Zunz, *Reliving the Past*, p. 72.

31. Lynn Jamieson, "Limited Resources and Limiting Conventions: Working-Class Mothers and Daughters in Urban Scotland, c. 1890–1925," in Jane Lewis, ed., *Labour and Love* (London: Basil Blackwell, 1986), pp. 49–69.

32. Hareven and Langenbach, *Amoskeag*, pp. 267–268.

33. Weinberg, *The World of Our Mothers*. See also "Longing to Learn."

34. DuBois et al., *Feminist Scholarship*, pp. 181, 188.

35. One of the formative studies was Carroll Smith-Rosenberg, "The Female World of Love and Ritual: Relations between Women in Nineteenth-Century America," *SIGNS* 1 (Autumn 1975): 1–29.

36. Heidi Hartmann, "The Family as the Locus of Gender, Class and Political Struggle: The Example of Housework," *SIGNS* 6(1981): 366–394; Louise Tilly and Miriam Cohen, "Does the Family Have a History? A Review of Theory and Practice in Family History," *Social Science History* 6 (1982): 131–179. Interestingly, Micaela Di Leonardo discovered in her anthropological research among Californians of Italian ancestry that women were more willing than men to discuss family feuds and crises—men tended to repeat formulaic statements asserting family unity. See Di Leonardo, "The Female World of Cards and Holidays," p. 444.

37. Zunz, *Reliving the Past*, p. 76.

38. Rayna Rapp, Ellen Ross, and Renate Bridenthal, "Examining Family History," *Feminist Studies* 5 (Spring 1979): 175, 188.

39. Joan Scott also challenges the validity of a history that assumes a fixed

distinction between men and women. See Scott, *Gender and the Politics of History* (New York: Columbia University Press, 1988), pp. 6, 10, 16–17.

40. See, for example, Smith-Rosenberg, "The Female World of Love and Ritual."

41. See the critique of Bodnar in Gabaccia, "*The Transplanted*: Women and Family in Immigrant America."

42. John Bodnar, Michael Weber, and Roger Simon, *Lives of Their Own: Blacks, Italians and Poles in Pittsburgh, 1900–1960*. (Urbana: University of Illinois Press, 1982).

43. Jon Gjerde, *From Peasants to Farmers: The Migration from Balestrand, Norway, to the Upper Middle West* (New York: Cambridge University Press, 1984).

44. Gjerde, *From Peasants to Farmers*, pp. 195, 200, 211, passim.

45. In fairness to Gjerde, we seldom learn how men thought either: what we learn is what they *did*.

46. Gary Mormino and George Pozzetta, *The Immigrant World of Ybor City: Italians and Their Latin Neighbors in Tampa, 1885–1985* (Urbana: University of Illinois Press, 1987).

47. Ibid., pp. 288–290.

48. Morawska, *For Bread with Butter*, pp. 174, 232, 292.

49. For example, Kerby A. Miller, *Emigrants and Exiles* (New York: Oxford University Press, 1985); Arthur Hertzberg, *The Jews in America* (New York: Simon and Schuster, 1989); John J. Bukowczyk, *And My Children Did Not Know Me: A History of the Polish-Americans* (Bloomington: Indiana University Press, 1987); Roger Daniels, *Asian America* (Seattle: University of Washington Press, 1988). In *The Chinese Experience in America* (Bloomington: Indiana University Press, 1986), Shih-shan Henry Tsai includes women only peripherally. Only Takaki, *Strangers from a Different Shore*, makes a serious attempt to include women's perceptions of their lives and of the effect women had upon the different Asian immigrant cultures. Like Daniels and Tsai, Takaki discusses the Chinese in America as a basically male society, but he then goes back to China to explain the role of women in Chinese culture and why they might not have wanted to emigrate even had this path been open to them. He compares the effect upon the lives of the American Chinese of *not* having a family life with those of the Chinese immigrants into Hawaii, where women were included and family life was possible.

50. On Jews, see Baum, Hyman, and Michel, *The Jewish Woman in America*; and Ewen, *Immigrant Women in the Land of Dollars*. On the Chinese, Loo and Ong, "Slaying Demons with a Sewing Needle"; Anne M. Butler, *Daughters of Joy, Sisters of Misery: Prostitutes in the American West, 1865–90* (Urbana: University of Illinois Press, 1985); Hirata, "Free, Indentured, Enslaved," and "Chinese Immigrant Women in Nineteenth-Century California," in Carol Ruth Berkin and Mary Beth Norton, eds., *Women of America, a History* (Boston: Houghton Mifflin, 1979), pp. 224–244; Ruthanne Lum McCunn, *A Thousand Pieces of Gold: A Biographical Novel* (San Francisco: Design Enterprises of San Francisco, 1981); Judy Yung, " 'A Bowlful of Tears.' " On the Japanese, in addition to the work of Sylvia Yanagisako (see note 13), see Glenn, "The Dialectics of Wage Work," and *Issei, Nisei, War Bride*; Ichioka, "Ameyuki-San" and "*Amerika Nadeshiko*"; Matsumoto, "Japanese-American Women during World War II." On Asian-American

women, see the bibliography compiled by Vicki Ruiz, in DuBois and Ruiz, *Unequal Sisters*.

51. This was less true after 1930, when women immigrants began to outnumber men. An argument can be made that it is also important to view immigrant men in more of a family context than is customary.

52. On this point, see Rosaldo and Lamphere, *Woman, Culture and Society*, pp. 8, 36.

53. Although there is a growing literature on the role of immigrant women in small businesses, this is not included in the general studies. See, for example, Ivan H. Light, *Ethnic Enterprises in America: Business and Welfare among Chinese, Japanese and Blacks* (Berkeley: University of California Press, 1972); Edna Bonacich and John Modell, *The Economic Basis of Ethnic Solidarity: Small Business in the Japanese-American Community* (Berkeley: University of California Press, 1980). More recently, in Ivan Light and Edna Bonacich's *Immigrant Entrepreneurs: Koreans in Los Angeles, 1965–1982* (Berkeley: University of California Press, 1989), women are mentioned only once in the index, and the text notes that although more than 60 percent of Korean immigrants were women, fewer women than men were entrepreneurs. However, in the conclusions, the authors note that because so many Korean women work and bear the double burden of wage work and housework, many families had great problems (p. 431). This is not, however, considered in the text.

54. On this point, see Sinke, "A Historiography of Immigrant Women," pp. 132–133.

55. As Joan Scott has observed (see *Gender and the Politics of History*, p. 206, n. 32), "There is a difference between describing a society's attribution of status to particular groups and reflecting that status without comment or ignoring it entirely. In the first case, the historian takes the construction of inequality as part of the story to be recounted; in the second, he or she accepts inequality as a 'natural' or inevitable fact, and, in effect, removes its construction from historical consideration." The only early general study of ethnic history to include women's roles was Maxine Seller's *To Seek America: A History of Ethnic Life in the United States* (New York: Jerome W. Ozer, 1977). A new revised edition has just been published.

56. DuBois et al., *Feminist Scholarship*, pp. 185–186, 189.

57. See "Statement of Purpose," and Joan Hoff-Wilson and Christie Farnham, "Editors' Note and Acknowledgments," in *Journal of Women's History* 1 (Spring 1989): 8, 11.

58. Leonore Davidoff and Catherine Hall, *Family Fortunes: Men and Women of the English Middle Class, 1780–1850* (Chicago: University of Chicago Press, 1987). Although this book is not about immigrants or the working class, it still raises valid questions applicable to immigration history.

59. For an explanation of the significance of Davidoff and Hall's work to literary critics as well as to historians, see Judith Newton, "*Family Fortunes*: 'New History' and 'New Historicism,' " *Radical History Review* 43 (Winter 1989): 5–32.

60. Gabaccia, "*The Transplanted*: Women and Family in Immigrant America."

61. This is feasible when it is possible to do oral histories among members of the immigrant group.

62. Sherry Ortner, "Is Female to Male as Nature Is to Culture?" in Rosaldo

and Lamphere, *Woman, Culture and Society*, p. 69; Louise Lamphere, "Strategies, Cooperation, and Conflict among Women in Domestic Groups," in ibid., pp. 99–100; Jane Collier, "Women in Politics," in ibid.

63. Cecile Dauphin et al., "Women's Culture and Women's Power: An Attempt at Historiography," *Journal of Women's History* 1 (Spring 1989): 66, 68, 83.

64. Scott, *Gender and the Politics of History*, pp. 6, 10.

65. Joan Kelly-Gadol, "The Social Relations of the Sexes," *SIGNS* 1 (1976): 809–823.

66. Scott, *Gender and the Politics of History*, pp. 16–17.

67. "Politics cannot be separated from the culture and social arrangements in which it is grounded and which in turn it shapes." Marilyn J. Boxer and Jean H. Quataert, *Connecting Spheres: Women in the Western World, 1500 to the Present* (New York: Oxford University Press, 1987), p. 102. See also Scott, *Gender and the Politics of History*, pp. 16–17; Linda Kerber, "Separate Spheres, Female Worlds, Woman's Place: The Rhetoric of Women's History," *Journal of American History* 75, 1 (1988): 9–39.

68. On this point, see Sinke, "A Historiography of Immigrant Women," pp. 130–131.

69. Hyman, "Immigrant Women and Consumer Protest."

70. Paula Hyman, "Culture and Gender: Women in the Immigrant Jewish Community," in David Berger, ed., *The Legacy of Jewish Immigration* (New York: Brooklyn College Press, 1983 [distributed by Columbia University Press]), p. 164. See also Hyman, "Gender and Jewish History," in *Tikkun* (January 1988): 35–38.

71. Zunz, *Reliving the Past*, pp. 82, 92.

72. George Pozzetta, "Immigrants and Ethnics: The State of Italian-American Historiography," *Journal of American Ethnic History* 9 (Fall 1989): 67–95.

73. On this point, see Gabaccia, *"The Transplanted*: Women and Family in Immigrant America," p. 248.

74. Weinberg, *The World of Our Mothers*; see also Weinberg, "Jewish Mothers and Immigrant Daughters."

75. As opposed to the specific consideration of women's lives alone.

76. Yans-McLaughlin, *Family and Community*; Gabaccia, *From Sicily to Elizabeth Street*; Smith, *Family Connections*; Anker, "Women, Work and Family" and "Family, Work and Community"; Kleinberg, *The Shadow of the Mills*; Deutsch, *No Separate Refuge*. Deutsch's study includes both immigrant women from Mexico and ethnic women of Hispanic descent whose families had lived in the Southwest for many generations.

77. See Yans-McLaughlin, *Family and Community*.

78. Smith, *Family Connections*; Anker, "Women, Work and Family."

79. Gabaccia, *From Sicily to Elizabeth Street*.

80. Nancy Foner, *Jamaica Farewell: Jamaican Migrants in London* (Berkeley: University of California Press, 1978). See also Pedraza, "Women and Migration."

81. Kleinberg, *The Shadow of the Mills*, p. 230.

82. Deutsch, *No Separate Refuge*, p. 61.

2

Sociology and Immigrant Women

Rita J. Simon

This chapter brings together two topics that are currently fashionable intellectually and professionally: immigration and women. Twenty-five years ago, neither topic aroused much interest in the scholarly and professional marketplace. From different sources and for different reasons, both have emerged as important research and public policy issues. As Nancy Foner observed, "Migrant women have emerged from academic invisibility.... Female migrants ... have become a recognized presence."[1]

Immigration as a topic for research has emerged largely because public policymakers, after a long hiatus, are debating immigration issues, and new standards and policies are being enacted. Indeed, the U.S. Congress on October 27, 1990, passed the first major immigration bill since 1965. The bill represents the first comprehensive revision of legal immigration in sixty-six years. It would increase the number of immigrants admitted per year from 540,000 to 700,000 for at least the first three years, and it would more than double the number of immigrants allowed entry because of their job skills. In addition, more than half of the visas would be set aside for families of U.S. citizens and permanent residents.

Social scientists and public policy analysts began focusing on immigration some thirty years ago when the first group of Cuban refugees was admitted to the United States following the Castro takeover in Cuba. The Cubans were among an early group of refugees to be admitted to the United States in the post–World War II era. Shortly before the Cubans were admitted, a few thousand Hungarians came in under refugee auspices following the 1956 revolt. After the first group of Cubans, Vietnamese, Soviet Jews, more Cubans, and other Hispanics from Central American countries were admitted as refugees in the 1970s and 1980s. In addition to refugees, there have been growing numbers of immigrants coming across the border from Central American countries and Mexico and from the Philippines, Korea, and other Asian countries.

The establishment of a Presidential Commission on Immigration in 1981 to study the social, economic, and cultural impact of immigrants on American society and to make recommendations about numbers and conditions of admission also contributed to an intellectual reawakening of the importance of immigrants to American society. Thus, over the past decade, studies resulting in numerous monographs and articles on immigrant entrepreneurs, on the adjustment and absorption of refugees, on the social mobility of various immigrant groups, on language facility, and on immigrant children's academic success have appeared in great numbers.

Along with a revitalization of intellectual interest in immigration, there has also been a good deal of ferment at the societal and community action level. Great numbers of organizations, almost all of which have assumed a restrictive or anti-immigrant stance, have appeared on the scene. The major explicit argument made by most of these organizations has been that more people are bad for the country. Immigrants are people, and people pollute and endanger the environment. Also creeping into some of the anti-immigrant rhetoric have been subtle warnings that have racist overtones, for example, in the use of phrases such as "the browning of America." The print and electronic media have also paid much more attention to immigration in recent years, albeit often in negative terms, with descriptions of illegals crossing our borders, taking jobs from natives, carrying diseases, or distributing drugs.

Tracing the development of interest and work on women migrants by sociologists involves recognition of the importance of the appearance of a women's movement in the United States in the late 1960s. In part, as a function of the visibility of that movement, interest in topics about women, funding for research on women's issues, and publications dealing with all aspects of women's lives skyrocketed. Any topic concerning women was considered intellectually interesting and important, and highly marketable. Thus, universities developed women studies curricula, and publishers organized series and produced monographs on women in the work force, in politics, and in education. Professional societies arranged sessions on various aspects of women's roles and statuses in the United States and the rest of the world. The spate of recent work by sociologists on women migrants can be explained easily by the enormous popularity that any topic on women receives, but coupled with the renewed interest in immigration, it is all the more obvious why sociologists have been paying so much attention to patterns of female migration.

With these explanations as background, it is important to note that the current sociological studies of immigrants tend to have a somewhat different focus and to employ different methods than the work done during the earlier rich period of immigration research in the 1920s and 1930s. Many of the studies emanating from that period were done by the Chicago school of sociology. Scholars from that school focused on patterns of adaptation, acculturation, and assimilation by different immigrant communities into the larger American society. The methods for studying these communities were often observational and relied on life histories in the form of letters, diaries, and direct first-person accounts that explained transitions and passages in individual lives, in families, and in larger units. Studies were done of conflicts between immigrant parents and their first-generation American-born offspring. Accounts were reported of how quickly and in what form different immigrant communities became Americanized through loss of accents, change of names, style of dress, choice of foods, and movement into nonethnic neighborhoods. The unit of analysis was often the family or an entire immigrant community that had recently established itself in an urban neighborhood. Thomas and Znaniecki's *The Polish Peasant in Europe and America* is one of the classics that emerged from that era.[2]

The revival of interest in immigrants in the 1970s and 1980s did not restore the earlier research agenda either substantively or methodologically. The issues today tend to be different than they were sixty and seventy years ago, and the methods have changed as well. Today, economic issues are more likely to be the dependent variables. Thus, data on labor force participation, educational background, job skills, work ethic, income, and mobility are collected through surveys or from sources such as the census. The focus is more on individual behavior, which is then aggregated, than on families or whole communities. There are fewer observational studies, and researchers are less dependent on subjective accounts.

When women are the focus, economic variables still play an important role. But fertility patterns and changing roles within the family and vis-à-vis the host society are special topics for female migrants. The methods employed are usually the same whether the target population is male or female, and the unit of analysis also tends to be the individual, irrespective of gender.[3]

In the sections that follow I discuss some of the major issues that have been researched about female migrants in the past two decades using data that bear primarily on immigration into the United States. A fact that often goes unnoticed or unreported is that more women than men have immigrated to the United States over the past sixty years, from the 1930s to the present. The predominance of female migrants over males is a phenomenon unique to the United States. In none of the other major receiving nations, for example, Canada, Australia, New Zealand, and Israel, does this pattern prevail. The female predominance in immigration to the United States is portrayed in Table 2.1.

The predominance ranges from 51.4 percent to 74.9 percent. The latter occurred in 1947 and is attributable largely to the migration of war brides, that is, wives of U.S. servicemen stationed overseas following the Second World War. From January 1946 through December 1948, 112,882 war brides were admitted to the United States. They accounted for almost 25 percent of all immigration for these three years.

But the countries from which over 50 percent of the migrants entering the United States are women are not limited to a small sample or a short period of time. As shown in Table 2.2, over seventy countries are represented, spread over many parts of the world. European, Asian, and Latin American countries are represented. The countries that fall below 50 percent are more likely to be in Africa and the Middle East. Indeed, the countries sending the largest number of female immigrants tend to be among those from which the largest numbers of male immigrants come as well: Mexico, the Philippines, and Korea are cases in point.

Like their male counterparts, most female migrants are under 35 years of age. Between the ages of 15 and 29, female migrants tend to outnumber males, especially within the 20-to-24 age category. A higher percentage of female than male migrants tend to be married: 71 percent as opposed to 66.4 percent.

Although at the time of arrival a much smaller percentage of female than male migrants are likely to report an occupation or labor market experience (77.4 percent for men compared to 34 percent for women), once women are in the United States, female immigrant participation in the labor force increases dramatically, for example, in 1970, 46.5 percent compared to 41.6 percent of native U.S. women. Looking at a breakdown of the occupations reported by natives and immigrant women, immigrant women are almost twice as likely to report professional occupations as are native women. Table 2.3 compares immigrant and native women by specific occupational categories.

Note that immigrant women are more likely than native women to be represented in the highest and lowest occupational categories. For example, 28.1 percent of immigrant women were employed as professionals compared to 16.1 percent of native female labor force, and 13.9 percent of immigrant women worked as domestics as opposed to 2.6 of native women. The same pattern appears, although not as dramatically, when comparisons are made between male immigrants and natives. For example, we see that 22.4 percent of male immigrants work in professional positions as opposed to 5.1 percent of natives, and 12 percent of male immigrants are employed as laborers as opposed to 7.3 percent of male natives. The greater concentration of both female and male

Table 2.1
Immigration to the United States, by Sex, 1930–1979

	Both Sexes	Males	Females	Percent Female
1930-39	699,375	312,716	386,659	55.3
1930	241,700	117,026	124,674	51.6
1931	97,139	40,621	56,518	58.2
1932	35,576	13,917	21,659	60.9
1933	23,068	9,219	13,849	60.0
1934	29,470	12,101	17,369	58.9
1935	34,956	14,010	20,946	59.9
1936	36,329	14,775	21,553	59.3
1937	50,244	21,664	28,580	56.9
1938	67,895	29,959	37,936	55.9
1939	82,998	39,423	43,575	52.5
1940-49	856,608	332,317	524,291	61.2
1940	70,756	33,460	37,296	52.7
1941	51,776	23,519	28,257	54.6
1942	28,781	12,008	16,773	58.3
1943	23,725	9,825	13,900	58.6
1944	28,551	11,410	17,141	60.0
1945	38,119	13,389	24,730	64.9
1946	108,721	27,275	81,446	74.9
1947	147,292	53,769	93,523	63.5
1948	170,570	67,322	103,248	60.5
1949	188,317	80,340	107,977	57.3
1950-59	2,499,268	1,157,864	1,341,404	53.7
1950	249,187	119,130	130,057	52.2
1951	205,717	99,327	106,390	51.7
1952	265,520	123,609	141,911	53.4
1953	170,434	73,073	97,361	57.1
1954	208,177	95,594	112,583	54.1
1955	237,790	112,032	125,758	52.9
1956	321,625	156,410	165,215	51.4
1957	326,867	155,201	171,666	52.5
1958	253,265	109,121	144,144	56.9
1959	260,686	114,367	146,319	56.1

Table 2.1 (continued)

	Both Sexes	Males	Females	Percent Female
1960-69	3,213,749	1,427,308	1,786,441	55.6
1960	265,398	116,687	148,711	56.0
1961	271,344	121,380	149,964	55.3
1962	283,763	131,575	152,188	53.6
1963	306,260	139,297	166,963	54.5
1964	292,248	126,214	166,034	56.8
1965	296,697	127,171	169,526	57.1
1966	323,040	141,456	181,584	56.2
1967	361,972	158,324	203,648	56.3
1968	454,448	199,732	254,716	56.0
1969	358,579	165,472	193,107	53.9
1970-79	4,336,001	2,036,292	2,299,709	53.0
1970	373,326	176,990	196,336	52.6
1971	370,478	172,528	197,950	53.4
1972	384,685	179,715	204,970	53.3
1973	400,063	186,320	213,743	53.4
1974	394,861	184,518	210,343	53.3
1975	386,194	180,741	205,453	53.2
1976	398,613	184,863	213,750	53.6
1976	103,676	48,283	55,393	53.4
1977	462,315	216,424	245,891	53.2
1978	601,442	286,374	315,068	52.4
1979	460,348	219,536	240,812	52.3

Source:

1911-32: U.S. Department of Labor, <u>Annual Reports of the Commissioner General of Immigration</u> (Washington, D.C.: U.S. Government Printing Office, 1911-1932).

1933-77: U.S. Immigration and Naturalization Service, <u>Annual Reports of the Immigration and Naturalization Service</u> (Washington, D.C.: U.S. Government Printing Office, 1941-1977).

1978-79: U.S. Immigration and Naturalization Service, <u>Statistical Yearbooks of the Immigration and Naturalization Service</u> (Washington, D.C.: U.S. Government Printing Office, 1978-1979).

Table 2.2
**Distribution of Countries of Origin of Immigrants to the United States, by
Percent of Female Immigrants, Fiscal Years 1972–1979**

	Percent Female	Total Immigration
Finland	72.4	2,638
Germany	72.1	51,878
Thailand	68.7	37,025
Japan	66.8	38,363
Panama	64.3	17,619
Pacific Isl. Trust Terr.	64.2	1,551
Iceland	62.6	1,093
Sweden	62.4	4,914
Korea	60.8	225,339
Nicaragua	60.8	10,101
Honduras	60.5	13,537
Philippines	59.9	289,429
Belgium	59.7	3,133
Brazil	59.7	10,675
Singapore	59.4	1,964
Australia	59.0	11,417
El Salvador	59.0	26,490
Denmark	58.5	3,509
Malaysia	58.0	3,494
Costa Rica	57.9	9,607
France	57.7	13,851
New Zealand	56.9	4,148
Netherlands	56.6	8.385
Colombia	56.2	59,829
Paraguay	56.2	1,206
Guatemala	55.7	19,629
United Kingdom	55.6	97,274
Canada	55.5	88,108
Belize	55.3	5,797
Montserrat	54.9	1,575
Cuba	54.8	140,119
Grenada	54.8	6,206
Poland	54.6	35,910
Ireland	54.5	11,510
Austria	54.4	3,635
Norway	54.0	3,175
Bermuda	53.9	1,596
Indonesia	53.8	4,831
Bolivia	53.0	5,062
Ecuador	53.0	39,047
China (Taiwan and Mainland)	52.8	160,454
Barbados	52.7	16,550

Table 2.2 (continued)

	Percent Female	Total Immigration
Trinidad and Tobago	52.7	49,492
Dominican Republic	52.5	118,147
Switzerland	52.5	5,066
Venezuela	52.4	5,544
Guyana	52.3	30,035
Peru	52.3	23,991
Haiti	52.3	44,721
Macau	52.2	1,810
Hong Kong	52.0	40,438
Jamaica	51.8	108,454
Burma	51.6	7,570
Cape Verde	51.6	4,560
Chile	51.4	14,078
USSR	51.4	31,951
St. Kitts Nevis	51.3	5,229
Anguilla	51.1	1,045
St. Vincent and Grenadines	51.1	3,678
Antigua-Barbuda	50.8	4,803
Kenya	50.8	3,582
Bahamas	50.5	3,447
Czechoslovakia	50.5	7,304
Netherlands Antilles	50.5	2,202
Vietnam	50.4	134,160
Zimbabwe	50.4	1,018
British Virgin Islands	50.2	2,561
Dominica	50.1	3,519
Tanzania	50.0	2,467
Turkey	50.0	14,599
Uruguay	49.9	6,487
Fiji	49.7	5,299
Spain	49.7	23,962
Yugoslavia	49.6	33,952
Argentina	49.5	20,321
Portugal	49.5	84,394
Sri Lanka	49.5	3,230
Western Samoa	49.4	3,097
Malta	49.3	2,010

Table 2.2 (continued)

	Percent Female	Total Immigration
St. Lucia	49.2	3,512
South Africa	49.2	9,124
Cyprus	49.0	3,610
Mexico	49.0	530,378
Zambia	49.0	1,127
Italy	48.7	102,528
Uganda	48.3	2,930
India	48.0	139,834
Hungary	48.0	9,213
Romania	47.8	13,924
Angola	47.7	1,229
Egypt	47.7	19,019
Laos	47.3	8,572
Morocco	47.0	3,575
Tonga	46.0	4,371
Greece	45.9	73,104
Kuwait	45.4	1,234
Israel	45.2	21,343
Syria	45.1	10,730
Iraq	44.6	19,515
Ethiopia	44.4	2,774
Kampuchea	44.1	5,604
Jordan	43.1	23,668
Lebanon	43.1	27,843
Pakistan	42.5	24,857
Bangladesh	42.0	3,322
Iran	41.0	33,331
Bulgaria	40.5	1,854
Liberia	40.0	1,858
Afghanistan	34.4	1,258
Ghana	34.1	3,854
Nigeria	32.3	6,420
Yemen (Sanaa)	13.2	4,446

Source: Unpublished tabulations based on Immigration and Naturalization Service's Public Use Tapes for immigrants (complete enumeration) for fiscal years 1972-1979.

Note: Data are by country of birth. Table includes all countries with 100 or more immigrants admitted to the United States during the period.

Table 2.3
Percent Distribution of Occupations of 1979 Employed U.S. Workers and Reported At-Entry Occupations of Fiscal Years 1972–1979 Immigrants, by Sex

	U.S. Employed			Percent Female
	Both Sexes	Males	Females	
White Collar	50.9%	41.2%	64.4%	52.7%
Professional, technical and kindred workers	15.5	15.1	16.1	43.3
Managers and administrators	10.8	14.0	6.4	24.7
Sales workers	6.4	6.0	6.9	45.1
Clerical and kindred	18.2	6.1	35.0	80.3
Blue Collar	33.1	46.3	14.6	18.4
Craft and kindred	13.3	21.5	1.8	5.7
Operatives	11.3	11.6	10.8	39.9
Transport operatives	3.7	5.9	.7	.7
Nonfarm laborers	4.8	7.3	1.3	11.3
Service	13.2	8.5	19.8	62.3
Service, except private household	12.1	8.5	17.2	59.1
Private household	1.1	--	2.6	97.5
Farm workers	2.8	3.9	1.2	18.0
Farmers and managers	1.5	2.3	0.3	9.6
Farm laborers and supervisors	1.3	1.6	0.9	27.5
Total number (in thousands)	98,824	57,607	41,217	41.7

Table 2.3 (continued)

	Immigrants			Percent Female
	Both Sexes	Males	Females	
White Collar	44.1	40.0	52.0	40.4
Professional, technical and kindred workers	24.3	22.4	29.1	39.5
Managers and administrators	7.6	9.6	3.7	16.8
Sales workers	2.4	2.5	2.2	31.7
Clerical and kindred	9.8	5.5	18.0	62.9
Blue Collar	36.5	43.4	23.3	21.9
Craft and kindred	12.0	17.2	2.1	5.9
Operatives	13.6	11.4	17.9	45.1
Transport operatives	1.9	2.8	0.2	3.1
Nonfarm laborers	9.0	12.0	3.2	12.2
Service	14.7	10.2	23.4	54.4
Service, except private household	9.8	10.0	9.5	33.2
Private household	4.9	0.2	13.9	96.7
Farm workers	4.6	6.3	1.3	9.8
Farmers and managers	.3	0.4	1.3	14.2
Farm laborers and supervisors	4.3	5.9	0.1	9.5
Total number (in thousands)	1,432	941	491	34.3

Source: U.S. Department of Labor, 1983, Tables 16 and 26. Unpublished tabulations based on the U.S. Immigration and Naturalization Service's public-use tapes for immigrants (complete enumeration) for fiscal years 1972-1979.

Note: Percentages may not add to 100 percent due to rounding.

Table 2.4
Percentage of the Population (Aged 25 Years or Over) with High and Low Education: U.S. Natives and Immigrants, 1980

	Natives	Immigrants, Arrived 1970–1980
Four-year college education	8.7%	9.7%
Five or more years college education	7.5	12.5
Less than five years elementary school education	2.9	12.8

Source: Julian Simon, <u>The Economic Consequences of Immigration</u> (Cambridge, Mass.: Basil Blackwell, 1990), p. 39.

immigrants at the extremes of the occupational hierarchy is a reflection of the immigrants' educational backgrounds. Like their occupational distributions, male and female immigrants are more likely to be represented at the extremes of high and low years of schooling than are natives, as seen in Table 2.4.

Data from the 1976 Survey of Income and Education show that adult immigrants who arrived between 1965 and 1974 had three-quarters of a year less education than the average number of years reported by natives in the labor force.

In sum, much of the sociological discussion of female immigrants in the 1970s and 1980s has focused on demographic and labor force characteristics. Those characteristics have been compared against male immigrants and female natives. Data on fertility patterns of immigrant versus native women have been examined, largely as one indication of the importance of culture as a differential characteristic among immigrant cohorts. The argument is usually phrased as follows: Women in less developed countries give birth to more children than women in Western European countries and the United States. For how long after female immigrants arrive in the United States are the differences in fertility patterns between foreign-born and native women likely to continue? To the extent that they exist throughout the subject's childbearing years and are passed on to future generations of daughters, cultural traits would be deemed important. But suppose the gap between the immigrant women's birth rates and those of natives grows increasingly smaller and suppose it is nonexistent in the next generation. Such a trend would diminish the importance or persistence of cultural differ-

Table 2.5
Children per 1,000 Women in the United States, 1970

Age	Native Women, Native Parentage	Foreign-Born Women	Native Women, Mixed/ Foreign Parentage
15-24	364	413	306
25-44	2,565	2,141	2,522
45-64	2,530	2,534	2,177
65-74	2,479	2,518	2,064
75+	2,762	3,284	2,390

Source: U.S. Bureau of the Census. 1980 Census of Population. (Washington, D.C.: U.S. Department of Commerce, 1982).

Table 2.6
Children per 1,000 Women in the United States, 1980

	Native	Foreign-Born		
		Total	Immigrated 1970-1980	Immigrated before 1970
Age 25-44	2,652	2,509	2,571	2,478

Source: U.S. Bureau of the Census. 1980 Census of Population. (Washington, D.C.: U.S. Department of Commerce, 1982).

ences. The data in Tables 2.5 and 2.6 show that foreign-born women in the 25–44 age categories have fewer children than native women and that native women of mixed or foreign-born parentage in all age categories (except age 25–44) have fewer children than foreign-born or native women. Cultural differences, thus, do not seem to persist and are thus not likely to have long-term implications.

To review the picture that has begun to form of immigrant women in the United States, we have found that most of them arrive when they are between the ages of 15 and 29 years of age. They have a bimodal educational distribution such that more of them are at the higher and lower educational levels than are native women. Once they have migrated to the United States, they are more likely to work outside their homes than are native women. Over 70 percent are married at the time of arrival. They have about the same number of children as native women.

A theme that is distinctive to work that has been done on female migrants concerns the basis for the double and triple oppression/discrimination models. Briefly, the thesis these models set forth is that women immigrants move from traditional cultures to modern cultures and that prior to their migration, they never worked outside their homes. The oppression or discrimination model posits that as migrant workers women are oppressed by virtue of their class, by virtue of their status as foreigners, and by virtue of their gender. They are oppressed vis-à-vis natives, vis-à-vis employers, and vis-à-vis men. Are there data that bear out or support these assumptions?

A review of the literature indicates a more complex situation. Studies of Muslim female migrants to France; Turkish migrants to Germany; and Mexican, Jamaican, Cuban, and Vietnamese migrants to the United States suggest that women enhance their roles and statuses as a function of their migration. Yolanda Prieto explains Cuban women's high labor force participation as follows:

The strongest factor behind the intense economic activity of Cuban women (as that of Cubans in general) is the combination of middle-class values and a strong anti-Communist ideology. These strong beliefs, common to refugees from socialist countries, are manifested in a strong work ethic and aspirations for social mobility. Primarily to compensate for the lost rewards in their home country, these migrants justify the massive entrance of women into paid production.[4]

Muslim women take on more public ceremonial roles in their host country than they performed in their country of origin. In her account of Algerian families in France, Sossie Andezian described the changes in the roles of Algerian wives in part as a function of the absence of mothers-in-law and other individuals that make up the traditional extended female kinship network. According to Andezian, Algerian wives assume a greater role in the decisions concerning their children's education and health, their children's matrimonial choices, and their own relations to the host society and their home country. The Algerian women participate in and have access to a public world that had previously been reserved primarily for men. It is the Algerian women in France who must contend with various services such as education and health in government agencies, for the hours of such agencies are such that their husbands, who are working outside their homes, do not have the time to attend. These women learn that they cannot rely on husbands, who are often equally illiterate and who have little leisure time to interact with the French bureaucracy. The women have also assumed roles as religious leaders, butchers who sell lawful meat, shopkeepers of ritual clothes, tenants of public baths necessary for purification rites, and singers of ritual chants who perform during feasts and familial events (e.g., births, circumcisions, weddings). In Andezian's words,

Contrary to the belief that Algerian women in France are increasingly enclosed in the domestic world, immigration has placed them in contact with the exterior world almost of necessity.... Immigration reveals that the production of sense and the creation of a new symbolic order is widely due to the participation of women.[5]

In her account of East African Sikh women in London, Parminder Bhachu describes their extensive involvement in community and religious activities. She contrasts the stereotypes of the submissive and secluded Asian women against the East African Sikh women in London and emphasizes the freedom they have and the time they spend on women's activities. Bhachu credits their involvement in public activities to the women's participation in the labor force, about which she writes:

Although migrant women are mostly in the "dirtiest and lowest paid jobs,"... wage labor has a strong impact on both the negotiation of power within the domestic sphere and on specific traditional patterns. Asian women in Britain have acquired greater control over cash than they ever had in the past, whether in India or East Africa.... The women ... constantly emphasized their delight at the acquisition of a potent commodity like money, which previously they had to look to their men folk to attain.[6]

Turkish women in Germany become more actively involved in the education their children receive in the German school system than they do in their homeland.[7] Mexican women migrants to the United States participate more prominently in immigrant community affairs than they participated in public life in Mexico.

In Nancy Foner's account of the situation of Jamaican women in New York and London, she emphasized the "new kind of freedom" that many of these women claim to enjoy in their new lives. Especially women in white-collar occupations reported opportunities to develop their potential "in a way that would not have been possible for them as women at home." Foner describes the new opportunities they see "to expand their cultural horizons through the theater, concerts, and films, and of the opportunities in New York to pursue their interests and lead their lives without the eyes and censure of the local community so closely upon them."[8]

These are some examples of enhanced private and public status that

Table 2.7
Mothers' and Daughters' Expectations about the Highest Degree Daughters Will Attain, by Ethnic Community

	Mothers		
	Soviet	Vietnamese	American
Less than B.A.	20%	52%	40%
B.A.	44	36	30
More than B.A.	36	12	30
	Daughters		
	Soviet	Vietnamese	American
Less than B.A.	18%	42%	42%
B.A.	38	34	34
More than B.A.	44	24	24

female migrants achieve as a function of their emigration. Contrary to popular assumptions, many female migrants to more developed countries have worked outside their homes in their country of origin. Nevertheless, the likelihood is that they will join the labor force in their host country in much greater numbers. And, while their wages in the first few years of their migration will be lower than those of female natives, there are studies that indicate that women migrants enter the labor force in their host countries sooner than male migrants emigrating from the same country and that the women earn more in wages than the men. Indeed, it is the changes in roles within immigrant families that often provide female migrants with higher status and more visibility in their host community than they achieved in their countries of origin. The enhancement in status that the migrant women obtain reverberates onto the next generation.

Studies I have done on the expectations that Soviet and Vietnamese women migrants have for their daughters show that they are higher, or as high as, the expectations and aspirations that native mothers hold for their daughters in the United States.[9] The surveys were conducted of Vietnamese and Soviet refugees within two years after their arrival in the United States in the 1970s. All of the respondents (100 in each community), including the United States citizens, were living in Chicago

Table 2.8
Mothers' and Daughters' Expectations about Daughters' Future Work, by Ethnic Community

	Mothers		
	Soviet	Vietnamese	American
Professional	58%	24%	10%
White Collar	10	14	28
Skilled	6	8	–
Unskilled/ Service	–	–	–
No Answer/Don't Know	26	34	24

	Daughters		
	Soviet	Vietnamese	American
Professional	56%	36%	34%
White Collar	14	18	26
Skilled	10	12	6
Unskilled/ Service	–	–	–
No Answer/Don't Know	20	32	34

at the time of the survey. Table 2.7 describes the educational aspirations and Table 2.8 the occupational aspirations immigrant and native mothers and daughters have for their daughters' futures. Among the mothers who wanted their daughters to be professionals, the Soviet and Vietnamese mothers were more likely to want them to be engineers and doctors; the native mothers hoped their daughters would become teachers and nurses, more traditional female occupations.

CONCLUSION

While this chapter has focused heavily on the United States, many of the findings about female migrants would generalize to other immigrant-receiving societies such as Canada, Australia, and New Zealand. For example, women immigrants are more likely to be in the labor force than are native women in all of those countries, and they are more likely to assume public roles in their host countries than they did in their countries of origin. The female migrant is an important research topic because immigration and women are highly marketable as well as intellectually challenging topics for study. Both issues have important and far-ranging public policy implications.

NOTES

1. Nancy Foner, "Sex Roles and Sensibilities: Jamaican Women in New York and London," in Simon and Brettell, *International Migration*, pp. 133–152, 133.

2. William Thomas and Florian Znaniecki, *The Polish Peasant in Europe and America*, ed. Eli Zaretsky (Urbana: University of Illinois Press, 1984).

3. Julian L. Simon, *The Economic Consequences of Immigration* (Cambridge, Mass.: Basil Blackwell, 1989).

4. Yolanda Prieto, "Cuban Women in New Jersey," in Simon and Brettell, *International Migration*, pp. 95–113, 110.

5. Sossie Andezian, "Women's Roles in Organizing Symbolic Life: Algerian Female Immigrants in France," in Simon and Brettell, *International Migration*, pp. 257–258, 265.

6. Parminder K. Bhachu, "Work, Dowry and Marriage among East African Sikh Women in the United Kingdom," in Simon and Brettell, *International Migration*, pp. 229–241, 231.

7. F. James Davis and Barbara S. Heyl, "Turkish Women and Guestworker Migration to West Germany," in Simon and Brettell, *International Migration*," pp. 178–197.

8. Foner, "Sex Roles and Sensibilities," pp. 145–146.

9. Rita J. Simon, "Refugee Women and Their Daughters: A Comparison of Soviet, Vietnamese, and Native-Born American Families," in Carolyn L. Williams and Joseph Westermeyer, eds., *Refugee Mental Health in Resettlement Countries* (Washington: Hemisphere Publishing, 1986), pp. 157–172.

3

Anthropology and the Study of Immigrant Women

Caroline B. Brettell and Patricia A. deBerjeois

In 1970, the meeting of the American Ethnological Society focused on the topic "Migration and Anthropology."[1] In his introduction to the volume of proceedings, Leonard Kasdan rightly observed that although migration had long been recognized as an important factor of change in a number of social science disciplines, anthropology had not defined it as a topic of research with high priority. However, changes in the world in the 1950s and 1960s brought migration onto the center stage of the discipline. In a range of areas where ethnographers had traditionally worked among native or peasant populations, for example, Africa, Latin America, and Asia, they began to document the process of outmigration from the villages of the rural countryside to the growing urban centers where new employment opportunities were expanding rapidly.[2] The interest in migrants and immigrants grew in conjunction with the development of both peasant studies and urban anthropology.

By 1975, two of the volumes that were published in the series that emerged from the Ninth International Congress of Anthropological and Ethnological Sciences treated migration and its relationship to processes of urbanization, development, and ethnic group formation.[3] Though the chapters in these volumes deal with a number of issues in a wide variety of migratory contexts, only passing references, if any, are made to the role of women in migration. Indeed, there is no entry in either index for "women" or "female." As numerous scholars have pointed out, the assumption was that women, if they left their home society at all, did so as passive followers rather than as active initiators. Furthermore, the modernization theories that were still prevalent at the time stressed emigration or outmigration as matters of individual choice rather than as household strategies with which women were intimately involved.[4]

Stimulated, no doubt, by the publication in 1974 of Rosaldo and Lamphere's path-breaking *Women, Culture and Society*, a book that brought gender as an analytic concept into the mainstream of anthropology, the journal *Anthropological Quarterly* published a special issue, "Women and Migration," in January of 1976. In each of the papers in the volume, migrant and immigrant women are not only viewed as actors in the migration process but also are set into networks of exchange of people, goods, services, and information. The authors demonstrate that women are as influenced as men by the forces of colonialism, socialism, and capitalism.

Despite Leeds's claim in the closing essay of this special issue that women were being spuriously reified as a unit of analysis, from this point on a number of anthropologists chose to address the experiences of migrant and immigrant women in a range of receiving societies, including Europe and the United States.[5] Using a variety of research methods (participant observation, the collection of life histories and case studies, in-depth interviews, etc.) to access how the women themselves understand their lives and the challenges posed by migration, they focused on how these experiences might differ from those of men and how geographical mobility, both within and across national boundaries, might alter not only culturally rooted understandings of what it means to be a woman, but also various other aspects of culture that individuals and families bring with them as they migrate or emigrate.

In this chapter, we will review the anthropological contribution to the study of immigrant women, addressing ourselves in particular to research on a range of immigrant populations in the United States.[6] Taking our lead from some of the analytic models that have emerged in feminist anthropology, we first discuss the work roles of immigrant women, how these intersect with domestic and familial roles, and the implications of this intersection for changes in the status of women. From there we move to a consideration of the significance of kinship and other social relationships that are instrumental in the process of adaptation for immigrant women. We then deal with research that broadly treats the question of culture change. After a brief overview of the factors that continue to tie a given migrant population to its ethnic roots over generations, we turn our attention to the wealth of studies within medical anthropology that have contributed to our understanding of immigrant women in the United States. Finally, we address the impact of the state on the lives of immigrant women.

PUBLIC AND PRIVATE, PRODUCTION AND REPRODUCTION: BALANCING WORK ROLES AND DOMESTIC ROLES

As a result of their inquiry into the question of whether women are universally subordinate to men, cultural anthropologists have contributed the domestic/public model to feminist theory. Embedded in this model are the notions that male activities in the public sphere are more highly valued, that men have formal authority over women while women exert informal influence and power within the domestic domain, and that women's status is lowest where these spheres are highly differentiated and where women are isolated from one another.[7] A parallel model emanating from Marxism analyzes the interrelationship between production and reproduction.[8] Feminist theorists have stressed that the way in which women's reproductive labor intersects with their productive labor is crucial to their position in society.

Although these models have been subjected to rigorous criticism for their lack of historical or cultural specificity, they have nevertheless influenced anthropological study of immigrant women in the United States.[9] They have led researchers to explore whether wage earning serves to enhance the power and status of immigrant women within their households and to investigate whether greater sharing of household activities emerges as a result of the work obligations of women. While the latter question obviously pertains to all wage-earning women, the notion is that immigrant women often not only face a clash of cultures, but may also be deprived of the support networks of kinship and community that existed in the countries they left behind.

Chai explicitly applies the conceptual scheme of domestic/public to an analysis of Korean immigrant women in Hawai'i.[10] Middle-class and well-educated, Korean immigrant women were relegated to the domestic sphere in their home society. In Hawai'i they must adjust to the economic demands of immigrant life by taking waged work outside the home. Husbands offer more help in the household than they did in Korea, but this is in part a function of age cohorts, and in many cases husbands retain ultimate authority over family decision making. However, some Korean women, according to Chai, begin to question their husbands' right to dominate them. "Women's wage earning," she concludes, "may lead to a more flexible division of labor, decision making and parental responsibility, as well as to less sex segregation in social and public places."[11] She also observes that as Korean immigrant women tire of the menial jobs to which they are relegated in the public domain of the larger society, they revert to working in family-owned businesses and construct their own public domain with its own ladder of achievement within the Korean ethnic community. Workplace and home are combined and permit these women to spend more time raising successful children who will achieve social and political status within the majority culture.

The decision to combine work roles with domestic roles, and thereby fuse the reproductive with the productive, has been documented for a number of other immigrant women in North America. Meintel, for example, shows that Portuguese women with young children tend to turn to work as cleaning women or to home piece work because the hours and conditions of work are both more flexible and less stressful.[12] She observes, however, that such an option is possible only if these women are in stable marital relationships with partners who earn a good income. Another option is described by Lamphere for Colombian and Portuguese immigrant families in New England.[13] Given the constraints of the local economy, wives and mothers are forced into the productive sphere of waged work in textile factories. As a result, reproductive labor within the household is reallocated and husbands take on many household chores that are normally defined as female tasks. In addition, husbands and wives work different shifts in order to accommodate child care. Nevertheless, some cultural conceptions, such as the belief that the male should remain the head of the household, are more resistant to change despite the economic contributions of women.

A similar disjunction between norms and behavior has been described for Haitian immigrant women in New York. Cultural definitions and expectations for sexual roles have changed less rapidly than the economic gains made by women. Furthermore, the financial independence of women exacerbates antagonism between the sexes. Haitian immigrant women put in a double day, working eight hours on the job and then coming home to housekeeping, cooking, and child care. If their husbands help, it is with reluctance because the *foye* (home) is the domain of women and it is there that a woman's primary responsibilities are located. The world of men is the *lari*—the street and beyond.[14]

If Haitian women have not experienced a dramatic reallocation of household tasks as a result of the demands made upon them by waged work, Dominican women, who are largely employed in the New York garment industry, have. Pessar describes a definite move to a more egalitarian division of labor and distribution of authority within the Dominican household.[15] She quotes one Dominican woman who comments that "we are both heads." Dominican immigrant men are willing to help out with household chores, especially child care and shopping, though their role decreases as a daughter becomes old enough to help her mother. The more cooperative domestic arrangements that emerge within many Dominican immigrant households, as well as the fact that migration does not rupture the social sphere in which women are self-actualized, are the major factors influencing the greater desire of Dominican women, by comparison with men, to remain in the United States.[16]

Within many immigrant Dominican households, income pooling, something that rarely occurs in the Dominican Republic, means that no distinction is made between the "essential" earnings of the male and the "supplementary" earnings of the female. However, this is not always the case. For example, Mexicana farm workers differentiate the "important" crops harvested by men from secondary "women's crops." Mexicana women "never express that their agricultural work is economically equivalent to men's." Instead when women work with their husbands, they define it as "*ayudandole a el.*"[17] It is in this "helping" context that women's waged work is ideologically acceptable. This is particularly the case when the household rather than the individual is defined as the basic productive (as well as reproductive) unit of the immigrant family.[18] Chavira argues that Mexicana women's roles in subsistence as well as their manipulation of the subsidy programs and other bureaucratic resources that are made available to them give them a position of power within their families.

Pessar cautions us to be aware of variations in household culture and organization that will influence individual attitudes toward women's work in the immigrant context, the sharing of domestic responsibilities, and the desire to remain abroad or return to the home country. Some Dominican immigrant men are reluctant to modify their patriarchal attitudes and behavior.[19] This intransigence is the major cause of marital breakdown. Nevertheless, a significant proportion of Dominican immigrant women feel they are better off. They perceive waged work positively because it brings both economic and personal benefits. This is a conclusion also reached by Foner in her work on Jamaican women in New York.[20] Independence and financial control are viewed as definite advantages and are a strong deterrent to return migration.

Although they are dealing with a seasonal Mexican female migrant population, Guendelman and Perez-Itriago document similar positive subjective assessments of life abroad that are rooted in the contrast between family roles in California and those that pertain in Mexico. As one of their informants put it, "in California my husband was like a *mariposa* meaning a sensitive, soft, responsive butterfly. Back here in Mexico he acts like a distant macho."[21] Many of the seasonal migrant women express an interest in returning to the United States in order to resume more cooperative relationships. Yet some, according to Fernandez-Kelly, are constrained by the pressures of caring for many children, especially if migration means facing the vagaries of undocumented illegal status in the United States.[22]

The anthropological research on immigrant women that has been stimulated by the analytical oppositions between domestic and public arenas or between production and reproduction indicates a set of complex and varied responses to the necessity of balancing work life with home life. In some cases greater equality between men and women is the result and in others it is not, and the differences must be explained by a close examination of cultural factors and economic constraints. Meintel and associates observe that "when changes in task-sharing and decision-making occur in conjunction with women's wage earning, they are likely to be found in areas which are most directly affected by women's employment: e.g., child care as opposed to housework, and financial decisions as opposed to those concerning freedom of movement and contraception."[23] It is common for anthropologists to emphasize the disjunction between behavior and norms, a disjunction that seems to have a powerful influence in the pace of change in various spheres of life for immigrant families. Cultural norms that continue to label men as principal providers and women as housekeepers and dependents are powerful deterrents to more egalitarian domestic arrangements. Nevertheless, in some situations immigrant women, like women elsewhere around the world, are able to exercise informal power.

If a number of immigrant women in the United States assess their increased earning capacity, their improved standard of living, and their greater opportunities to work and achieve upward mobility positively, they perceive other facets of immigrant life negatively. For many, the most negative results of migration are the temporary or permanent loss of a kinship support system and the absence of leisure time. It is thus to the social world of immigrant women both within and beyond the domestic sphere that we now turn.

HUSBANDS, WIVES, AND IMMIGRANT SOCIAL NETWORKS

"Strategy" and "process" have replaced "structure" as underlying concepts within anthropology.[24] Social networks, first examined with seriousness by ethnologists working in urban Africa in the late 1960s and the 1970s, have thus become a key focus of research on social organization. Anthropologists recognize the value of networks to migrants. These networks consist of friends or relatives of the migrant who are already in the destination area or those who are return migrants.[25] They serve as communication links between the sending and receiving communities. This seems especially important in international migration where the distances involved make adequate information harder to obtain.

There are two general types of networks. One serves the purpose of chain migration, where individuals channel their efforts to reunite extended family groups.[26] The other type is community based and operates to support newcomers as they adjust to the demands of their new environments.[27] Immigrant women are frequently found at the center of these networks. They both initiate and maintain them. They are the "nodes" that connect people, and generally they do it so subtly and unobtrusively that the significance of their actions is sometimes little recognized even by themselves.[28]

Though deeply embedded in migration processes around the world, kin-based migration networks that foster chain migration have proliferated as a result of the United States Immigration Act of 1965, which had as its aim the reuniting of families. The new law made it possible for individuals to "call over" other family members one at a time. Chavez, for example, writes of an unmarried El Salvador woman who first called her niece and two years later her mother and her nephew.[29]

There are two distinct problems with the reunification policy. It takes a long time to bring over an entire family, and in many cases the definition of family that the law proscribes is not broad enough to fit the concept of family held by certain ethnic groups. As a result, complex strategies to bypass the laws and restrictions that perpetuate family separation have been devised and carried out.[30] In many cases these include marriages of convenience or the adoption of children. Often the migrations can only be managed in stages, with the newcomer first going to Canada or Mexico or to U.S. cities other than their final destination. Women have an active part in the decision process that determines the order of migration of absent members, and they hold down jobs that fund the moves. Stafford tells us that women continue to play an important role in Haitian chain migration schemes, helping themselves and others through the difficult adjustment process.[31]

Community-based networks take shape in both sending and receiving areas. Mexican men from the Nayarit region who leave their wives behind make sure that a network of wife helpers (usually drawn from among the husband's kin) is in place to help with short-term loans, repairs to the household, bills, the care and sale of animals, the purchasing of materials and other tasks normally carried out by the husband.[32] When a man returns, part of what he has earned will be spent on gifts for members of this help network. This cements the obligation. However, as time passes and the woman becomes more self-sufficient, she relies less and less on these help networks. She becomes a *mujer fuerte* and gains esteem and social prestige while her husband is absent.

A substantial number of Dominican immigrant women are single parents who want to provide a better life for their children than is possible in their home countries. They must make use of networks at both ends of their migration trail. If they have young children who must be cared for, they may choose to leave them behind with their maternal grandmother. Once in this country, women usually live in extended family groupings that are composed of blood or marital kin who provide one another with financial and emotional support. Forming networks within their own groups, these women belie the stereotype of the passive Latin woman. They are not patiently waiting to be helped by husbands or brothers but are assuming active leadership roles, taking charge of their own lives and helping kinswomen do the same.[33]

Korean immigrant women in Hawai'i also spend a period of cores-idence with kin and, contrary to tradition, it is usually the relatives of the wife rather than those of the husband.[34] Laotian women, accustomed to carrying out daily tasks on a communal basis, form networks with kin and nonkin living nearby to help them cope with the loss of the support systems they had in Laos.[35] These networks are cooperative in nature and without accurate record keeping succeed in remaining balanced. Whether employed outside the home or not, the women share in caring for each other's children. They plan and carry out food shopping and preparation together. They provide for each other's social needs and serve as channels of community information.

Women have social license not available to men to share their personal concerns and worries with each other. These discussions take place in-formally as women gather at social and religious functions, or around a common worktable on the job. While outsiders may view these as gossip sessions, they actually serve as occasions for passing on valuable infor-mation and widening the range of an individual's contacts. O'Connor, for example, writes about the female-centered networks that emerge among Mexican immigrants, many of them undocumented, in Santa Barbara as a result of their labor force participation in local nurseries.[36] Based on the idea of *confianza* that is traditionally characteristic of kin and fictive kin relations in Mexico, these networks within the workplace provide the framework within which immigrant women seek help from formal agencies or mobilize themselves for social action. According to O'Connor, this represents a dramatic change from Mexico, where "women rarely work outside the subsistence economy, . . . have little knowledge of formal political or legal entities beyond local municipal affairs, . . . and participate in the social networks of their husbands and fathers [rather than] instigate network relationships of their own."[37]

While the bulk of research on the networks of migrant and immigrant women deals with the larger kin group or the workplace, some studies consider how the role changes experienced by male and female immi-grants are related to changing patterns in their social relationships. Ac-cording to a theory proposed by Bott, couples share a social network and perceive each other as companions in direct proportion to how they normally divide conjugal tasks. If conjugal roles are separate, so also are social and kin networks. When roles overlap or become cooperative in nature, social and kin networks do also.[38] An instance that might lend support to this theory can be seen in the experience of Korean women in Hawai'i.

In Korea the lives of men and women run on separate but parallel tracks. Labor is strictly divided, with men performing economically related tasks outside the home and women responsible for motherhood and other tasks inside the home. Each has distinct networks with which they interact and socialize on a daily basis. In Hawai'i women must hold jobs outside the home and many couples have made adjustments in the ways domestic duties are assigned. Men and women both are separated from their customary social and support ties and need to rely on each other. They spend more time together both in domestic tasks and in social activities. A majority of women, though by no means all, report enhanced marital relationships.[39]

A similar situation is reported by Lamphere, Silva, and Sousa in their work on Portuguese immigrants in New England. The realignments in household division of labor resulting from women's work outside the home have drawn nuclear families closer, while ties to extended families and friends become less important.[40] Conversely, Bloch argues that the economic pursuits of Polish immigrants divide family members, sending each off in a different direction every day. The family unit becomes fractionalized as its members develop distinct sets of friends and a variety of interests, returning home at night too tired to reconnect with each other. Polish women express feelings of isolation, feel that they are overworked, and fear that they have lost touch with their children. They seem at a particular disadvantage compared to women of other ethnic groups because they are unable to draw support from friends and kin. Bloch reports that they operate on a basis of suspicion and competitiveness with both family and nonfamily members. Where other groups see increased opportunity for all flowing from information exchange and cooperative efforts, the Poles see in these behaviors only the possibility of losses of personal advantages. They therefore are fearful and secretive in their dealings with those from whom others draw support.[41]

A different outcome is experienced by middle-class Cuban women. These women view the role of wife as primary. Children are valued and loved, but the focal point of a Cuban woman's life is her husband and her relationship to him. In the United States, Cuban women are entering the work force in increasing numbers, and operating within it competently and aggressively, but they have not let this influence their interactions with husbands inside the home. What they have done, however, is to take on an additional role, one that was carried out by a man's mistress in Cuba, where showing off a beautiful mistress gave status to a man and did not dishonor his wife. Since United States customs do not provide the same approbation for such behavior, the Cuban wife fills it and thereby earns her husband the status he would otherwise be denied. Women who in Cuba were able to become slightly plump must diet in the United States to maintain the image of youth and beauty necessary to fulfill this role.[42]

Anthropological research has demonstrated that the balance contained within male-female relationships is upset by the migratory experience. Both men and women must adjust to the demands of changing roles inside and outside the home. Relationships with children change also. In some cases prolonged separation of children from parents becomes necessary, and in others parents find that the demands of operating and financing households in the United States leaves little time and/or energy for the sort of interaction with children that would have taken place in their home communities. New social networks may be forged or old ones sustained. These networks may or may not be shared by husband and wife. The networks of immigrant women are crucial for disseminating information not only about employment opportunities, but also about various institutions of the host society. One of these institutions is the health care system, and it is to these issues that we now turn.

HEALTH, ILLNESS, AND THE IMMIGRANT WOMAN

The study of how cultures change is fundamental to anthropology, and a number of processes by which this occurs have been delineated. Culture change is clearly of central importance in the study of immigrants, although research in this area often analyzes a group or population according to their participation in traditional practices. Considered are things such as the meanings involved in continuing to serve symbolic foods and whether or not these foods are prepared with traditional ingredients or with the use of substitutes that maintain the symbolic value but may lose authentic taste quality. Native language use and the efforts that are made to teach the original language to succeeding generations provide another arena for assessing change. Language is often at the core of expressions of ethnic identity.[43] Of interest also are the methods used to hand down traditional songs and dances.[44] Studies measure the number of ethnically based voluntary associations that are active within the community and the rate of participation in them by its members. Religious practices conducted in the ethnic vernacular and social activities that bring together the ethnic group are yet another indicator of cultural cohesion.[45] Many of these studies are not primarily focused on women, but they deal with domains of family life that are centered around women. Thus the way that immigrant women respond to cultural difference is of utmost importance to any understanding of how immigrant families adapt to a new way of life. One female-centered domain where both cultural differences and adaptation are significant is that of family health.

Major contributions to the study of health issues among immigrants have been made by medical anthropologists. Medical anthropology emerged as a subfield of the discipline in the mid-1960s, although the issues that scholars in this field address (ethnomedicine, cultural conceptions of disease, human reproduction, etc.) have a longer history within anthropology, many of them subsumed within ethnographic studies of religion, research on culture and personality, or investigations of international public health systems.[46] In directing their attention to the adaptation of immigrants in the United States, medical anthropologists have demonstrated that the health of migrants is worse than that of nonmigrants,[47] and that many suffer from significant stress disorders that are not necessarily alleviated over time.[48] Clearly the impact of migration on health issues has a gender component. Research on gender and health can be subdivided into three areas: studies of the relationship between ethnomedical and biomedical orientations toward sickness and healing, studies of mental health and stress, and studies of the use of the health care system.

Indigenous Health Beliefs and U.S. Health Care

Immigrants and refugees, even those who have been in the United States for some time, either continue folk healing methods or juxtapose their own medical beliefs and practices with those of the United States.[49] Scholars who have conducted research in this area emphasize that health care professionals must adopt a transcultural perspective.

Bell and Whiteford show that Tai Dai women hold different concepts of illness causality than do Euro-Americans.[50] They emphasize food, temperature changes, and supernatural forces to a greater degree. Samoan migrants in Los Angeles retain a belief in the concept of *aitu*, the ghost spirit who punishes the living by bringing on a variety of physiological and mental illnesses.[51] For Samoan immigrant women, *M'ai aitu* is a culturally appropriate and patterned way to cope with anxiety and stress. DeSantis shows that while Cuban immigrant women in Florida have a biomedical orientation to illness and health care that is similar to that of Western health care professionals (illnesses and their associated symptoms are identified by their biomedical names), Haitian women are more ethnomedically oriented and tend to "give folk interpretations of biomedical explanations regarding pathophysiological processes." She associates these differences with (1) the educational and health care systems in the countries of origin, (2) the socioeconomic and political situation that affects immigrants in the localized receiving community, (3) household structure and function, and (4) beliefs about child behavior (the study focused on children's illnesses).[52]

Many immigrant and refugee women combine orientations and therefore remedies. Thus, the Cuban women discussed by Kirby use prescription tranquilizers in conjunction with herbal teas and other home remedies in their search for a cure for "*nervios*."[53] Cohen claims that Latina women frequently seek consultations with native pharmacists from their home country to supplement the care that they receive from the U.S. system.[54] Sargent, Marcucci, and Ellison show that Khmer women increasingly seek prenatal care at U.S. hospitals and clinics and tend to deliver their babies in hospitals. However, they also continue to follow traditional postpartum protective measures and to consult the indigenous midwife (*chmop*).[55]

Scholars in a number of disciplines have studied fertility patterns among immigrant women, mostly demonstrating a decline after migration.[56] Anthropologists have tended to focus on the cultural factors that influence attitudes toward childbirth, pregnancy, and other female health issues.[57] Morse and Park document cultural variations in perceptions of the pain that is associated with childbirth and explain them according to whether or not childbirth is viewed as natural or not.[58] In another article on the Khmer community in Dallas, Sargent and Marcucci demonstrate how pregnancy is culturally and socially constructed. The Khmer, like many other cultural groups, believe in humoral concepts and use them to diagnose pregnancy, treat symptoms, and control diet during pregnancy.[59] Similar humorally based attitudes are described for Indochinese women in California. They influence their preference for formula over breast milk.[60] Korean immigrant women in Honolulu have trouble communicating their anxieties about *naeng*, a folk illness rooted in ideas about a cold womb, to clinicians. Frequently, humoral and cosmopolitan lore are synthesized as an explanation for personal affliction.[61] Finally, Engle, Scrimshaw, and Smidt have worked on sex differences in attitudes toward newborns among Mexican immigrants in the Los Angeles area. Although they discovered an absence of preference among mothers (especially by comparison with fathers), they also suggest that "the more acculturated women express less positive attitudes toward their newborns," and the relationship was slightly stronger for girls than boys.[62]

Mental Health and Stress

A certain amount of stress is associated with the experience of immigration. A number of scholars, both sociologists and anthropologists, have examined variations in mental health by gender.[63] Friedenberg and associates show that Argentine immigrant women in New York are more demoralized across socioeconomic strata than are males, especially those who are nonworking or without household help to assist in child care.[64] In a study of Hmong refugees in Minnesota, Westermeyer and associates show that men experience greater stress during the initial phase of migration because of a loss in power and status and an inability to cope adequately with the public domain. However, as their employment situation and linguistic capabilities improve, their symptoms decrease. By contrast, women in the initial phase experience less psychological distress than men because they continue in their traditional domestic roles and do not have to deal with the obligations of financial support. The exceptions are women who become employed: "They reported more Phobic Anxiety symptoms...due to the new and relatively nontraditional roles as wage workers outside the Hmong community."[65] However, mental illness and stress increase for women over time, particularly as they become concerned about the Americanization of their children. Women heading their own household experience constant stress, a fact also noted by Cohen for single Latina immigrant women who have settled on the East Coast of the United States.[66]

Vega and associates also focus on the initial migration phase, and argue that depression symptom levels of Mexican immigrants are higher among those who have been in the United States for less than five years.[67] They find a positive correlation between depression and disrupted marital status, serious life events, poor physical health, and being a single head of household. Depression is negatively correlated with educational and income levels, and there seems to be no relationship according to the number of children. They argue that for women in particular "family structure and normative expectations are unstable and deeply conflicted. ...The effort to maintain traditional cultural role expectations within the context of a highly urbanized and affluent social system could be expected to increase stress and economic marginality."[68] When migrant women maintain contact with their support network of kin in Mexico, they are much better adjusted.[69]

The conflicts between motherhood and breadwinner roles create significant stress for a number of immigrant women in the United States. Among Latin American women in San Francisco, illness, whether mental or physical, validates a claim to maternal identity.[70] Korean women in Hawai'i complain of a variety of health disorders from insomnia to chest pain, to loss of appetite and frigidity. Chai suggests that many of these complaints are psychosomatic and are an informal strategy used by these women to legitimize and reaffirm their roles as good wives and mothers in a situation where their inadequate English, limited knowledge of American culture, employment in degrading jobs, and the double burden of waged and domestic work leads to declining authority over their children.[71]

Finally, Kirby describes the solace from stress that Cuban women in South Florida find in increased use of minor prescription tranquilizers. This stress is a result of the conflict between the ideal sex roles defined by Cuban culture and the economic realities of immigrant life—particularly the need to take on waged employment and to juggle work, child care, and other household responsibilities.[72] Tranquilizers alleviate ailments associated with *nervios*—a mental health ailment described by other scholars of immigrant women in North America,[73] one that is commonly attributed to poor working conditions, low wages, and gender relations.[74] Use of tranquilizers, in Kirby's view, "may be indicative of an adaptive strategy for dealing with culture change, and not merely as an example of illicit drug abuse."[75]

Access to and Use of the Health Care System

A number of anthropologists have focused on the access to and use of the health care system by various immigrant and refugee groups in the United States. For many, contact with the system is minimal. In a study of Laotian Tai Dam female refugees in Iowa, Bell and Whiteford show: (1) that two thirds of Tai Dam women do not use and have never used birth control because of insufficient knowledge and cultural norms, (2) that language creates problems of communication with doctors, (3) that a quarter of Tai Dam women are not covered by insurance, and (4) that close to a quarter have never seen a dentist and almost half do not have a personal physician.[76] Mexican immigrant women tend to underutilize health facilities even for prenatal care.[77] Illegal status and both the lack of insurance and fear associated with it provides one explanation. Work factors may also be important. Fifty-five percent of a sample of Mexican immigrant women in one study had at least one illness episode during their stay in the United States, and more working than nonworking women reported illness.[78] This may not be the result of the harsh conditions of work per se but of the increased access to medical care through work, which may influence the reporting of illness.

Other research shows that women immigrants seek medical attention and assistance as a way to alleviate tension and stress—being sick is a culturally appropriate means of gaining sympathy and support. For Latin American immigrant women in San Francisco, "illness may provide the opportunity for involvement in one of the few truly recreational activities available to women—going to the doctor."[79] When immigrant women do seek access to the U.S. health care system, it is largely through their own social networks.[80]

Chavira characterizes their role as "subsidy providers" as one of the more important among Mexicana migrants in the midwestern United States. "Women always carry, handle, and store all the family's documents and handle all bureaucratic matters affecting the family. In these ways, women are responsible for the family's health and other business. They function, as well, as cultural brokers as they introduce the family to the medical bureaucratic culture."[81] By becoming the health experts, women gain prestige and authority in vital decisions about geographical movement.

Through their dealings with the health care system, immigrant women come into contact with one aspect of state bureaucracy. In the final section of this chapter we explore other aspects of this interaction as well as the significance of social class.

IMMIGRANT WOMEN, SOCIAL CLASS, AND THE STATE

The political economic perspective has attuned anthropologists to the way in which global processes and class relations influence everyday lives. Within feminist anthropology this has resulted in a rich body of data on the impact of national and international development projects on women and in an exploration of how the social position of women is affected by the social, economic, and political policies of states. Research has emphasized not only how national immigration policies influence the demography of international female migration, but also their insertion in the receiving society. A model that addresses a threefold oppression or a "triple invisibility" according to gender, class, and ethnicity has emerged from these concerns.[82] One scholar has described a fourth oppression stemming from internalized self-perceptions whereby an exploited position is accepted as normal and natural.[83]

Class is experienced in the context of a transnational division of labor that is in turn linked to local and generally segmented occupational structures that funnel immigrant women into a few sectors of the economy, the garment industry and domestic service in particular.[84] Safa, for example, argues that the job market explains why Hispanic immigrant women outnumber men in the New York area.[85] A decline in these jobs in recent years has forced them to scramble to find other ways to support themselves. Alternatively, Fernandez-Kelly and Garcia show how local and federal agencies, operating within the framework of capitalist government policies, contribute to the growth of an informal or underground economy that employs numerous Hispanic women in Los Angeles and Miami.[86]

While these macro political and economic concerns have occupied the attention of some anthropologists, others have focused more closely on internalized perceptions of class and particularly the experience of downward mobility that is voiced by immigrant women who defined themselves as middle class prior to their arrival in the United States. Brazilian women in New York who were used to employing servants are now employed as servants. They cope with this change in social position by defining their situation as short-term and temporary.[87] Haitian women who held professional or white-collar positions in their home country express enormous resentment about their loss in social status and the fact that their education and skills are not valued in a predominantly English-speaking society. One Haitian woman who found herself working in a leather goods factory in the United States commented, "The job I do is for an animal. It's the same day after day.... I used to be a schoolteacher in Haiti. Now I'm doing a job that doesn't even require me to think."[88] High status middle-class Korean women who were not employed outside the home prior to emigration generally work at menial jobs that are not commensurate with their education once they arrive in the United States.[89] They are forced to take on these jobs because of the discrimination faced by their husbands. Professionals, managers, and white collar workers in Korea, these men find themselves working as janitors, gardeners, painters, and dishwashers in the United States. The same is true among Soviet Jews and Vietnamese refugees.[90]

Interestingly, it is the studies of middle-class female immigrants that show waged work failing to enhance women's status. The major motive for international migration among Colombians is the proletarianization of the middle class; they face increasing unemployment and poverty in their own country.[91] Perhaps because they had waged employment in their home country, Colombian immigrant women do not gain self-esteem and autonomy in relation to their spouses because of their earnings. In the "least attractive categories in the labor market" of the United States, they are insecure about their position as workers and earn less than their husbands.[92] According to Boone, Cuban women in Washington, D.C., do not value labor in and of itself because it is an extension of their domestic roles and is expected of them.[93] Alternatively, another study argues that Cuban mores restricted women's activities to the home and that women gained prestige and high standing by remaining within the domestic domain.[94] This status is lost as a result of the necessity of employment in the United States. The meaning of this loss of status is perhaps best expressed in a statement made by a Cuban respondent in a study conducted in Hudson County, New Jersey. "I used to work as a doctor's secretary in Cuba. I could dress well and it was a respectable job. Here I have to do factory work.... Instead of improving myself in coming to the United States, I feel like I'm going backwards every day."[95] The contradictions in the research on Cuban immigrant women's attitudes toward work emphasize most blatantly the need to be precise about the social class background of immigrants.[96] This is nowhere more apparent than in a comparison between Cuban entrepreneurs in Miami and proletarianized Mexican women in Los Angeles. In one case, home work becomes a strategy to maximize earnings and reconcile the cultural and economic demands placed upon women; in the other it is an avenue to increasing vulnerability.[97]

While social class is significant, anthropologists are quick to emphasize that the exploitation and discrimination that immigrant women experience may result more from their foreigness and/or femaleness. Foner notes a number of factors that divide Jamaican women from other immigrant or working-class women and, conversely, unites them with Jamaican men in a common cause.[98] Among Dominican women, "the identification and satisfaction with improvements in life-style dampen the collective sentiments and solidarity that are potentially nurtured and ignited in the workplace."[99] These women view themselves as middle class and measure themselves against where they were when they left their home country. Their orientation, according to Pessar, is individualistic rather than collective, and as a result they shun unions, legislative processes, and collective community action.

Pessar's observations draw attention to the pitfalls of ascribing our own concepts of liberation and oppression to immigrant women, who either feel the inevitability of their situation or have a different set of standards by which to evaluate their success. Both these factors explain their comparatively low level of political consciousness. Although there are a few exceptions, generally where anthropologists and other social scientists have even acknowledged the stirrings of group-based political expression, they describe it as incipient or weak.[100] The fact that community and social organizations tend to be male oriented explains, in Gordon's view, the low level of collective action among Caribbean immigrant women.[101] Their social world is the interpersonal world of kin and neighbors. Another factor is the basic division in the working class along ethnic lines. Lamphere describes some of this resentment between older (Italian, Irish, French-Canadian) and newer (Portuguese, Latin American) female immigrant factory workers in a New England apparel plant. Much of it centers on accusations of "rate busting." The perception is that new immigrants work too fast and the piece rate is lowered such that all workers have to increase their output to make the same pay. Despite these divisions and tensions, a culture of resistance that crosses ethnic lines can develop, according to Lamphere, when unions base their organizational activities on the informal networks that are established among women who bring their social and familial roles to the workplace.[102] This humanized work culture may not emerge in every situation, but where it does it can provide a powerful base for collective action by immigrant women.[103] Certainly more research is necessary to unravel the possibilities for political consciousness among immigrant women more generally.

CONCLUSION

Anthropology is a diverse and holistic discipline that encompasses within it a wide variety of theoretical perspectives and an unlimited number of research problems that are both interesting and important. This breadth is reflected in the scholarship on immigrant women in the United States. While much of this research is carried out at the micro community level, today it is rarely without some recognition of the significance of macro economic and political forces. While feminist models have suggested new questions to address, the emphasis within anthropology on the insider's interpretation of events has meant that universal dichotomies are not applied categorically. What is perhaps less apparent in studies of immigrant women, though fundamental to the anthropological imagination, is the comparative perspective. Ethnologists have tended to focus on single cultural groups and as a result lose the context within which to delineate how culture as opposed to some other factor, such as class, influences the lives and experiences of immigrant women. However, from the perspective of anthropology, social classes also have culture. It is the concept of culture that leads us to appreciate the multiple voices of immigrant women.

NOTES

1. Robert F. Spencer, ed., *Migration and Anthropology* (Seattle: University of Washington Press, 1970).

2. Douglas S. Butterworth, "A Study of the Urbanization Process Among Mixtec Migrants from Tilantego in Mexico City," *America Indigena* 22, 3 (1962): 257–274; Abner Cohen, "The Migratory Process: Settlers and Strangers," in Abner Cohen, ed., *Customs and Politics in Urban Africa: A Study of Hausa Migrants in Yoruba Towns* (London: Routledge and Kegan Paul, 1969), pp. 29–50; Edwin Eames, "Some Aspects of Urban Migration from a Village in North Central India," *Eastern Anthropologist* 8, 1 (1954): 13–26; William Mangin, ed., *Peasants in Cities: Readings in the Anthropology of Urbanization* (Boston: Houghton Mifflin, 1969).

3. Brian DuToit and Helen I. Safa, *Migration and Urbanization: Models and Adaptive Strategies* (The Hague: Mouton, 1975) and *Migration and Development: Implications for Ethnic Identity and Political Conflict* (The Hague: Mouton, 1975).

4. For examples of studies that use the household as the major unit of analysis, see Janet E. Benson, "Households, Migration and Community Context," *Urban Anthropology* 19, 1 (1990): 9–29; Elizabeth K. Briody, "Patterns of Household Migration into South Texas," *International Migration Review* 21, 1 (1987): 27–47; Ina Dinerman, "Patterns of Adaptation among Households of U.S.-Bound Migrants from Michoacan Mexico," *International Migration Review* 12 (1978): 485–501; Patricia Pessar, "The Role of Households in International Migration and the Case of U.S.-Bound Migration from the Dominican Republic," *International Migration Review* 16, 2 (1982): 342–364; Charles Wood, "Structural Change and Household Strategies: A Conceptual Framework for the Study of Rural Migration," *Human Organization* 40, 4 (1981): 338–343.

5. Anthony Leeds, "Women in the Migratory Process: A Reductionist Outlook," *Anthropological Quarterly* 49, 1 (1976): 69–76; Parminder K. Bhachu, *Twice*

Migrants (London: Tavistock, 1985); Brettell, *We Have Already Cried Many Tears*; Hans C. Buechler and Judith Maria Buechler, *Carmen: The Autobiography of a Spanish Galician Woman* (Cambridge, Mass.: Schenkman, 1981); Nancy Foner, *Jamaica Farewell: Jamaican Migrants in London* (Berkeley: University of California Press, 1978); Lisa Gilad, *Ginger and Salt: Yemeni Jewish Women in an Israeli Town* (Boulder: Westview Press, 1989); Charity Goodman, "Immigration and Class Mobility: The Case of Family Reunification Wives in East Germany," *Women's Studies* 13 (1987): 235–248.

6. In this chapter we use migrant and immigrant interchangeably, though we are always talking about women who are crossing an international boundary. In general, we are dealing with the literature on relative newcomers to the United States, but occasionally studies of second- or even third-generation ethnic groups are included. We have included some research on refugee groups. These populations are the focus of increasing attention by anthropologists, and they often experience problems similar to those of economic migrants. Finally, where we thought it relevant, we have made reference to some studies of immigrant women in Canada.

7. Rosaldo, "Women, Culture and Society," pp. 17–43.

8. Claude Meillassoux, *Maidens, Meals and Money* (Cambridge: Cambridge University Press, 1981); Gayle Rubin, "The Traffic in Women: Notes on the Political Economy of Sex," in Rayna Reiter, ed., *Toward an Anthropology of Women* (New York: Monthly Review Press, 1975), pp. 157–210.

9. Felicity Edholm, Olivia Harris, and Kate Young, "Conceptualizing Women," *Critique of Anthropology* 3 (1977): 101–130; Olivia Harris, "Households as Natural Units," in Kate Young, Carol Wollcowitz, and Roslyn McCullagh, eds., *Of Marriage and the Market* (London: CSE Books, 1981), pp. 49–68; Henrietta L. Moore, *Feminism and Anthropology* (Minneapolis: University of Minnesota Press, 1988); Susan Carol Rogers, "Women's Place: A Critical View of Anthropological Theory," *Comparative Studies in Society and History* 20 (1978): 123–162; Michelle Zimbalist Rosaldo, "The Use and Abuse of Anthropology: Reflections on Feminism and Cross-Cultural Understanding," *SIGNS* 4, 3 (1980): 497–513; Sylvia Junko Yanagisako and Jane Collier, *Gender and Kinship: Toward a Unified Analysis* (Stanford, Calif.: Stanford University Press, 1987).

10. Chai, "Adaptive Strategies of Recent Korean Immigrant Women in Hawaii," and "Freed from the Elders but Locked into Labor."

11. Chai, "Freed from the Elders but Locked into Labor," p. 229.

12. Deirdre Meintel, "The New Double Workday of Immigrant Workers in Quebec," *Women Studies* 13 (1987): 273–293.

13. Lamphere, "From Working Daughters to Working Mothers"; "Working Mothers and Family Strategies: Portuguese and Colombian Women in a New England Community," in Simon and Brettell, *International Migration*, pp. 266–283; Lamphere, *From Working Daughters to Working Mothers*.

14. Stafford, "Haitian Immigrant Women," p. 186.

15. Pessar, "The Role of Households in International Migration"; Pessar, "The Linkage between the Household and Workplace Experience"; Pessar, "The Role of Gender in Dominican Settlement in the United States," in Nash and Safa, *Women and Change*, pp. 274–294; Pessar, "The Dominicans"; Pessar, "The Constraints on and Release of Female Labor Power."

16. Pessar, "The Role of Gender in Dominican Settlement," p. 276.

17. This concept of helping—women help men outside the home and men help women within it—has been described for other immigrant groups. See Goody, "Introduction to Female Migrants and the Work Force"; Alicia Chavira, "Tienes Que Ser Valiente: Mexican Migrants in a Midwestern Farm Labor Camp," in Melville, *Mexicans at Work*, pp. 64–73, here, p. 69.

18. Briody, "Patterns of Household Migration."

19. Pessar, "The Dominicans," p. 123.

20. Foner, "Sex Roles and Sensibilities."

21. Guendelman and Perez-Itriago, "Double Lives," p. 268.

22. Fernandez-Kelly, "Mexican Border Industrialization."

23. Meintel, "Migration, Wage Labor and Domestic Relationships: Immigrant Women in Montreal," *Anthropologica* 26, 2 (1984): 135–169, here, p. 162.

24. Sherry B. Ortner, "Theory in Anthropology since the Sixties," *Comparative Studies in Society and History* 26, 1 (1984): 126–166.

25. Gonzalez, "Multiple Migratory Experiences"; Daniel O. Price and Melanie M. Sikes, *Rural-Urban Migration Research in the United States*, Center of Population Research Monograph (Washington, D.C.: National Institute of Child Health and Human Development, 1975).

26. Nancy B. Graves and Theodore Graves, "Adaptive Strategies in Urban Migration," *Annual Review of Anthropology* 3 (1974): 117–151.

27. Janet E. Benson, "Households, Migration and Community Context," *Urban Anthropology* 19 (1990): 9–29; Steven J. Gold, "Differential Adjustment among New Immigrant Family Members," *Journal of Contemporary Ethnography* 17 (1989): 408–434.

28. Smith, "Networks and Migration Resettlement"; Cohen, "The Female Factor in Resettlement"; Stafford, "Haitian Immigrant Women"; Sylvia Junko Yanagisako, "Women-Centered Kin Networks in Urban Bilateral Kinship," *American Ethnologist* 4 (1977): 207–226.

29. Chavez, "Coresidence and Resistance."

30. Stephen M. Fjellman and Hugh Gladwin, "Haitian Family Patterns of Migration to South Florida," *Human Organization* 44, 4 (1985): 301–312; Vivian Garrison and Carol I. Weiss, "Dominican Family Networks and United States Immigration Policy: A Case Study," *International Migration Review* 13 (1979): 264–283.

31. Stafford, "Haitian Immigrant Women."

32. Ahern, Bryan, and Baca, "Migration and La Mujer Fuerte."

33. Cohen, "The Female Factor in Resettlement."

34. Chai, "Adaptive Strategies of Recent Korean Immigrant Women in Hawaii," and "Freed from the Elders but Locked into Labor."

35. Muir, *The Strongest Part of the Family*.

36. O'Connor, "Women's Networks," p. 82.

37. Ibid., p. 85. See also Lamphere, "Bringing the Family to Work," and Zavella, "Abnormal Intimacy," for additional discussions of how networks affect women's consciousness among migrant and immigrant populations.

38. Elizabeth Bott, *Family and Social Network* (New York: Free Press, 1971).

39. Chai, "Adaptive Strategies of Recent Korean Immigrant Women in Hawaii," and "Freed from the Elders but Locked into Labor."

40. Louise Lamphere, Filomena M. Silva, and John P. Sousa, "Kin Networks and Strategies of Working-Class Portuguese Families in a New England Town," in Linda Cordell and Stephen Beckerman, eds., *The Versatility of Kinship* (New York: Academic Press, 1980), pp. 219–249.

41. Bloch, "Changing Domestic Roles among Polish Women."

42. Boone, "The Uses of Traditional Concepts."

43. Susan H. Buchanan, "Language and Identity: Haitians in New York City," *International Migration Review* 13, 2 (1979): 298–313.

44. Molly G. Schuchat, "Hungarian-Americans in the Nation's Capitol," *Anthropological Quarterly* 54, 2 (1981): 89–93.

45. Liucija Baskauskas, "Multiple Identities: Adjusted Lithuanian Refugees in Los Angeles," *Urban Anthropology* 6, 2 (1977): 141–154.

46. Thomas M. Johnson and Carolyn F. Sargent, *Medical Anthropology: Contemporary Method and Theory* (New York: Praeger, 1990).

47. Paul T. Baker, Joel M. Hanna, and Thelma Baker, eds., *The Changing Samoans* (New York: Oxford University Press, 1986); Robert Hackenberg et al., "Migration, Modernization and Hypertension," *Medical Anthropology* 7 (1983): 45–71.

48. William W. Dressler and Henrietta Bernal, "Acculturation and Stress in a Low-Income Puerto Rican Community," *Journal of Human Stress* 8 (1982): 32–38; Joseph Westermeyer, John Neider, and Tou Fu Vang, "Acculturation and Mental Health: A Study of Hmong Refugees at 1.5 and 3.5 Years Postmigration," *Social Science and Medicine* 18 (1984): 87–94.

49. Arthur J. Rubel, "Concepts of Disease in Mexican-American Culture," *American Anthropologist* 62 (1960): 795–814; M. Estellie Smith, "Folk Medicine among Sicilian-Americans in Buffalo, New York," *Urban Anthropology* 1, 1 (1972): 87–106.

50. Bell and Whiteford, "Tai Dam Health Care Practices."

51. Ineke M. Lazar, "Culture-Bound Illness in a Samoan Migrant Community," *Research Review* 6 (1988): 3–4.

52. DeSantis, "Health Care Orientations of Cuban and Haitian Immigrant Mothers, " pp. 76, 79.

53. Kirby, "Immigrants, Stress and Prescription Drug Use."

54. Lucy M. Cohen, *Culture, Disease and Stress among Latino Immigrants* (Washington, D.C.: Research Institute on Immigration and Ethnic Studies, 1979).

55. Sargent, Marcucci, and Ellison, "Tiger Bones, Fire and Wine."

56. Harbison and Weishaar, "Samoan Migrant Fertility"; Ford, "Fertility of Immigrant Women"; Ford, "Diverse Fertility."

57. Nancie Gonzalez, "Giving Birth in America," in Simon and Brettell, *International Migration*, pp. 241–253; Wanda R. Trevathan, "Childbirth in a Bicultural Community: Attitudinal and Behavioral Variation," pp. 216–227 in Michaelson, *Childbirth in America*.

58. Janice M. Morse and Caroline Park, "Differences in Cultural Expectations of Perceived Painfulness of Childbirth," in Michaelson, *Childbirth in America*, pp. 121–129.

59. Carolyn Sargent and John Marcucci, "Khmer Prenatal Health Practices and the American Clinical Experience," in Michaelson, *Childbirth in America*, pp. 79–89.

60. Fishman, Evans, and Jenks, "Warm Bodies, Cool Milk."

61. Kendall, "Cold Wombs in Balmy Honolulu," p. 373.

62. Engle, Scrimshaw, and Smidt, "Sex Differences in Attitudes towards Newborn Infants," p. 142.

63. Cohen, *Culture, Disease and Stress.*

64. Judith Friedenberg, Graciela Imperiale, and Mary Louise Skovron, "Migrant Careers and Well-Being of Women," *International Migration Review* 22 (1988): 208–225.

65. Westermeyer, Bouafuely, and Vang, "Hmong Refugees in Minnesota," p. 241.

66. Cohen, *Culture, Disease and Stress.*

67. Vega, Kolody, and Vallé, "Relationship of Marital Status, Confidant Support and Depression."

68. Vega et al., "Depressive Symptoms," p. 650.

69. Vega et al., "Migration and Mental Health."

70. Lewin, "The Nobility of Suffering."

71. Chai, "Adaptive Strategies of Recent Korean Immigrant Women in Hawaii," and "Freed from the Elders but Locked into Labor."

72. Kirby, "Immigrants, Stress, and Prescription Drug Use."

73. Kay and Portillo, "Nervios and Dysphoria."

74. Pamela Dunk, "Greek Women and Broken Nerves in Montreal," *Medical Anthropology* 11 (1989): 29–45.

75. Kirby, "Immigrants, Stress and Prescription Drug Use," p. 293.

76. Bell and Whiteford, "Tai Dam Health Care Practices."

77. Leo R. Chavez, "Households, Migration, and Labor Market Participation: The Adaptation of Mexicans to Life in the United States," *Urban Anthropology* 14 (1985): 301–346; Chavez, Cornelius, and Jones, "Utilization of Health Services by Mexican Immigrant Women."

78. Guendelman and Perez-Itriago, "Double Lives."

79. Lewin, "The Nobility of Suffering," p. 155.

80. Cohen, *Culture, Disease and Stress.*

81. Chavira, "Tienes Que Ser Valiente," p. 71.

82. Paule Marshall, "Black Immigrant Women in Brown Girls, Brownstones," in Mortimer and Bryce Laporte, *Female Immigrants*, pp. 1–13; Melville, "Mexican Women in the U.S. Wage Labor Force," in Melville, *Mexicans at Work*, pp. 1–11.

83. Mirjana Morokvašić, "Women in Migration: Beyond the Reductionist Outlook," in Annie Phizacklea, ed., *One Way Ticket: Migration and Female Labour* (London: Routledge and Kegan Paul, 1983), pp. 13–31; Morokvašić, "Migrant Women in Europe: A Comparative Perspective," in *Women on the Move: Contemporary Changes in Family and Society* (Paris: UNESCO, 1984), pp. 111–132; Morokvašić, "Cash in Hand for the First Time: The Case of Yugoslav Immigrant Women in Western Europe," in Charles Stahl, ed., *International Migration Today: Emerging Issues* (Paris: UNESCO, 1988), pp. 155–167.

84. Chavez, "Households, Migration and Labor Market Participation"; Rusty Neale and Virginia Neale, "As Long as You Know How to Do Housework: Portuguese-Canadian Women and the Office-Cleaning Industry in Toronto," *Resources for Feminist Research* 16 (1987): 39–41.

85. Helen I. Safa, "The Differential Incorporation of Hispanic Women Migrants in the United States Labor Force," in *Women on the Move*, pp. 159–173.

86. The informal economy is defined as the exchanges of transactions that occur among individuals or units of production that are totally outside the boundaries sanctioned by state or federal legislation. Fernandez-Kelly and Garcia, "The Making of an Underground Economy," p. 65. See the article for further clarification.

87. Margolis, "From Mistress to Servant." Not all immigrant women in the United States come from poor rural backgrounds and have minimal levels of education. Many have worked as professionals prior to their departure. Others have been recruited for their professional qualifications. This latter statement is perhaps most true for those women (Koreans, Filipinos, Caribbeans) who, in rather dramatic numbers, have come to North America to fill the shortages in the nursing profession.

88. Stafford, "Haitian Immigrant Women," p. 181.

89. Chai, "Adaptive Strategies of Recent Korean Immigrant Women in Hawaii," and "Freed from the Elders but Locked into Labor."

90. Steven J. Gold, "Differential Adjustment among New Immigrant Family Members," *Journal of Contemporary Ethnography* 17 (1989): 408–434.

91. Maria Garcia Castro, "Work Versus Life: Colombian Women in New York," pp. 231–259 in Nash and Safa, *Women and Change*, mentions familial difficulties, particularly the repression of sexuality, as a major motive for the migration of younger single women.

92. Castro, "Work Versus Life," p. 243.

93. Boone, "The Uses of Traditional Concepts."

94. Kirby, "Immigrants, Stress and Prescription Drug Use."

95. Prieto, "Cuban Women," p. 106.

96. As Safa, "Differential Incorporation of Hispanic Women," argues, the ideology of confinement to the home is a class ideology because it is only operative among elite women. See Gonzalez, "Multiple Migratory Experiences," for personal accounts of Dominican immigrant women of different class backgrounds.

97. Fernandez-Kelly and Garcia, "The Making of an Underground Economy."

98. Foner, "Sex Roles and Sensibilities."

99. Pessar, "The Dominicans," p. 123.

100. Melville, "Mexican Women Adapt to Migration"; Prieto, "Cuban Women and Work."

101. Monica Gordon, "Caribbean Migration: A Perspective on Women," in Mortimer and Bryce LaPorte, *Female Immigrants*, pp. 14–55.

102. Lamphere, "Bringing the Family to Work."

103. O'Connor, "Women's Networks"; Zavella, *Women's Work*.

Part II

The Immigrant Women of the Past

4

The International Marriage Market and the Sphere of Social Reproduction: A German Case Study

Suzanne Sinke with Stephen Gross

In 1855 August Frank wrote a letter to his nieces, trying to convince them to come to America: "If you come here, I will see to it that each of you gets a good husband who lets you have nice dresses."[1] The refrain of finding a husband in America appeared not only in personal letters, but also in emigration manuals: "Industrious and calm girls who are at least reasonably good looking can be sure that they will receive several proposals of marriage in the first year."[2] As historians have examined European migration patterns in the late nineteenth century, an era characterized by the expansion of industrialization, they have placed immigrants in the context of production as actors within the international labor market. The forces of production in a world capitalist system are important considerations, but just as important are the forces of reproduction. Reproductive activities are an essential counterpart to productive activities, and they operate on an international scale as well. What the international labor market was to the productive system, the international marriage market was to the reproductive system.

Reproduction and production, while complementary, do not move in tandem. The process of migration often disrupts the relationship between them, because women, at least in Western society, have handled the bulk of reproductive activities. By looking at American immigration in relationship to the international system of reproduction, historians can not only gain insight into the experience of women migrants but also learn how migration can alter the balance between productive and reproductive forces.

There is an exceedingly long and diverse literature defining reproduction in relation to production. Much of it springs from Engels's *The*

Origin of the Family, Private Property and the State, in which reproduction is largely confined to the physical reproduction of individuals and the relations of production. Recent feminist critiques of this position have diverged from those focused on the relation of patriarchy to unpaid labor in the home—and thus a strictly material basis for women's oppression—to those that posited another system of oppression based on sex hierarchy in the domestic (reproductive) sphere, such as the dichotomous model of Zillah Eisenstein in *Capitalist Patriarchy and the Case for Socialist Feminism*.[3] Most of these descriptions shared a rather limited definition of reproduction, one based on specific functions of reproducing individuals and/or providing the unpaid production and consumption components of society that went along with production.

Reproduction as I use it here is much broader; it entails biological and social components. Biological reproduction includes bearing children and the activities necessary for physical sustenance: nurturance and meeting basic physical and psychological needs. Social reproduction refers to some of the same activities, but delves more deeply into the way in which one carries out these activities.[4] It also goes beyond meeting basic needs to incorporate activities meant to replicate family, community, ethnic, or other cultural patterns. These activities are much harder to tie to an economic model, for while one can label them the requirements for replication of the labor force and analyze them for economic value, they operate in a realm of culture and society that does not base status or even identity merely on economic factors, and in actuality they go much beyond the "needs" of any particular production system.[5] Social *re*production is a misnomer, because it is social production—that is, it is the creation as much as re-creation of certain cultural settings and societal norms. They are no more fixed than are more traditional definitions of production.

During migration, both individuals and nations have recognized the social and biological facets of reproduction. Disease control represents one aspect of biological reproduction, one that has played a constant role in migration regulations. Whether an eighteenth-century ship quarantined for cholera, a nineteenth-century migrant turned back for trachoma, or a twentieth-century visitor denied admittance because of AIDS, through such health restrictions government officials have sought to regulate certain biological components of migration. In these cases, the question is how to protect the American population from contamination.

U.S. immigration policy around the turn of the century exemplifies another attempt to avoid contamination, this time in the form of "inferior" races. Policymakers articulated their arguments in distinctly biological terms, using the fear of race suicide to legislate bans on Asian migrants and then to enact the national-origin quota system.[6] The national-origin quota system of the 1920s responded not only to the fear that the character of American stock would change for the worse should too many of the "inferior" sorts remain, but also to the myth that the new groups had higher fertility rates than native-born white women, so the new groups would constitute the majority within a few generations.[7] Nativist fears of race suicide were largely unfounded. While immigrant women experienced higher fertility levels than white women of native-born parents, their daughters, the so-called second generation, had fewer children than their nonethnic counterparts.[8]

While policymakers often based biological arguments on the fear of intermixture of groups, a converse fear often fueled arguments on issues of social reproduction—specifically, that undesirables would not mix with "Americans" and hence would continue to live in a world replicating the homeland, a world that adhered to values other than the American standard. Thus immigrants from southern and eastern Europe represented a threat in the eyes of policymakers as much for their cultural traditions as for their blood.

Today immigration historians have largely (and rightfully) abandoned the biological focus of the 1920s with its racist overtones, but the debate concerning social reproduction remains couched in terms that reflect the evolutionary theory of that era: acculturation and assimilation. Those who wish to stress cultural continuity within ethnic groups may refer to "ethnogenesis," or the construction of ethnicity. Is "social reproduction" simply another name for examining these phenomena? Certainly, to some degree, for many of the same issues of re-creating institutions and adapting to new ones come into question. Yet the concept of social reproduction is not linear; it does not assume progress in one direction toward becoming one with the culture of the new land as do acculturation and assimilation.[9] Neither does it focus singly on aspects of society that replicate old world ways or that immigrants identify as specific to their ethnicity. It distinguishes itself further from some students of ethnogenesis by its inclusion (and stress) on household or private activities of a reproductive nature. But like ethnogenesis, social reproduction places the emphasis on the immigrants as active participants in the process of creating culture and defining their own identities within the parameters of their circumstances. Furthermore, social reproduction complements existing literature on economic forces of migration by demonstrating to a greater degree how women fit into the picture. It does not deny women's or men's productive roles; it does show how traditional roles could not exist without each other, and how reproductive jobs came to America just as did productive ones. Women as well as men took part in the economic migration, as part of the work force headed for another land. Yet there were many women who arrived as the spouse of someone, women whose primary economic role was keeping their place to live in order, procuring and preparing food, bearing and raising children, and making life a little more pleasant for the husband. This was one of very few economically viable options available to women in the late nineteenth century.

The roles—the breadwinner and the bread baker—which Western culture frequently aligned as complementary gender roles, changed in the process of migration, but they did not disappear. How immigrants rearranged their reproductive tasks in a society where women were absent or scarce differed. For the nineteenth-century male "bird of passage," the food and shelter might come in the form of a boarding house, the social life in the local bar, and the female company in the bordello. But how many wanted to continue in this pattern indefinitely? The necessity of women, more specifically wives, to re-create a society appeared more clearly. The question then became where to find a mate.

Just as the international labor market served to advance capitalism, so too the international marriage market served to maintain existing forms of patriarchy. The parallels between the two markets are many. Prospective workers sometimes received work contracts (formal or informal) before emigrating, sometimes they received general invitations for work among family or friends, and sometimes they received more general news of good opportunities for work. Likewise, women were sometimes married in absentia or on very short notice to immigrant men who sought wives, sometimes they received news of specific individuals looking for spouses, and sometimes they received more general news of good marital prospects.[10] For both the labor and marriage markets, persons sometimes migrated for other reasons, but then ended up getting married or taking a job nonetheless. Further, both markets responded to changes in conditions in both the sending and receiving areas.[11]

The immigrant letters I have consulted from Germans in the late nineteenth and early twentieth century illustrate these patterns. I read over a thousand letters by German immigrants, and did a closer evaluation of about three hundred to see how these individuals, particularly the women, viewed their gender roles.[12] One of the interesting differences in letters written to men and women was that while both men and women would receive news of job opportunities in America, women would also receive news of marriage opportunities. Stephen Gross, a colleague, then examined the 1900 and 1910 Public Use Samples of the federal manuscript censuses, seeking to uncover the workings of the marriage market. There were 1,200 German women in the 1900 sample, and 2,600 in the 1910 sample.[13]

Let us look more closely at this German-American group to see how the marriage market operated. As Figure 4.1 shows, males outnumbered women in the German-American migration throughout the turn-of-the-century period, although the fluctuations in the number of female im-

Figure 4.1
Male and Female German Emigrants, Aged 21 to 50, 1872–1910

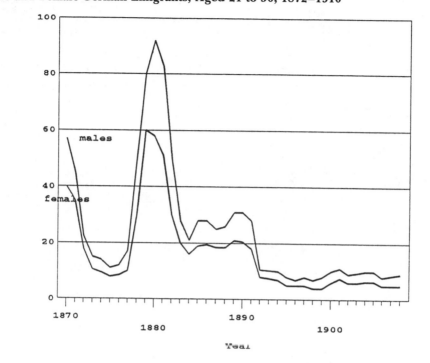

migrants closely paralleled those in the number of men.[14] Sex ratios in and of themselves are not reliable indicators of the number of single individuals immigrating, especially since the number of women immigrating in family systems approximated that of men and since people immigrating in families always comprised a large proportion of German immigrants (see Table 4.1). With the public use samples, we could choose those who were single at migration and control for age (see Table 4.2). The correlation of the number of single women to the percentage of women marrying demonstrated the marriage market in effect.

It is impossible to ascertain motive for migration from census data, thus we cannot determine the percentage of women who immigrated with the intent of marrying. The impressionistic evidence from letters indicates that the number was quite small, though marriage possibilities formed an important secondary consideration among young women. Yet whatever their reasons for coming to America, the percentage of German immigrant women who found a mate of the same ethnic background in America during the period 1870 to 1910 was very high. Among immigrants who were single at migration, endogamy registered

Table 4.1
Percentage Female of German Immigrants According to Various Sources,
1871 through 1910

	German Data[1]	American Data[2]	Public Use Sample Data[3]
1871–1880	42.9	41.0	39.6
1881–1885	43.2	41.6	40.0
1886–1890	45.0	44.1	39.8
1891–1895	45.0	*	42.2
1896–1900	44.7	45.3	40.6
1901–1905	42.0	39.4	38.7
1906–1910	41.5	40.1	41.0

Sources:

1. Walter F. Willcox, ed., International Migrations (New York: National Bureau of Economic Research, 1929), vol. I, pp. 298–699.

2. Willcox, ed., International Migrations, Vol. I, pp. 418–437.

3. Michael Strong et al., User's Guide: Public Use Sample, 1910, United States Census of Population. (Philadelphia: University of Pennsylvania, Population Studies Center 1989).

* U.S. data is missing for 1893 through 1895. The percent female for 1891 and 1892 was 40 percent.

around 95 percent for German women, while it fluctuated closer to 50 percent for German men (see Table 4.3).

For a late-nineteenth-century German immigrant woman, a key to fulfilling her role in life was marriage. Women and men identified themselves to friends and relatives uniformly in terms of being married or single, and they used this category as one, if not the most important, way to identify others. They also, with few exceptions, left no doubt as to their preference for (eventual) marriage. "I am still staying with [brother] Joseph. But I will get married the end of this summer; I think that will be best."[15] Some stressed the advantages of marriage: "It will be good if he gets married, then he will stay in one position longer, he changes too often."[16] However they viewed it, immigrants generally saw marriage as an option in America.

In Germany, marriage chances contracted with economic conditions.

Table 4.2
Single German Emigrants According to Sex, and Percentage Female of Single German Immigrants According to Age, 1871 through 1910

	Percentage Single	
	Male	Female
1881–1890	68.5%	31.5%
1891–1900	63.8	36.2
1901–1910	67.5	32.5

	Percentage Female		
	age 16-30	age 31-45	age 46-60
1871–1880	38.6%	39.1%	*38.7%
1881–1885	38.1	51.8	*58.1
1886–1890	37.9	52.3	*51.8
1891–1895	37.5	46.5	*51.4
1896–1900	36.9	37.1	*50.8
1901–1905	34.1	36.0	*25.7
1906–1910	35.5	50.2	*57.9

Source: For percentage single, F. Burgdörfer, "Migration Across the Frontiers of Germany" Walter F. Willcox, ed., International Migrations (New York: National Bureau of Economic Research, 1929), vol. II; for percentage female, Michael Strong et al., User's Guide: Public Use Sample, 1910, United States Census of Population. (Philadelphia: University of Pennsylvania, Population Studies Center 1989).

*Under 20 cases. Percentages have been adjusted to reflect .01 maternal mortality per birth.

People sometimes chose to postpone marriage because of economic uncertainty, waiting until an inheritance or property arrangement allowed the necessary financial basis for a household. Fears of pauper marriages also engendered a variety of laws against marriage for those without a set requirement of money or goods, or for those without a permanent residency in a particular area, notably seasonal farm workers and day laborers. These laws often had the contradictory effect of increasing the

Table 4.3
Percentage of In-Group Marriages for German Immigrant Women and Men, Single at Immigration, 1871 through 1910

	Women	Men
1871–1880	93.77%	53.60%
1881–1885	96.86	59.60
1886–1890	98.57	47.90
1891–1895	98.34	46.75
1896–1900	95.38	45.88
1901–1905	96.15	61.23
1906–1910	96.00	65.22

Source: Michael Strong et al., User's Guide: Public Use Sample, 1910, United States Census of Population. (Philadelphia: University of Pennsylvania, Population Studies Center 1989).

rate of illegitimacy. Regardless of the numbers involved, there was still a stigma attached to illegitimacy that both drove those with "uneheliche Kinder" (illegitimate children) from their homeland and pushed others to avoid that fate by improving their economic circumstances in America.

The Klinger family from Württemberg offers an example. According to a law passed in 1852, couples were required to have goods or cash to the value of 150 Gulden in order to wed. Daniel Klinger and his partner, Marie Friederike Kaiser, came to America with two illegitimate children and one more on the way in the late 1850s. Even with the assistance of previously emigrated siblings, they had to rely on the German home town to help pay Kaiser's passage, indicating that the couple did not have the cash to marry (and also that emigration was an alternative to continued support of the poor for the municipality).[17] This experience, and that of Daniel's parents, who also lived together and conceived illegitimate children until they could afford to marry, informed Daniel's advice regarding his younger sister: "[Rosina should] take care not to get involved with someone because she will get a husband here and women are more highly regarded in America than in Germany."[18]

Marriage was one of the few economic options open to women, along with religious service or life as a servant in someone else's home. Hence it was not surprising that immigrants tried to lure their single (and widowed) female friends and relatives to America by discussing "good" marital prospects. Some writers noted that in America a woman did not need a dowry to marry well: "You write that Roessle is not married yet and lacks sufficient wherewithal, in America one doesn't need anything, because the husband has to buy everything, here everything is totally different, because one doesn't need a dowry."[19] Others mentioned eligible bachelors by name: "Don't you want to come to us in America? Or do you have a sweetheart there. You could marry Frank Rauch."[20] But the most common approach was to summarize nuptial prospects in general terms, sometimes a little exaggerated: "One can get married any day here."[21]

Even if immigrants did not intend to lure others, they frequently noted the consequences of unbalanced sex ratios in their German-American communities. One woman agonized over the lack of household help, especially after her niece decided not to emigrate. "Girls are really rare here because as fast as they arrive they get married."[22] Further, the experience of certain immigrants, such as Engel Winkelmeier, brought hope to those caught in deteriorating economic conditions. Winkelmeier came from a day laborer's family in eastern Westphalia. She immigrated to America in 1867 with her sister Margarethe. Both sought and immediately found jobs as servants in German households, only to switch shortly thereafter to better-paid positions in American families. Two years after her arrival, when she was thirty-two, Engel Winkelmeier married a man of the same age from her region of Germany. They moved out of the city to a farm, raised children, and at least as far as the surviving letters indicate, did reasonably well economically.[23] For daughters of day laborers in Germany, this constituted a step up in the world, one of which the Winkelmeiers could boast, and one that the women recommended to friends.

Not only women above the average age at marriage, but also widows could take part in this international marriage market. After Pauline Gauss, a native of the Berlin area, lost her husband, she decided to join her uncle in America. She and her two children immigrated to Iowa, where she married Johan Wendt three months after arrival. In this case it appears she planned to emigrate specifically because Wendt wanted a wife to help run his farm. In any case, one year after her arrival in America, Pauline Gauss suggested a similar route to someone in Germany: "If Mrs. Palm is not [re]married yet then she can come here[;] there are many good men who want wives."[24]

Few immigrant women reported anything vaguely related to romantic love in their descriptions of fiancees or new husbands. These individuals viewed marriage as companionate only insofar as they shared work.[25] The kind of information they provided tended to focus on the man's financial worth and/or profession first, then where he was from and whether he was a "good" husband (a description upon which few elaborated). For example, Minnie Decker wrote a friend: "I have to tell you that things are going exceptionally well for me, because I have gotten such a good husband, we live happily and in satisfaction together."

Table 4.4
Percentage of German Immigrant Women and Men (Aged 15 + at Immigration) Marrying within 2 Years after Immigration, 1871 through 1910*

	Women	Men
1871–1880	63.1%	28.3%
1881–1885	72.1	33.5
1886–1890	56.3	29.8
1891–1895	53.3	22.6
1896–1900	58.3	24.3
1901–1905	62.9	35.7
1906–1910	63.5	32.5

Source: Michael Strong et al., User's Guide: Public Use Sample, 1910, United States Census of Population. (Philadelphia: University of Pennsylvania, Population Studies Center 1989).

*The decrease in mean years between immigration and marriage is partially a product of selection bias. The distortion, however, should be minimal after 1890, since mortality would not have been that drastic.

Decker included a wedding picture, but no further information about her husband other than that he was German and they had a business. She did, however, list *all* her wedding presents and describe her home furnishings in detail.[26]

This material litany appeared also in the writings of Margarethe Schiefer. Schiefer wrote her parents to announce that she had "taken the opportunity" to get married three weeks after she arrived in a small German-American town in Michigan. Her husband included a letter of introduction for his new in-laws, indicating that it would be nice to get to know them and that he was from the same region of Germany.[27] While such a whirlwind courtship may not have been the standard, marriage within the first two years was. For women over age fifteen who were single at the time of migration, the percentage of those marrying within the first two years averaged around 60 percent from 1896 to 1910. Moreover, the percentage rose consistently after 1891.[28] (See Table 4.4.)

Among the immigrant letters, I found only one that indicated that a German-American woman in her twenties could not marry despite wanting to, in this case a young woman who was mentally impaired.[29] Thus it is not surprising that Margarethe Winkelmeier wrote in a letter to her family that all the girls who had come to America from their village had married—all, that was, except for her. Perhaps as a way of explaining why she was still single, Winkelmeier went on to state that she really did not want to marry yet, and then reported that she had been ill recently and had lost some of her hair.[30]

Winkelmeier's insistence that she preferred to decide herself about marriage illustrated another aspect of the German-American marriage market. Despite the replication of communities of people from the same area, a consequence of chain migration, the tradition of men choosing their mates and fathers influencing such decisions for daughters lost some of its power as the chances for marriage increased and the distances between family networks widened. Women, likewise, could support themselves much better on American wages than on German ones, and hence could wrest more freedom out of a still strongly patriarchal system. American influence, at least in popular parlance, also contributed to this loosening of social control patterns. A German newspaper for emigrants noted that women were more independent in America, girls could marry whomever they wanted, divorce was easy, and the father was no longer the representative of the household.[31] While the argument may have been overstated, the reality of considerable independence is substantiated by immigrant letters. And some women reported their own choices of mates, at times to the dismay of other family members.

Barbara Reuss immigrated to America to join (and serve) an uncle and his family. After a time she moved to the farm of a German-American woman: "This good woman who is our landlady came to America 20 years ago as a poor girl and now is a very rich woman."[32] Reuss soon got to know the family, and had thoughts of marrying one son. The letters are unclear whether she or he felt it was inappropriate to marry without a dowry. In any case, Reuss changed her mind and decided "a girl doesn't need anything here if the guy has a little something, then they get ahead."[33] Reuss then married another son, a saddlemaker, with the blessings and considerable financial assistance of her mother-in-law. Her uncle wrote his version of the occurrence, which illustrated his impatience with the young woman's independence: "The entire wedding doings were carried out in secret. . . . If Barbara had stayed with us for another year, I would have made sure myself that she had married well. But it happened."[34] The uncle had a variety of complaints against the bridegroom, including a club foot, a "zealous" Catholicism, and a financial dependence on his mother. However, the uncle conceded that the young man was, perhaps, not so bad and that they had married in a proper Catholic ceremony, which should please Reuss's parents.

A somewhat more ambiguous case was that of Barbara Klinger, who got pregnant shortly after her arrival in New York. Her lover refused to marry her, but under pressure from Klinger's siblings, agreed to pay something toward the welfare of the child and mother. Klinger turned the baby over to her sister soon, and headed west to marry. Her destination was a rural area of Indiana populated by a number of German-Americans known to the family. Her sister's letters indicate that Klinger may have changed her mind about whom she wanted to marry in the course of the trip or in the early days of her stay in Indiana. "[Barbara] wrote in her last letter that she was going west with Wagner at the end of October to Hetzel and Albeck. She wrote us in her first letter that Albeck had asked her to marry him and that she had promised to do so[;] in her last letter she wrote that she will marry Hetzel, and now we don't know which of them she married, or if she didn't marry either of these two."[35] A later letter reported that it was Gottlieb Hetzel whom Klinger had married. When Hetzel died a few years later, Klinger remarried, this time to another local German-American farmer.[36]

This is not to say that most or even many immigrant women made choices about husbands. Perhaps we can best picture this as a situation in which men still did the choosing, but women were more free than they had been in the past to say no, and still have a sufficient chance to get married to someone else. That most single female immigrants could and did find a suitable mate within the first years of their arrival attests to both the strength of the ideal of marriage, its economic advantages, and the opportunities America offered along these lines.

Staying out of trouble, which Barbara Klinger did not do, was one way of assuring that marriage chances would not decline. Young women traveling alone had both the freedom and the risks of making choices about their company. "Dear Sister-in-law[, K]eep to yourself during the trip and don't get involved with the young people at most with a married family and keep totally away from the sailors."[37] The refrain of protecting young women appeared in various publications offering information for emigrants. On the one hand, there was a risk of men who tricked women with false promises of marriage or jobs that turned out to be in brothels. As the *Deutsche Auswanderer Zeitung* reported, women should be admonished that no matter what a man said, sea air was not an effective contraceptive, and unwanted pregnancy could lead to poverty, prostitution, or infanticide.[38] On the other hand, young women traveling without zealous chaperones could choose their own companions on shipboard, and in some cases romances that resulted did lead to long-term commitments.

One of the interesting things to note about German immigrant patterns of marriage is that they run counter to those of several other ethnic groups. German immigrant women married and began raising families when others were immigrating to get jobs or postponing having children after marriage. Among the German brides, the mean years between marriage and birth of the first child decreased around the turn of the century, indicating that women were less likely to delay getting pregnant after marriage. We actually anticipated that marriage would become less rather than more important over time for German women as job opportunities for women increased. This was the case among several other immigrant groups, notably Irish and southern and eastern Europeans, but among the Germans the percentage of women working went from 14.8 percent in 1900 to 13.6 percent in 1910.[39] Why? One reason was a shift in migration patterns. In the period from 1880 to 1895 German immigrants tended to live in the eastern part of the United States or in large cities. After 1895 this trend changed; Germans more often lived in rural areas, with a concentration in the Midwest.[40] Likewise, a shift in the areas of emigration, back to the mid-nineteenth-century pattern from west to southwestern Germany, may have attracted a more conservative group. Further, those in rural areas could engage in farming, which for most German immigrants was an occupation for a family—at the least for a couple. This translated into the "need" for a wife about which many men in rural America wrote.

German men had a different role in the international marriage market than did women. Because of skewed sex ratios among the group they wished to wed—German women of similar regional and religious background—they often had to return to the old country to find a "suitable" spouse. Some asked for help in this endeavor. In one case an immigrant man wrote to his aunt, asking her to find a wife for him: "My demands for a young woman are very limited, a developed figure with passable face is sufficient, everyone wants industriousness and a good disposition, social position and class make no difference. Wealth is good and none perhaps better. Concerning religion I could go along with anything except a Catholic."[41]

The same plea but from a different religious background appeared in the letter of one of the first missionary priests in Stearns County to his superior: "Everyone wants to get married, but no girls. Do not forget your promise! But only those that are to your honor and no English people, because otherwise the parishes will be disrupted."[42] By 1865 only 33 weddings had taken place in his parish, and of the 16 brides for whom data is available, the median age at marriage was 19, with 6 under the age of 17. In comparison, Knodel's study of mean age at marriage for women in several communities was 25.5 for women overall (28.3 for men), thus substantially higher than for German women in the United States.[43] Age at marriage was less for German immigrant women than for women who stayed in Germany, according to calculations from the Public Use Sample as well. (See Table 4.5.)

For men, the lack of available spouses along with the new setting often meant having to improvise concerning living arrangements. Boarding was a common phenomenon, but an expensive one if one was not used

Table 4.5
Mean Age at Marriage and Percentage Married at Immigration for German Immigrant Women, 1871 through 1910*

	Mean Age of Women		Married at Immigration
	Married before Immigration	Married after Immigration	
1871–1880	22.63	22.62	36.57%
1881–1885	22.58	23.61	44.32
1886–1890	22.14	24.08	41.81
1891–1895	22.72	22.87	50.29
1896–1900	22.44	24.48	33.33
1901–1905	21.89	23.66	46.91
1906–1910	21.95	25.23	63.33

Source: Michael Strong et al., User's Guide: Public Use Sample, 1910, United States Census of Population. (Philadelphia: University of Pennsylvania, Population Studies Center 1989).

*Women aged 15 and above at immigration and married only once.

to paying for cooking, cleaning, and other household tasks. One writer noted that he and his five male roommates living in a house outside of St. Paul, Minnesota, gained quite a bit of attention from their friends. Their house was called the "bachelor hole," and "many people make fun of us, but it does well for our pocketbooks."[44] Specifically, it was less than half as expensive as staying in a boarding house. Some immigrant men simply lived with the consequences of not having someone to do household chores. Thus one immigrant wrote that he had bought a house, but he lived like a "typical bachelor. Dear heaven! my laundry! holes and tears! and the socks!! and the floor!! and the pillow!! Do not come for a while."[45]

The need for someone to carry out domestic tasks was especially acute for widowers. Henry Miller, for example, felt he could not care for his two-year-old daughter after the death of his wife. When a friend recommended Elisabeth Deist, a German-American woman slightly older than Miller, he agreed to meet her. Deist, the daughter of a local farmer, made a good first impression, as did Miller. They met at the friend's house and decided immediately to get married. She went home with him that night. Even Miller commented to his parents that the speed at which one could get married in America was astounding. The marriage of convenience proved advantageous to Miller in many ways, not least of which was receiving money from his new father-in-law.[46]

The legal simplicity of marriage in America in comparison with most German states was perhaps more striking than Miller realized. The Millers fulfilled the basic requirements of common-law marriage by agreeing to marry and beginning to cohabit.[47] Thus they achieved in one day what many Germans could not achieve in years because of various restrictions. American conditions combined with a variety of legal traditions to produce the common-law marriage. Without sufficient officials to carry out weddings, and in the face of various religious and cultural differences concerning marriage, American lawmakers opted for a variety of possibilities. At the end of the nineteenth century, residents of the United States could choose a civil ceremony, a religious ceremony, or a common-law arrangement, or any combination of them. Restrictions on marriage commonly dealt with miscegenation, bigamy, and age at marriage, rather than with property or residency requirements (as in German states). If the letters are any indication, most immigrants married in official ceremonies, which they duly reported to their relatives.

Not all men were as fortunate as Henry Miller in finding a suitable woman available when they wanted to marry. If they did not go back to the old world, immigrant men sometimes faced the prospect of marriage with a woman from another ethnic background, an option that many of them, at least in their letters, found distasteful.[48] To have to marry an American was particularly repulsive to many. In response to a question about American women, one man wrote to his sister: "[They do] nothing besides rocking in a rocking chair all day, and to pass the time a little reading or sewing. That is their occupation, that is their work."[49]

Could this comparative "laziness" have had to do with the shortage of women? Certainly many commentators noted that men had to treat women better in America than in Germany.[50] While German men were typically appalled at American women, German female immigrants viewed American native-born white women with a mixture of jealousy and disgust: "Women don't have much [experience] here. The husband has to take care of things and it is easy for the wife."[51] The impact of American views on German-American patterns, however, was evident. Immigrants encouraged their female friends to marry in America specifically because the men treated the women better. "Come to America, you will have a better time here than in Germany and if you get even a halfway good husband you won't have to bother so much as in Germany."[52] Katharina Stier, writing to her sister, illustrated both an awareness of American laws concerning women and the changing standard toward divorce that appeared in the early twentieth century: "How is Pauline? Hopefully she is healthy again, what will she do now? She won't go back to her terrible husband again will she? He will certainly have to support her if she decides to get a divorce, and will also have to make provision for the children, if the laws in Germany are like those here in America, or are they different there."[53] American women's behavior and its influence on German-American women's views constituted one reason for men to return to Germany to find a mate, and the improvements in trans-Atlantic travel made this a more feasible option over time.

Another option men often discussed was marriage for money. Though men and women rarely referred to dowries in their letters, men did recognize the advantages of a woman of means. Some sought to wed German-American women or American women who had a bit of capital. Young widows often fell in this category. Valentin Pruehs wrote to his brother: "I should marry a 25 year old widow. She has 20 acres of woods very near the city but I don't know what I should do because she has a child and is Protestant."[54]

While men sometimes had to return to Germany temporarily to find spouses, one study of long-term return migration indicates that women may have gone to America at least partly to marry and then return. Once in America, women were much less likely to return to the old world than men, but those who did tended to fit in two categories: impoverished or newly married. While young men often returned after amassing a nest egg, single women who returned did so with few financial resources. So while a German man might go to America to earn some money and return, a German woman would rarely do so.[55] On the other hand, women who migrated when they were single sometimes returned to Germany with their husbands shortly after marriage, and in these cases, the couple generally had a reasonable amount of capital.[56] People who married after migration tended to follow German age-at-marriage patterns, while those who married before migration (in Germany), did so at an earlier age. (See Table 4.5.)

What do all these figures, letters, and stories tell us about the sphere of social reproduction? First, they confirm the existence of an international marriage market, whether on a conscious or unconscious level. Second, they demonstrate that migration disrupted the balance between productive and reproductive activities. Women encountered better chances to marry in America than in Germany, and men found more chances to earn sufficient funds to support a family. Among German women in the late nineteenth and early twentieth centuries, the decline in the age at marriage and the decrease in the proportion of women employed outside the home indicate the shift in balance toward reproductive activities. So long as women handled the bulk of household activities, and so long as men constituted a larger percentage of the migrant stream than women, then the "need" for women to carry out reproductive tasks would push them into this sector. For other groups, particularly those with fewer economic resources, women were not taken out of the work force, but instead earned their living in the reproductive/service sector. These women often benefited from the imbalance in productive and reproductive roles through better wages for household work. Hence the international marriage market may have functioned quite differently for groups other than the Germans. However, if their experience was the more typical, then the international marriage market functioned to support a separation of spheres in America, albeit in different form than the prevailing white bourgeois norms.[57] That could also help explain why it became harder to support notions of domesticity when the sex ratios of the migration stream changed in the early twentieth century.

NOTES

1. August Frank to nieces, Milwaukee, 22 September 1855, in Louis Frederick Frank, comp., *German-American Pioneers in Wisconsin and Michigan; The Frank-Kerler Letters, 1840—1864*, trans. Margaret Wolff, ed. Harry H. Anderson (Milwaukee: Milwaukee County Historical Society, 1971).

2. Traugott Bromme, *Hand- und Reisebuch für Auswanderer nach den Vereinigten Staaten von Nord-Amerika* (Bayreuth: Buchner, 1848), p. 57; quoted in Wolfgang Helbich, Walter Kamphoefner, and Ulrike Sommer, *Briefe aus Amerika: Deutsche Auswanderer Schreiben aus der Neuen Welt 1830–1930* (Munich: C. H. Beck, 1988), p. 499

3. For a brief overview of this literature, see Beechey, *Unequal Work*, chapter 4, "On Patriarchy."

4. This may be confusing to those familiar with Marxist feminist writing, which uses social reproduction in a more materialistic fashion. I use it this way because the tasks involved are reproducing society, though not necessarily in the same form as before. These are tasks that men and women have shared—tasks that other researchers would term cultural adaptation and cultural continuity. To divide these tasks from "productive" ones is an artificial distinction largely based on the sex-gender system.

5. Using reproduction in this expanded definition allows one to incorporate ideas that otherwise seem incompatible: cultural analysis that grants a large degree of agency to historical actors, and forms of analysis drawing on post-structuralism and socialist thought that paint a highly deterministic picture of societies. My approach is to see actors making choices within certain parameters. David Levine, in *Reproducing Families: The Political Economy of English Population History* (Cambridge: Cambridge University Press, 1987), p. 8, describes this: "individuals' choices of action were limited and defined by the context in which they acted, the context in which they thought, the context in which they planned and the context in which they made their choices. It is in this sense that individuals faced a determinate set of choices, not of their own choosing." I prefer to stress that despite the parameters, there were choices, and those choices could make a large difference both in individual lives and in collective experience.

6. The fact that the government first hindered Asian women from migrating in order to prevent these groups from establishing a permanent base in the U.S. population and thus "infecting" it with an "undesirable" racial component yet still allowed Asian men to come as workers for a time clearly demonstrates the separation of production and reproduction issues in policy-making.

7. Over a long period of time, a major biological change did take place in North America owing to migration. Scholars from the *Annales* tradition have documented how with the arrival of Europeans in the Americas, blood types changed. A related development, one gained at the price of epidemics that decimated the native Americans, was a population more resistant to a wider range of diseases. See, for example, Alfred W. Crosby, Jr., *The Columbian Exchange: Biological and Cultural Consequences of 1492* (Westport, Conn.: Greenwood Press, 1972).

8. The decline in fertility for the second generation is attributable to delays in leaving home and consequently delays in finally marrying. In short, familial obligations and specifically obligations to parents deterred early marriage and childbearing for these women. Miriam King and Steven Ruggles, "American Immigration," *Journal of Interdisciplinary History* 22 (Winter 1990): 347–369.

9. If anything, social reproduction as a term goes in the opposite direction, because it is *re*-production rather than simply production.

10. Japanese picture brides form the most striking example in the first category. See Alice Chai's chapter in this volume.

11. When economic conditions improved in Germany, the women who immigrated tended to be older. See Table 4.2.

12. Most of the letters I consulted are found in the Bochum Immigrant Letter Collection (hereafter BLC). For additional information on the Bochum collection, see Wolfgang Helbich, "The Letters They Sent Home: The Subjective Perspective of German Immigrants in the Nineteenth Century," *Yearbook of German American Studies* 22 (1987): 1–20. See also the two books published from the collection: Wolfgang Helbich, *America ist ein freies Land . . . : Auswanderer schreiben nach Deutschland* (Darmstadt: Luchterhand, 1985), and Helbich, Kamphoefner, and Sommer, *Briefe aus Amerika*. I would like to thank the Ruhr Universität, Bochum, for the opportunity to use the letter collection, and members of the research team, especially Professor Wolfgang Helbich, Cornelia Vogt, and Ulrike Sommer, for their assistance.

In addition to the Bochum collection, I consulted a number of published collections, which included: Frank, *German-American Pioneers*; C. Carnahan Goetsch, "The Immigrant in America: Assimilation of a German Family," *Annals of Iowa* 42 (1973): 17–27, 114–125; Joseph Ruff, "The Joys and Sorrows of an Emigrant Family," *Michigan History Magazine* 4 (April–July 1920): 530–574; Peter Schwinn, " 'Man hat hier ein schönes Leben: Ein Marburger Auswanderin schildert ihre Ankunft in der Neuen Welt," *Hessische Heimat* 33 (Fall/Winter 1983): 104–108.

13. The 1900 sample includes approximately one in every 760 individuals, and the 1910 data set is significantly larger, including one in every 250 respondents. Stephen Gross created a subsample from the larger public use samples which consisted of all German-born females for whom date of immigration was listed. He supplemented these data with published German data from Walter

F. Willcox, ed., *International Migrations* (New York: National Bureau of Economic Research, 1929).

14. The magnitude of immigration fluctuated dramatically through this period, peaking in the early 1880s at roughly 150,000 people per annum and then declining after 1893 to less than 20,000 people annually. In part this reflects regional shifts in sending areas, as the German source areas shifted from the West and Southwest to the East and North after midcentury. Later, after 1885 or so, the sending areas shifted back again slightly.

15. Veronika Rapp to uncle and aunt, Chicago, 1 March 1885, BLC.

16. Kaethe Stier to sister and family, Chicago, 29 November 1913, BLC.

17. Helbich, Kamphoefner, and Sommer, *Briefe aus Amerika*, p. 503.

18. Daniel Klinger to family, Albany, 16 August 1857, in Helbich, Kamphoefner, and Sommer, *Briefe aus Amerika*, p. 522.

19. Barbara Monn to brother and sister-in-law and children, Marine City, Mich., 4 September 1871, BLC.

20. Augustine Weber to Ludwina (Bleuel), St. Paul area, 16 April 1893, BLC.

21. Quoted in Schwinn, " 'Man hat hier ein schönes Leben,' " p. 107.

22. Barbara Monn to brother and sister-in-law and other relatives, Marine City, Mich., 16 February 1870, BLC.

23. Helbich, Kamphoefner, and Sommer, *Briefe aus Amerika*, pp. 535–554.

24. Pauline Wendt to brother-in-law, Manson, Iowa, 15 May 1890, BLC.

25. With one significant exception—some bourgeois immigrants. Few well-to-do individuals emigrated, but even though this group is probably overrepresented among the immigrant letters (since its members were more likely to be literate), there were few letters that spoke in romantic terms.

26. Minne Decker to Marie, Secaucus, N.J., 16 March 1888, in Helbich, Kamphoefner, and Sommer, *Briefe aus Amerika*, pp. 586–587.

27. Johan Georg Schiefer to in-laws, 10 August 1852, BLC.

28. The figures for Germans who were over age fifteen and still single at migration who then married within the first two years in America were:

	Women	Men
1891–1895	53.3%	22.6%
1896–1900	58.3%	24.3%
1901–1910	62.9%	35.7%
1906–1910	63.1%	32.5%

These figures include all marriages, regardless of spouses' ethnicity, in the Public Use Sample.

29. See the correspondence of Anna Maria Averbeck to friends, Eldorado, Wisc., 1890s, BLC.

30. Margarethe to father, brother, sister-in-law, Indianapolis, 6 December 1870, BLC.

31. "Die Familie in Europa and in den Ver. Staaten," *Deutsche Auswanderer Zeitung*, 15 March 1858, p. 43.

32. Barbara (Reuss) Meister to parents and siblings, Metamara, Michigan, 20 September 1869, BLC.

33. Ibid.

34. J. G. Zeller to brother-in-law, Spring Bay, Michigan, 21 May 1869, BLC.

35. Anna Maria Schano to parents, Albany, 23 January 1856, in Helbich, Kamphoefner, and Sommer, *Briefe aus Amerika*, p. 518.

36. Ibid., p. 534.

37. Friedrich Breitwieser to sister-in-law, New York, 1 December 1858, in Helbich, Kamphoefner, and Sommer, *Briefe aus Amerika*, p. 524.

38. "Ermahnung, namentlich an auswanderende ledige Frauenzimmer," *Deutsche Auswanderer Zeitung*, 17 August 1857, p. 254.

39.

Employment	1900	1910
British/Scots	29%	48%
Irish	44%	47%
Scandinavian	28%	10%
German	25%	22%
Central Europe	18%	12%
Other Europe	17%	25%

The source is Michael Strong et al., *User's Guide: Public Use Sample, 1910, United States Census of Population* (Philadelphia: University of Pennsylvania Population Studies Center, 1989).

40. This may help to explain the puzzling phenomenon of why women appear to work less in a period of expanding job opportunities for women.

41. Otto Kollmann and Ludwig Naumann to aunt, Calemonty, Wisc., 8 June 1850, in Helbich, *Amerika*, p. 137.

42. Bruno Riess OSB to Boniface Wimmer OSB, 1 October 1856, Abbey of St. Vincent, Latrobe, Pa., quoted in Howard Brice, *Saints Peter and Paul, Richmond—100 Years* (n.p., 1956), p. 31.

43. John E. Knodel, *Demographic Behavior in the Past: A Study of 14 German Village Populations in the 18th and 19th Centuries* (Cambridge: Cambridge University Press, 1988), pp. 132–133. See also Knodel, *The Decline of Fertility in Germany, 1871–1939* (Princeton: Princeton University Press, 1974).

44. Aquilin Flügel, September 1884, BLC.

45. John Kerler, Jr., to Veronica Kerler, Holland, Mich., 19 October 1851, in Frank, *German-American Pioneers in Wisconsin and Michigan*.

46. Henry Miller to parents, siblings, and their spouses, Meyer Mill, Pa., 30 July 1871, in Helbich, Kamphoefner, and Sommer, *Briefe aus Amerika*, p. 211.

47. Lawrence M. Friedman, *A History of American Law* (New York: Simon and Schuster, 1973), pp. 179–180.

48. The fact that many women returned to Germany shortly after marriage adds credence to this view. On the patterns of return migration, see Walter Kamphoefner, "Volume and Composition of German-American Return Migra-

tion," pp. 293–313 in Rudolph J. Vecoli and Suzanne M. Sinke, eds., *A Century of European Migrations, 1830–1930* (Urbana: University of Illinois Press, 1991).

49. Peter Greggers to sister, Charleston, Ill., 29 March 1857, quoted in Helbich, *Amerika*, p. 130.

50. See, for example, "Die Familie in Europa and in den Ver. Staaten," *Deutsche Auswanderer Zeitung* (Bremen), 15 March 1858.

51. Pauline Wendt to Schwager and family, Manson, Iowa, 7 March 1899, BLC.

52. Katharina Salker to sister Margarethe Loewen, n.p., n.d., BLC.

53. Katharina Stier to sister and family, Chicago, 4 December 1914, BLC.

54. Valentin Pruehs to brother, St. Joseph, Mich., 10 April 1870, BLC.

55. This contrasts strongly with other immigrant groups, where women coming back from America often had substantial monies. This appears to be the case for many Irish, Swedish, and Finnish women. I suspect that long-term domestic service was the key to this difference. In terms of percentages, domestic service played a much greater role among these groups than among the Germans.

56. Kamphoefner, "Volume and Composition of German-American Return Migration."

57. The difference lay partially in different patterns of work division according to gender, i.e., German-American men and women defined many jobs as possible or expected for women, while native-born communities (above poverty level) defined them as male only. A second difference arose from the class position of immigrants and the changing face of industrialization. Immigrant women arrived at a time when the economy was shifting, so that their job opportunities were more likely to be in the reproductive/service sector (paid or unpaid) than in direct production. Likewise, most arrived without the resources to join what they considered a "leisured" American middle class. Their later experiences rarely erased this impression.

5

Catholic Sisterhoods and the Immigrant Church

Deirdre Mageean

Roman Catholic nuns, or sisters, have been part of American life and immigrant communities since the eighteenth century. From those early times to the twentieth century, they have been the labor force that staffed the major charitable and educational institutions of the Catholic Church. For the millions of immigrant members of the church, it was women religious who tended to their many needs and taught and preserved their faith. Their communities were present in cities and towns throughout the country, in small rural settlements on the plains, and in mission settlements for Native Americans.

Understanding the role of nuns in American society requires an understanding of their European culture and origin, the immigrant communities in which they served (and recruited), and the adjustments to American life that these communities were forced to make. In this chapter these issues are addressed for some Irish religious communities in the United States, communities either founded in Ireland or brought to the United States from Ireland.

Over the course of the nineteenth century the numbers of women religious grew from under forty to more than forty thousand.[1] Through their numbers and the extent of their involvement in many activities, nuns represented Catholicism to many Americans. As such, it was they and their convents that were the frequent targets of nativism and anti-Catholic mobs, but it was also they who, through their many charitable and educational works, won over hearts and minds that were initially opposed to them and what they stood for. By the end of the century they outnumbered priests four to one and were a significant presence in every diocese.[2]

Until recently, conventional historical studies have either ignored or downplayed nuns' contribution to immigrant communities and settlements. Despite their numbers and their myriad activities, nuns are "invisible women" in church history and in American social history. Official church publications such as the *Official Catholic Directory* scrupulously record the names, locations, and accomplishments of male clergy while neglecting or giving scant coverage to women religious. Parish histories frequently only note the name and numbers of the religious community, while community histories and biographies tend to concentrate purely on the religious roles of the women concerned. As one author commented concerning the coverage of nuns in secular and church history, "Catholic sisters are traditionally pictured as silent representatives of female purity or as extensions of the church hierarchy."[3] The nature of convent life, the distinctive dress, and the frequent desire of nuns to go about their work silently and unobtrusively no doubt contributed to the perception of women religious as socially peripheral or aloof from society and its concerns. However, to regard nuns as being on the fringes of nineteenth- and twentieth-century American society or to assess only their religious roles is to overlook the significant contribution they made as migrant women and as builders of the immigrant communities they served.

ORIGINS OF MIGRANT NUNS

Of the twelve communities of nuns who established convents in America during the period 1790–1829, five originated in America while the remainder were founded from European motherhouses. The one exception was the ill-fated Ursuline convent, which was established in Boston in 1820 by two Irish girls who had been trained in Canada.[4] Interestingly, all of the communities founded in America survived and flourished, while only one of the communities founded in Europe achieved stability and success.[5] The causes of failure of the European communities lay largely in their inability to adapt their customs and rules to the American environment. One of the major problems was economic survival. The European orders, particularly those that were contemplative and did not engage in remunerative work such as teaching and nursing, traditionally financed their activities from endowments and dowries. In the United States, there was no wealthy aristocracy to support the convents and the level of dowry required of those entering the orders was generally well above the means of American families.[6] Additionally, contemplative orders were singularly ill-suited to life in America, where there was a great need for charitable services. Several orders were also faced with the demands of a rule that had been developed for European conditions but that put excessive demands on nuns who were faced with the rigors of pioneer life and the extra burdens of supporting their communities through work.[7] The communities that survived were those that established rules that, from their foundation, took account of the particular demands of life in America and those that quickly adapted to their new environment.

A good example of this adaptation was the community of Visitation nuns founded in 1799 by Alice Lalor from Kilkenny in Ireland. Lalor, along with two wealthy and educated widows whom she met on the ship from Ireland to the United States, settled in the then village of Georgetown, near the future capital. The group of women lived a religious life according to a rule devised by a priest from Philadelphia. Over time the women felt the need for a more formal constitution and rule, but it was twenty years before they adopted the rule of the Visitandines, a cloistered order with its origin in France. When they examined the Visitandine rule, their twenty years of experience in teaching and nursing in America made them realize that they had to adapt the rule in order to continue their teaching, to escort their pupils in public, and to do their own marketing of the goods they produced.[8] The early days of these nuns were ones of poverty and privation. Often, too, their survival as a community seemed in doubt, as postulants were slow to come forth and their numbers had to be supplemented from France. However, as their school became established, a number of their pupils passed from the classroom to the novitiate, and the community became more secure. This recruitment of young women to the religious life from the ranks of pupils attending schools run by the religious orders increasingly became a major source of new members for the communities. The Georgetown community of Visitandines survived through adapting to the demands of life in America, while other orders returned to Europe because of their inability to acquire sufficient dowries from American girls. Still others found their numbers decimated by death and disease as a result of adherence to austere rules drawn up in another culture.

Between 1830 and 1860, the Catholic church in America grew rapidly, its numbers swollen by the great increase in immigrants from countries such as Ireland and Germany. For most of these migrants, the church was a central social as well as religious institution, and as the immigrants crowded into American cities, the demands on the Church to provide schools, and orphanages grew rapidly. Hard-pressed bishops faced with a shortage of personnel turned to European Catholic countries in search of women religious. During this period many new foundations were founded both from motherhouses in Europe and from within America. Given the large influx of Irish immigrants during this time, it is not surprising that requests for assistance were particularly directed to Ireland. Fortunately for the American clergy, the response was forthcoming.

Three Irish orders were particularly successful and effective among immigrant communities. The first, founded in Philadelphia in 1833, was the Sisters of Charity of the Blessed Virgin Mary. The other two were Irish orders, the Sisters of Mercy, who established their first community in Pittsburgh, Pennsylvania, in 1843, and the Sisters of the Presentation of the Blessed Virgin Mary, whose first American location was San Francisco in 1854. In order to understand the scope and success of the work undertaken by these orders in America, we need to examine their origins.

An order that grew directly out of a response to an appeal for Catholic workers was the Sisters of Charity of the Blessed Virgin Mary. The order was founded in Philadelphia in 1833 by four young Irish women who had begun their communal life in Dublin. Their founder was Mary Francis Clarke, who, like many foundresses, came from an educated and middle-class background. Clarke and her companions lived as a community and opened a small school in Dublin for children of the poor in that city. They ministered to the victims of the 1831 cholera outbreak in Dublin, but their primary mission was in providing Catholic education to children. Their coming to America was in response to news that they had heard of a need for religious instruction among the children of Irish immigrants in Philadelphia. Clarke and four companions decided to leave their well-established school in Dublin and work where the need was perceived as being greater. Shortly after arriving in Philadelphia, they were organized into a religious community. The community quickly grew, and the schools that they established flourished. Only one year after their formalization into a religious community, they responded to an appeal to establish a school in Dubuque. At that time, the diocese comprised the entire territory of Wisconsin and the northern part of Illinois. Dubuque eventually became the motherhouse of the order, and from there the order spread into Chicago, Milwaukee, St. Louis, and other parts of the Midwest and West Coast.

The Sisters of the Presentation of the B.V.M. and the Sisters of Mercy were two of the many new female religious communities set up in Ireland between 1776 and 1875.[9] Over these one hundred years, the conditions for Catholics gradually improved as the penal laws were gradually dismantled and, later (1829), Catholic emancipation was granted. A sense of political, collective identity emerged and was strengthened by the revival of the Catholic Church. While these conditions created an environment that was conducive to the growth of religious communities, the foundation of many of the orders was as much a response to the social problems consequent on economic change in Ireland. Both orders considered here had their origins in social work among the poor and disadvantaged, albeit social work that was motivated by religion.

The first Irish order to grow from such social work was the Presentation Sisters founded in 1775. The foundress was Honoria ("Nano")

Nagle, born in 1728 into a well-to-do Cork family. Like many girls of the time from a similar social background, she was educated in France. On completion of her studies, she returned to Ireland and was introduced to society. However, she was struck by the condition of those whose world was in stark contrast to her own, and she resolved to dedicate herself to service to the poor. Of her own means, she established free schools, an asylum for aged and infirm women, and a home for working women in Cork.[10] Nagle was instrumental in the establishment in Cork of a foundation of Ursulines from Paris, and she invited them to take over the schools that she had founded. However, the Ursulines were an enclosed order, and their rule prevented them from running the schools. Nor could they engage in the various works of charity that Nagle felt were needed in the city. Some twenty years after initiating her work with the poor, Nagle founded her own order—a sisterhood that was not enclosed and could carry out its works of charity among the poor and disadvantaged as well as educate children. As Clear has noted in her work on Irish nuns, an unenclosed sisterhood was without precedent in Ireland. Furthermore, Nagle's group was the first sisterhood to have a specific social purpose.[11] Nagle believed firmly that the road to salvation was through good works such as teaching and ministering—works that would have been impossible if the order had been enclosed. Unfortunately, Nagle died in 1784 before the community was formally changed to a religious congregation and officially approved by the church. When the order was formally approved in 1805, it was with solemn vows and enclosure—quite different from the original ideals of its founder—and the nuns confined themselves to teaching in their free schools. Ironically, the order found it easier to maintain internal cohesion within the new framework. They attracted considerable numbers to their community, and the order quickly spread throughout Ireland. It was not until the order established its foreign missions in Canada and the United States that enclosure was challenged.[12]

In the 1820s a second order with a specific social purpose, the Sisters of Mercy, was founded in Dublin. The founder of the sisters was Catherine McAuley, an upper-middle-class woman who inherited a sizeable fortune and used her wealth to provide services for the poor. In 1824 she bought property in Dublin City and established a school for poor and working girls and a refuge for orphans and unemployed servants. Mercy House quickly became something of a social service center. It had seventy inmates and twelve teachers and helpers, including one Frances Ward, who was later to introduce the order to the United States. The scope and extent of the group's work increased dramatically. By the end of 1828, the women were given permission to visit the city hospitals and sick, and the workers began to make plans for establishing their own hospitals.[13]

McAuley's original intent was to establish not a religious order but a group of female social workers. They called themselves the Sisters of Mercy, lived a communal life, and dressed in similar clothes. In addition to their works, their daily routine included meditation and prayer. They adopted a rule by which to live, and over the years they evolved into a religious community. The decision was not forced on them by any bishop; rather the decision was made by the workers in Mercy House. However, a factor that may have influenced their decision was the opposition and resentment of local clergy and other religious to their active work and independence. As a religious institution, they were guaranteed more cooperation. However, they still had to overcome the barriers that had hitherto prevented sisters from engaging in active work.

The order quickly became popular, attracting many recruits, and its institutes, schools, and hospitals spread throughout the country. It was the first order to carry out nursing in the hospitals of the poor law unions and its members ran the cholera hospital in Dublin during the cholera outbreak of 1831. In 1839 they established a convent in London, and it was from there that a group of sisters went, in 1854, to care for the soldiers of the Crimean War. The active involvement in the works of mercy, the distinctive feature of the order, made it particularly attractive to bishops in America, who needed help in their rapidly growing dioceses.

That the American bishops who called upon the various Irish orders were successful is testimony not just to the sense of mission that many of these communities possessed, but also to the ever-growing pool of women religious within Ireland. The number of nuns in Ireland increased eightfold between 1841 and 1901, a time when the Catholic population nearly halved.[14] The increase in religious vocations at this time was not peculiar to Ireland; there was a general increase in many of the European countries as the Catholic church enjoyed a revival. However, the increase in Ireland was dramatic, and the growth in the number of women religious in particular was spectacular. Hence we need to look to factors beyond religious motivation for an explanation of this phenomenon.

Postfamine Ireland was a period of considerable economic, social, and demographic change in the society. Subdivision of land, low age at marriage, and high rates of marriage gave way to impartible inheritance, reduction in the marriage rate, and late age at marriage—a trend that had begun in parts of the country before the famine but that now spread throughout Ireland except in the more remote parts. With changes in farming from tillage to pasture and the loss of the domestic textile industry in many areas, women's economic contribution to the family was either reduced or taken over by men. Instead, women's economic worth was valued according to the dowry that they brought with them upon marriage. Marriages were frequently arranged, and partners were increasingly chosen on economic grounds. For many women, marriage was a loveless experience and one marked by hard work and continuous childbearing. Overall, the position of women deteriorated as they became more marginal to the economy. As a result of this reduction in economic status, they became increasingly dependent on and subordinate to males, whether married or unmarried. For those women who were unwilling to face these prospects, there were usually two options—to remain unmarried (which still meant remaining in a subordinate position), or to improve their social status by emigration. Increasingly, they chose the latter. In the decades after the famine, the proportion of Irish women emigrating steadily increased, such that by the end of the nineteenth century and into the early twentieth century women dominated the migration stream—a pattern unique among European migrants at that time.[15]

Throughout this same period, educational opportunities for girls improved considerably. Literacy rates for females increased, and more and more girls completed their secondary education. However, the possibilities of usefully employing their skills were low. Most opportunities for work outside the home were for working-class girls, either in domestic service or in factory work. Few opportunities existed for middle-class women who wished to pursue a professional career. For most middle-class women, marriage and motherhood was the next stage in life after attaining adulthood. Yet with the advances made in education, from the 1850s on the expectations of women were raised and they sought a degree of autonomy and activity that could not be found within marriage. An increasingly popular route for some of those women was found in the religious life.

PIONEER SISTERS

Active and unenclosed orders such as the Mercy nuns were attractive to such women. The decentralized structure meant that nuns could disperse and go wherever the need was greatest. Twelve years after their foundation, the Sisters of Mercy had twice as many convents as the older orders.[16] The women who became mother superiors of convents, especially those who led newly founded convents, were strong characters, good leaders and negotiators. These same qualities were common among the women who left Ireland to establish orders throughout America.[17] In many ways, the seven Sisters of Mercy, who in 1843 left their convent in Carlow, Ireland, in response to an appeal from the bishop of Pittsburgh to establish a community there, were typical of such women. Their leader, Mother Francis Warde, was from a well-to-do family and had been privately educated. At age thirty-three she had already served as superior in three new convents in Ireland. She was an intelligent, energetic, and capable woman with considerable administrative experience. The remainder of these "pioneer nuns" were from similar backgrounds, and despite their youth—most were in their early or middle twenties—they had considerable experience in education, nursing, and administration.[18]

In Pittsburgh the nuns were faced with a large but floating Catholic population, but they quickly got down to the task of visiting the sick and giving religious instruction to children. In 1844 they opened the first Mercy school in the United States, and the following year, a boarding school. In 1846, barely three years after their arrival in Pittsburgh, they responded to an appeal by the bishop of Chicago to establish a community in his rapidly growing diocese. Of the many cities throughout the United States that the Mercy nuns worked in, Chicago provides an excellent example of the range of activities in which these women engaged.

Once again led by the redoubtable Mother Warde, the new community quickly established itself in Chicago, where they were impressed by the needs of poor immigrant Catholics, most of whom were Irish. From their arrival, they became the pioneers of the Church's activities and laid the foundations of the many charitable and educational institutions in the city. The scope of their work is impressive by any standard. The sisters visited the sick in their homes and the prisoners in jail; they opened the first five parochial schools and the first night school for Catholic adults, the first convert classes for adults, the first orphanage, and the first academy. They nursed the sick in the city's Alm House and in the first county hospital; they took over the care of Chicago's first hospital and erected and maintained Chicago's first permanent hospital. They also founded a Catholic girls' high school, the first working girls' home, the first Catholic training school for nurses, the first Catholic women's college, and the first Magdalen asylum for troubled young women. They took charge of the cholera victims in 1849 and again in 1854 and rendered service in other epidemics.[19]

Not until 1856, ten years after their arrival, were they joined in Chicago by another order of nuns. But in those ten years they grew in numbers from the original five to thirty-five, this despite losing several members to contagious diseases contracted while nursing the ill. By 1896, when the sisters celebrated their golden anniversary in Chicago, they numbered 225. The majority were first- and second-generation Irish, and they recruited from within the Irish immigrant communities, where their presence was always visible through their schools and charitable organizations. Many histories and annual reports of Irish parishes in Chicago list with pride the many names of those who joined the Mercies, the B.V.M.s, and other orders.

We may well ask what attracted Irish women in Chicago and other cities to the life of a nun. The nuns had strong connections to the Irish communities, and there was a certain amount of empathy, as many of the nuns were Irish immigrants or the daughters of them. But the attraction to the religious life? It was not merely a question of piety, although women then, as now, are more pious than men. Like the migration process itself, the answers seem to lie in a combination of "push" and "pull" factors.

For many Irish women, the religious life must have appeared as an attractive alternative to what married life offered, with its high rates of widowhood, desertion, and abuse. The religious life also freed women from the drudgeries of domestic duties, repeated and often dangerous childbirth, and the subordinate role in marriage. However, to view nuns as mere refugees from the married state or to see convents as the solution to the high numbers of unmarried Irish women in the United States is to do a disservice to those women who "took the veil."[20] The religious life was an alternative to marriage, motherhood, and spinsterhood for good, positive reasons. Freed from many of the traditional constraints on women, nuns were able to exploit their marginal position in society and pursue active involvement in areas that at the time were considered unsuitable for women—such as nursing. They enjoyed opportunities open to few other women of the nineteenth century—administrative positions, principalships of schools, presidencies of colleges, and heads of hospitals. Within their many charitable institutions, there was ample scope for the talents of any woman, and there was frequently the opportunity for travel and adventure. They did "men's" work without waiting to be permitted.[21]

Convents offered their members power, respect, and long-term careers. They also offered a degree of autonomy, although bishops and priests frequently tried (sometimes with success) to cajole and force communities to do what they wanted. No doubt some bishops resented the control over personnel that many mother superiors had in schools, hospitals, orphanages, and other institutions under their domain. However, other bishops and priests had a healthy respect for the power of nuns. Communities would fight for their rights, and some bishops who took them on learned to their cost what the consequences could be. As the main providers of charitable services, nuns were in a powerful position. They could simply withdraw, and often did, from a parish or diocese if disagreements became major. As Ewens has pointed out, "There was always another bishop, just over the diocesan borders, who needed the services the sisters provided."[22]

Finally, nuns were never isolated from the company of other women. In the many tribulations they faced—the rigors of rural pioneer life, poverty, and difficulties in their work—they were able to help one another and offer companionship. What is less certain is the degree of solidarity they felt with women in general. Did they identify with secular women's movements?[23] There seems little doubt that in their charitable works and in their educational role they had a bias toward their own gender. Through their emphasis on the education of girls, they were at least partly responsible for the significant social mobility of second-generation Irish women.[24] Yet we still know little of their views on the cult of domesticity or the Victorian woman, whether they were aware of women's movements, or how their views on the social position of women could be reconciled with their views on the spiritual position of women. These are all areas worthy of further research.

We can, however, feel sure that women religious in nineteenth- and early twentieth-century American society were not socially peripheral women, nor were they women who were aloof from society's needs and concerns. They were a force in the immigrant church and a strong and visible presence in many ethnic communities. They also instituted and developed the chief charitable resources of many nineteenth-century American communities. As such, they deserve better than to be "invisible women" in church and social history. Rather, they should be studied both as immigrant women and as women who touched the lives of many immigrants.

NOTES

1. Mary Ewens, "The Leadership of Nuns."
2. Ibid., p. 101.
3. Susan Peterson, "A Widening Horizon: Catholic Sisterhoods on the Northern Plains, 1874–1910," *Great Plains Quarterly* 5 (1985): 125.
4. The Mount St. Benedict community and school in Boston were successful, but the community was forced to disband after the school was destroyed by a nativist mob in 1843. See Mary Ewens, *The Role of the Nun in Nineteenth-Century America*, pp. 148–151.
5. Ibid., p. 32.
6. From the late sixteenth century on, dowries brought by women upon entering the religious life provided financial support for the convent. The required dowry was used for the establishment and maintenance of those charitable activities for which the institute was founded. The amount required varied from convent to convent according to the financial structure of the house, but within the house the figure was usually inflexible. The amount required could be quite steep. For instance the Irish Ursulines who came to New York in 1812 set the figure at $2000—a considerable sum for those days. As might be expected, hardly any New Yorker could afford that sum, and the sisters, bereft of any other source of income, were forced to return to Ireland. See T. M. Kealy, "Dowry," *The New Catholic Encyclopedia*, vol. 10, pp. 1028–1029.
7. Ewens cites the case of a number of orders that had to modify their constitutions in order to eliminate midnight prayer. The duties of nocturnal

prayer on top of farming and teaching caused the death and illness of a number of their members. See her *Role of the Nun*, p. 114.

8. Rev. Joseph Code, *Great American Foundresses* (Freeport, Me.: Books for Libraries Press, 1968), p. 188.

9. Catriona Clear, "The Limits of Female Autonomy: Nuns in Nineteenth-Century Ireland," in Maria Luddy and Cliona Murphy, eds., *Women Surviving* (Dublin: Poolbeg Press, 1990), p. 27.

10. Elinor Tong Dehey, *Religious Orders of Women in the United States* (Hammond, Ind.: W. B. Conkey, 1930), pp. 544–545.

11. Clear, "Limits of Female Autonomy," pp. 27–28.

12. For a good history of the work of the Presentation nuns on the rural frontier, see Peterson and Vaughn-Robertson, *Women with Vision*.

13. Dehey, *Religious Orders of Women*, p. 286.

14. Clear, "Limits of Female Autonomy," p. 21.

15. For more on this see Diner, *Erin's Daughters*, and Nolan, *Ourselves Alone*.

16. Clear, "Limits of Female Autonomy," p. 34.

17. For a good introduction, see Code, *Great American Foundresses*.

18. Sr. Jerome McHale, *On the Wing—the Story of the Pittsburgh Sisters of Mercy, 1843–1968* (New York: Seabury Press, 1980), p. 18.

19. Dehey, *Religious Orders of Women*, p. 297; Brewer, *Nuns and the Education of American Catholic Women*, p. 29; Roger Coughlin and Cathryn Riplinger, *The Story of Charitable Care in the Archdiocese, 1844–1959* (Chicago: The Catholic Charities of Chicago, 1983), pp. 68–73.

20. For rates of marriage among the Irish in various communities see Diner, *Erin's Daughters*, pp. 48–49.

21. Sr. Elizabeth Kolmer, "Catholic Women Religious and Women's History: A Survey of the Literature," *American Quarterly* 30 (1978): 649.

22. Ewens, "The Leadership of Nuns," p. 107.

23. On this issue, see Peterson, "A Widening Horizon," pp. 125–132, and Kolmer, "Catholic Women Religious," pp. 639–651.

24. Mary Oates, "Organized Voluntarism: The Catholic Sisters in Massachusetts, 1870–1940," *American Quarterly* 30 (1978): 662.

6

Ideology, Ethnicity, and the Gendered Subject: Reading Immigrant Women's Autobiographies

Betty Bergland

But hark to the clamor of the city all about! This is my latest home, and it invites me to a glad new life. The endless ages have indeed throbbed through my blood, but a new rhythm dances in my veins. My spirit is not tied to the monumental past, any more than my feet were bound to my grandfather's house below the hill. The past was only my cradle, and now it cannot hold me, because I am grown too big; just as the little house in Polotzk, once my home, has now become a toy of memory, as I move about at will in the wide spaces of this splendid palace, whose shadow covers acres. No! It is not I that belong to the past, but the past that belongs to me. America is the youngest of the nations, and inherits all that went before in history. And I am the youngest of America's children, and into my hands is given all her priceless heritage, to the last white star espied through the telescope, to the last great thought of the philosopher. Mine is the whole majestic past, and mine is the shining future.

Mary Antin, *The Promised Land*[1]

Mary Antin emigrated to the United States in 1894 at the age of thirteen with her family from the village of Polotzk in the Russian Pale of Settlement to Boston, Massachusetts. She and her family thus joined the 35 million immigrants in the late nineteenth and early twentieth centuries leaving Europe for what many viewed as the Promised Land. Scores of these immigrants, like Mary Antin, wrote autobiographies chronicling the journey and new life in America, often describing this experience in epic terms through spatial and temporal metaphors. In the closing paragraph of her autobiography, the passage cited above, the Antin narrator represents the past of Polotzk, in the Russian Pale of Settlement, as a cradle, a metaphor signifying the geographic world and Jewish history she left, the monumental past to which her spirit no longer feels tied; while America is represented as a grand palace, its shadow covering acres, that ennobles this immigrant woman. Presumably, because this immigrant resides in the palace/America, she also inherits its "priceless heritage," as should all who inhabit that space. The repetition of this pattern of representing America and Americanness in an epic scope with spatial and temporal metaphors is suggested in titles of many immigrant autobiographies.[2] However, Mary Antin's autobiography has circulated widely in the culture in the twentieth century—thirty-four printings, two re-editions, in 1969 and 1985, and frequent reproductions in anthologies—which means the autobiography has served a paradigmatic function. This led Mary Dearborn in *Pochahontas's Daughters* to conclude that *The Promised Land* has become an "immigrant classic."[3]

The model represents a pattern of assimilation and movement from old world to new world and from Jewish immigrant to American citizen, but the model represents more. What has gone unnoticed in this classic model is the fact that the immigrant who speaks, the autobiographical "I," Autobiographical Antin, never leaves adolescence, nor does she leave the spaces of the schoolroom. As the Autobiographical Antin never leaves the time of adolescence and the space of the schoolroom, the readers cannot imagine what Americanness means concretely to the Historical Mary Antin or, generally, what it means to be an adult immigrant in the palace/America. This pattern can be found in both published and unpublished immigrant narratives throughout much of the century. One dramatic example is found in Angela Mischke's unpublished manuscript: emigrating with her family from Poland to Chicago in 1913, Mischke begins her life narrative with her arrival in America and reflects back on the journey and her early years in America; however, the narrative ends abruptly with her marriage and concludes with one paragraph devoted to the accomplishments of her grown children. Thus, the significant moments for this narrator remain the trans-Atlantic journey and her children, essentially preadolescent stages.[4] This pattern crosses ethnic, gender, and class boundaries. For example, Richard Rodriguez's *Hunger of Memory*, the narrative of a second-generation Mexican-American, ends with his leaving school, while Maxine Hong Kingston's *The Woman Warrior*, the celebrated narrative on growing up Chinese-American, includes adult women, but the autobiographical "I" remains in girlhood.[5] While the ethnic subjectivity narrated by the Antin Autobiographical "I" represents prevailing ideologies in 1912, the ethnic subjectivity of adolescent school-leaving also signifies ideologies found in the late twentieth century, evident in the more recent examples.

Focusing on the temporal and spatial positions of the autobiographical

"I" exposes the ideologies embedded in autobiographical narratives. Ideology here refers to unstated assumptions about the nature of reality accepted as natural or true.[6] The transformative moment for the cultural Other in the school-leaving of adolescence freezes the autobiographical subject in that moment, for both the narrator and the reader. If the autobiographical "I" of this ethnic subjectivity remains in adolescence, then adulthood—including all the gendered and ethnic complexities of adulthood—dissolves. The effect on the reader is to conceptualize the immigrant and foreigner as a child. By making this image the signifier of the Historical Antin, the Narrator in effect perpetuates a view of the cultural Other as a child. For the reader the further effect is to foreclose any imaginative possibilities of gendered and ethnic difference or adulthood. The model of the American transformed at the palace gate by virtue of articulating, "I am an American," reflects and reproduces that ideology. The abstract quality of that articulation implies that access to the palace, meaning realization of all the emancipatory promises of America, can be secured by all who utter these words; however, since Autobiographical Antin never moves beyond that frozen point, what this in fact means is that all difference is erased in the abstraction—ethnicity, gender, class, as well as adult struggles of sexuality, parenting, negotiating contradictory cultural narratives. In short, complex social, political, and economic relations of the larger society are erased.

The problematic effect on the reader of these absent subject positions intensifies if we imagine that autobiography represents an "authentic" voice. In the last twenty years, immigrant, ethnic, and women's historians have sought to document lives of silenced and marginalized groups. In seeking to capture the "authentic experience" of women, immigrants, or ethnics, they have turned to first-person narratives for what is often imagined as "authentic" voice—autobiographies, memoirs, diaries, journals, oral histories, reminiscences—as if some pure state of Polishness, Italianness, Germanness, Jewishness, or femaleness existed in them. However, the assumption that "authentic" ethnic voices speak an ethnic purity tends to essentialize the speaking "I," and by extension, the ethnic group; further, imagining a unified ethnic identity tends to blur complexities of subjectivity generated by different positions within ethnic groups linked to class, gender, regions, and historical moments.[7] Consequently, in assuming authenticity and essential group identity, we ignore the multiple and competing ideologies represented by different languages and discourses in which all immigrants found themselves, in both old and new worlds. Clearly, the world of the immigrant was not unlike the world of the illiterate peasant described by M. M. Bakhtin in *The Dialogic Imagination*, only perhaps more so:

Thus an illiterate peasant, miles away from any urban center, naively immersed in an unmoving and for him unshakable everyday world, nevertheless lived in several language systems: he prayed to God in one language (Church Slavonic), sang songs in another, spoke to his family in a third and, when he began to dictate petitions to the local authorities through a scribe, he tried speaking yet a fourth language (the official-literate language, "paper" language). All these are *different languages*, even from the point of view of abstract socio-dilectological markers.[8]

Bakhtin argues that when peasants recognized that these languages also represented different ideological systems and contradictory worldviews intimately linked to these languages, they could no longer live peacefully; at that point peasants had to choose an "orientation among them." How these multiple ideological contradictions were negotiated and an orientation was eventually chosen was determined both by possibility and by the consequences of available courses: immigrants could speak only what was linguistically and culturally possible, and generally spoke what would be culturally sanctioned. Like Bakhtin's illiterate peasants, immigrants were situated in contradictory ideologies, not only in language systems from the old world—the language of religious institutions, of local songs and folklore, of daily life, and of paper (state) language— but also the language systems of the new world. Contradictory ideological systems multiplied. For immigrant women, contradictions multiplied also because a patriarchal system of the old world permeated the new world: they were situated simultaneously and paradoxically both in the patriarchal old world and in a *radically different patriarchal* new world. (Patriarchy, understood here in its broadest sense, signifies a system that designates primary difference and meanings based on gender.)

Reading first-person ethnic and immigrant narratives, one must consider the multiple discourses/languages in which immigrants were permitted to speak and the meanings associated with these articulations. In order to understand an "I" who speaks, especially the voice of the immigrant woman, we must appreciate not only the historical circumstances surrounding immigration but also the ideologies of the language systems in which these women were situated, including patriarchal ideologies of the old and new worlds. We cannot assume that their words transparently reveal the historical subject. We need to understand how ideology secures certain subjectivities within the prevailing social order. I will argue in this chapter that autobiographies of immigrant women expose the ideologies in which these women lived and their effects.

One way of understanding immigrant women's autobiographies is through a chronotopic (literally time/space) analysis of the speaking "I." It exposes ideologies embedded in the narrative, enables us to see relationships between culture and consciousness, and distinguishes a gendered subject in the narrative.[9] If we read autobiographies chronotopically—that is, by situating the autobiographical subject in the time and place of the narrative and by placing the autobiographical subjects in their historical and discursive contexts—we can see the concrete effects of ideologies on subjectivities. A chronotopic analysis provides a meaningful strategy for going beyond literary, aesthetic, or historical analyses to illuminate ideological effects of American and ethnic discourses on immigrant women. While Mary Antin serves as the model of the immigrant autobiographical "I" situated in adolescent school-leaving, chronotopic analysis can reveal other positions found among immigrant autobiographies.

I will compare and contrast the temporal and spatial subject positions in three autobiographies of immigrant women. The first represents an identification with America—Mary Antin's *The Promised Land*. The second represents identification with patriarchal (ethnic and American) positions for women as wife and mother—Hilda Polacheck's *I Came a Stranger: The Story of a Hull-House Girl*. The third, Emma Goldman's *Living My Life*, represents a resistance to dominant ideologies for both gendered and ethnic subjectivities.[10] These three narratives, all written by Eastern European Jewish immigrants from the turn of the century, do not represent all immigrant narratives nor all chronotopic positions, but they serve representative functions. In the process of interpreting these autobiographies, we can see how ideologies embedded in the narrative and the subject positions they signify, can serve prevailing views and social relations. In the paradigmatic immigrant narrative, Autobiographical Mary Antin is situated in the schoolroom of the adolescent, the time and space of many immigrant autobiographies. If Antin's narrative is paradigmatic, then Goldman's represents an unparadigmatic autobiography—challenging prevailing ideologies by occupying public and forbidden spaces (public arenas and prisons) as an adult female. On the other hand, Autobiographical Polacheck aligns herself with the patriarchy and occupies primarily the space of the settlement house and home; representing female subjectivities, her autobiography was considered uninteresting for decades and was only recently published.

By illustrating how the ideological effects of discourses can be read into the autobiographical subjects, I hope to demonstrate the value of a chronotopic analysis for reading immigrant women's autobiographies. Where the autobiographical "I" situates the self in the temporal and spatial world is where the readers will imagine the historical figure. It is not self-evident what temporal and spatial arenas the autobiographer will occupy in the narrative, but those represented by the narrator signify subjectivities valued and suggest the ideological effects on historical subjects, given the discursive formations in which they were positioned.

Mary Antin's *The Promised Land* moves chronologically from the old to the new world, beginning in the Pale of Settlement in the late nineteenth century and ending in the new world when Mary Antin, as an adolescent schoolgirl, proclaims her transformation to American in a "second birth." The first half of the autobiography, comprising both a personal narrative and a communal history, begins:

When I was a little girl, the world was divided into two parts; namely Polotzk, the place where I lived, and a strange land called Russia. All the little girls I knew lived in Polotzk, with their fathers and mothers and friends. Russia was the place where one's father went on business. It was so far off, and so many bad things happened there, that one's mother and grandmother and grown-up aunts cried at the railroad station, and one was expected to be sad and quiet for the rest of the day, when the father departed for Russia. (p. 1)

The Narrator recreates her own youth within the context of a larger narrative of Jews in tsarist Russia. The community of "we" in the first half of the autobiography signified her immediate family, the extended family, the people of Polotzk, Jews within the Pale, and those within the historical community of Jews, and is distinguished from the "they" (gentiles, particularly Russians). The chronotopic positioning emerges from this "we." Thus, the spatial boundaries of Antin's universe, the topos, revolve around the safe and nonsafe: the "here" (Pale) usually remained safe, while the "there" (outside the Pale) generated fear. The Narrator writes, "I do not know when I became old enough to understand. The truth was born in on me a dozen times a day. . . . [I]t was the first lesson a little girl in Polotzk had to learn. . . . [W]e must not be found outside the Pale, because we were Jews" (pp. 4–5). Similarly, the chronos in the first half of the autobiography revolves around the same opposition: the "now" (of tsarist oppression) and the "then" (before oppression, when David was king and Jewish girls were princesses).

The chronos and topos both evoke a collective history. Gender differences existed in the Pale, both imposed from without by Russian racist policies, which conscripted Jewish men into the tsar's army, but not women, inflicting tortures, mutilations, and forced baptisms, and imposed from within by orthodox traditions that designated separate arenas for males (the Heder and synagogue) and females (the home, where the kitchen was "a girl's real schoolroom") (p. 34). Despite these distinct spatial arenas based on gender, the primary subjectivities of the old world narrative revolve around ethnic difference. Consequently, Narrator Antin in the old world linked the autobiographical "I" to historical, cultural, religious, and communal narratives, defining herself collectively inside Judaism—inside the Pale, inside a history that ennobled her, and inside a family—contrasted with an outside world of secular and oppressive rule. Within that world of spatial and temporal boundaries, Autobiographical Antin articulates an "I" that remains primarily a "we" in a collective time and space, and the primary marker of subjectivity remains ethnic.

In 1894, Mary (then Maschke) Antin, along with her mother and siblings, emigrated to Boston to join her father Israel Antin, who had left Polotzk three years earlier. The second half of the autobiography is set in America, where the autobiographical subject was "made over." The first chapter set in the new world repeats the title of the autobiography, *The Promised Land,* and focuses on the Americanization process, culminating with the day the father delivered the Antin children to school. The schoolroom, site of subsequent chapters, thus becomes the critical signifier of America and the central chronotope of the autobiography. The Narrator writes that the first day of school was "magnified a hundred times" in her memory and will be remembered long after "I forget my name" (p. 199). As identification of the Autobiographical Antin with America centers in the schoolroom, that site also signifies Americanization discourses. Americanization, understood generally as a process of assimilation to Anglo-Saxon culture, historically is attached to a specific movement at the turn of the century when mass immigration of thousands of non-Anglo, non-Protestant, non-English-speaking populations alarmed American gatekeepers, who feared civilization and the natural order of things were threatened. Xenophobes sought immigration restriction, while more reform-minded agents sought to halt the collapse of the moral order through education: the English language, Anglo-Saxon culture, Protestant virtues, and middle-class cultural values could redeem civilization and humanity, reformers thought American schools played a key role in this transformation of the alien into the American, and language, namely linguistic competence, often served as the critical sign of patriotism, morality, and humanity. Autobiographical Antin narrates the initiation into the discourse of the school, and especially of the teacher. George Washington served as a primary signifier of the Americanization discourse for Autobiographical Antin because he was a "king in greatness," and he and Antin were "fellow citizens"; Autobiographical Antin felt "nobly related" (p. 253). Autobiographical Antin occupies the space of the schoolroom for much of the remainder of the autobiography, along with spaces related to the school by virtue of the knowledges they represent, namely the Boston Public Library; the private library of Dr. Hale, the "grand old man of Boston"; and Hale House Settlement, where Antin is introduced to the Natural History Club and nature.

Like the school (both in the knowledges it contains and in the architectural order it signifies), the Boston Public Library represents ideologies of Americanization and Western rationality. While the Boston Public Library became known as "The People's Palace" after Oliver Wendell Holmes's dedicatory poem, the library's beaux arts architecture, associated with the classical ideals of ancient Greece and Rome, and its lavish construction (which made Holmes's label partially ironic) signify a democratic—that is people's—space. Nevertheless, the reference remains problematic, for it signifies an elite culture. The kind of knowledge elevated in the Boston library becomes clear when the Autobiographical Antin visits her sister Frieda and reads in Frieda's tenement kitchen not what might be called the people's stories—not Russian, Yiddish, or even American literature—but what the school and library taught should be read and valued: the classics, specifically, Cicero, Ovid, and Virgil (the sisters especially liked to read *The Aenid*). The elite nature of this knowledge is again reinforced when juxtaposed with Dr. Hale's library on Highland Street. Going to Hale's library before school and the Boston Public Library after school, Autobiographical Antin endured the slum: "Who would feel cramped in a tenement with such royal privileges as these," she proclaimed; "one could be happy a year on Dover Street [the slum] after spending a half hour on Highland Street [location of Hales's upper class home]" (pp. 345–346). The contradictions residing in this space signifying American cultural assimilation become explicit when we consider that these spaces—the school and the library—offered no meaningful residence in any sense; the knowledges they represented denied Antin, as woman, the franchise (legitimacy), and the economic insecurity of Dover Street contrasted with Highland Street speaks to the contradictions of the American promises the Autobiographical Antin affirms.

In the final chronotope of the autobiography the reader meets the Antin Subject in front of the Boston Public Library, an adolescent who has just returned from a Natural History Club outing at the sea, having been left on the steps of the library. Autobiographical Antin holds a specimen jar in hand from her nature collection, and reflects on being the "youngest of America's children." The final topos of the autobiography aligns the Antin Subject with two dominant epistemologies of Western culture—elite cultural knowledge housed in the Boston Public Library, before which she stands; and scientific rationalism, which collects, labels, and controls Nature, signified by the day's catch in the specimen jar. The school and library, the primary chronotopes of the autobiography and site of her narrative "rebirth," merge in this final image, and by aligning the speaking subject with these knowledges, the Narrator would secure the Autobiographical Antin as an American. However, the reader cannot imagine an Antin beyond the steps of the Boston library. Although the Historical Antin was nearly thirty when the autobiography was written (and she had studied at Barnard, married, borne a child, moved to New York), the "life" of the Autobiographical Antin ends with adolescent school-leaving on the steps of the Boston Public Library. The Antin Subject the reader thus meets in this autobiography is an adolescent who reached neither adulthood nor maturity; she is neither a sexual nor a social being; the Antin Subject is rooted in no specific place or community. Female subjectivities (along with marriage and parenthood) are erased in the final chronotope, along with ethnicity. Thus, the assertion of Americanness denies both gendered and ethnic difference.

Consequently, the meaning of rebirth as an American remains an abstract utterance, contradictory and without real meaning. We might argue that this explains why the work is frequently cited as a "classic immigrant autobiography." A few years after the publication of *The Promised Land* in 1918, the Historical Antin suffered from what was diagnosed as neurasthenia, from which she never really recovered. Surely, the psychic struggle of the Historical Antin is not unrelated to the enormous contradictions between the idealized American represented by the Autobiographical Subject, for whom adulthood, sexuality and difference remained unimagined and unimaginable, and the actual conditions of the Historical Antin—woman, wife (separated), mother, Russian Jewish immigrant, author. For Historical Antin, dominant cultural discourses provided no language for these positions, rendering them unimaginable; consequently, Narrator Antin lacked a language for articulating the contradictory positions of the Historical Antin. To suggest that the American-identified Autobiographical Antin represents the "real" Mary Antin denies the Historical Antin the contradictions and complexities of that life, while it renders the notion of the "classic immigrant autobiography" abstract and provides the reader no glimpse of what it might mean to be an adult American female and ethnic. The problem lies not in a deficient, essential Antin; rather, the problem is lodged in the ideologies to which she is attached.

The publication of *I Came a Stranger: The Story of a Hull-House Girl* in 1989 by the University of Illinois Press, in the Women in American History Series, marks an achievement for ethnic studies and women's history. Hilda Polacheck began writing her autobiography in 1953, and until her death in 1967 sought to publish her story because she believed it important to relate the way a Jewish immigrant from Poland became an American during a visit to Hull House.[11] Scholars in immigration literature and history have marked Mary Antin's narrative as paradigmatic; however, Polacheck's autobiography reveals dimensions of immigrant/ethnic/Jewish/female life that Antin's does not—most specifically life centered in the spaces of the settlement house and the private home. Autobiographical Polacheck addresses female subjectivity, namely as wife, mother, and widow in the home, and reveals further dimensions of ethnic and gendered subjectivity among immigrant women signified in the chronotopic arenas of Hull House and the family home. Not only does Polacheck give us a moving and significant narrative of immigrant ethnic life, exceptional for its attention to the very categories of gender and domestic life excised from the Antin autobiography (and many immigrant women's autobiographies that seek legitimation through identification with the father), but Polacheck provides us with the "only known description of Hull-House written by a woman from the neighborhood."[12] The publication of *I Came a Stranger* adds a new dimension to our understanding of Hull House: since the settlement house acts as the pivotal space of the narrative and shapes Polacheck's life, it serves as the central chronotope of the autobiography; Autobiographical Polacheck identifies with the reform discourses of the settlement house and particularly Jane Addams. This arena permits Autobiographical Polacheck comfortably to assume multiple positions as female (including wife and mother) and American, while remaining critical of dimensions of America.

Hilda Satt arrived in the United States in the early 1890s, at about the same time as Antin, and both their fathers celebrated the new world, yet Narrator Polacheck situates herself as an adult engaged in the contemporary world. Reform discourses of the settlement house align her with the socialist movement in Milwaukee and involvement with global issues of peace and justice—suggesting a social critique muted in Antin's autobiography—and they locate her outside the home in public spaces and monumental time; yet Autobiographical Polacheck is also positioned as a wife and mother within the spatial and temporal concerns of the home. Thus, Hilda Polacheck emerges as an immigrant woman, balancing contradictory discourses of Americanization and patriarchy within her life. The settlement house movement generally, and Hull House particularly, serve as a crucial chronotope for understanding the subjectivity represented by Hilda Satt Polacheck, and by extension other women influenced by the settlement house movement. Polacheck linked her economic and personal struggles to a larger arena as she witnessed Jane Addams engaged in struggles with individuals, the neighborhood, Chicago, the nation, and the globe. The spatial arenas in which Polacheck might thus imagine herself grew broader and provided a counter to the daily struggle of earning bread and to the individualized discourses Mary Antin found in the schools. Consequently, while Polacheck positions herself within traditional patriarchal discourses of wife and mother, she also emerges as a citizen of the world engaged in social and political issues.

The autobiography moves chronologically from Poland to Chicago, to Hull House, to Milwaukee, and back to Chicago. Hull House occupies the center of the narrative, a section consisting of seventy-five pages, roughly one-half of the autobiography. While Hull House becomes the metaphoric and concrete center around which the narrative revolves, Narrator Polacheck also positions the autobiographical subject primarily within domestic spaces: in the old world (pre–Hull House chapters) the home remains the primary site of religious observance and a safe place away from anti-Semitic attacks; in the new world (in the post–Hull House chapters) the home serves as a central space, representing not only a place where Polacheck is wife and mother, but a center of political engagement and domestic pleasure—a house transformed by Polacheck as a socialist.

Narrator Polacheck recounts the first visit to Hull House for a Christmas party in 1896. At first reluctant to join her Irish friend, Hilda responds that it had been unsafe in Poland for Jewish children to be out on Christmas; she is afraid that she could be killed. Reassured, she eventually decides to go. The Narrator writes:

It dawned on me that the people in this room had come from other countries. Yet there was no tension. Everybody seemed to be having a good time. No one seemed to care where they had come from, or what religion they professed, or what clothes they wore, or what they thought. As I sat there, I am sure I felt myself being freed from a variety of century old superstitions and inhibitions. (pp. 51–52)

The Narrator describes Addams's entry into the room; she welcomed guests and made them feel wanted: "I know that I became a staunch American at this party. I was with children who had been brought here from all over the world. The fathers and mothers, like my father and mother, had come in search of a free and happy life. And we were all having a good time at a party as the guests of an American, Jane Addams" (p. 52). The Narrator rejects a trivialization of the party and expands her meaning, stating that all the children there were poor and many were underfed or ill-dressed—but they did not fear one another. She gives Addams a tribute: "What greater service can a human being give to her country than to banish fear from the heart of a child? Jane Addams did that for me at that party" (p. 52). Linking the social space of Hull House with the friendliness of a party but also the potential to destroy fear of the stranger in the heart of a child, Narrator Polacheck represents Hull House as a site of pleasure and peace, and Jane Addams signifies personal and collective compassion. The hospitable space of Hull House provides the autobiographical subject with the possibility for making a meaningful home for herself as an adult in Milwaukee. Unlike Autobiographical Antin, who never reaches adulthood or occupies the domestic arena, Autobiographical Polacheck extends her subjectivity into adulthood and the transforming spaces of the home where she occupied domestic space, yet she also sees herself as a global citizen. Hull House provided a model of a friendly space in an otherwise hostile world, and its discursive practices, which acknowledged diversity, social and economic justice, and spiritual longings of the young, presented an expanded world vision where Hilda Satt Polacheck could take her place.

Only later, as an adult, does Polacheck return to Hull House, after a boring day at the factory, and this was the start of a new life for her. Hull House, she writes, became an "oasis in a desert of disease and monotony and monotony can become a disease" (p. 73). Hull House satisfied Polacheck's desire for knowledge through literature, the arts, music, writing, drama; it expanded her vision of the world through exposure to visitors from all over the world; it provided a social space for meeting others her age with shared interests; it offered a site in which debate and criticism of America was possible and encouraged; it stimulated opportunities for the future by encouraging her in reading, writing, and eventual attendance at the University of Chicago and subsequent employment at social institutions; it offered a gendered role model through the figure of Jane Addams and helped to cultivate bourgeois tastes, which made her a suitable mate for William Polacheck; finally, it provided a model for living in a socially and culturally diverse world by providing an example of tolerance and acceptance.

These settlement house discourses were embodied in Addams, who for Autobiographical Polacheck came to signify an acceptable subjectivity—as American, as woman—and mediated tensions around discourses of ethnicity and patriarchy. Though predominantly middle-class and Protestant, the discourses of Addams and Hull House encouraged tolerance, compassion, and social justice, and Polacheck defends Addams, describing her affectionately and with admiration. Thus Narrator Polacheck writes of Addams that she

gave me an abiding faith in the true principles of Americanism. She was a firm believer in freedom of speech, freedom of the press, and freedom of religion. As for freedom of speech, I cannot recall any time when anyone was denied the use of the hall for a meeting on political grounds. . . . Jane Addams was not a professional patriot. . . . She did not believe in the axiom, "My Country right or wrong." (p. 103)

Polacheck's exposure to reform discourses with the settlement house movement permitted critique, though not a radical critique, of America. Hilda married in 1912 and so gained citizenship, and she comments that women in America were second-class citizens since they could not vote: they paid taxes and had no voice. And she is critical of Addams. In the 1950s, Polacheck writes that Addams was perhaps too optimistic in thinking that a better world could be created within the economic conditions that prevailed. "We still have poverty; we still have slums; we still have injustice; we still have discrimination" (p. 104).

Ironically, while Addams legitimated a critical position as an American, she also permitted a space for Autobiographical Polacheck to assume gendered positions as wife and mother—erased in the Antin narrative and in many immigrant autobiographies. Polacheck includes her courtship and marriage, though both events are subsumed in chapter titles focused on public and dramatic moments: "The Forward Movement," and "The Walking Delegate." Addams's relationship to the patriarchy and gendered discourses suggests contradictions, yet for Polacheck the subjectivities of Jane Addams (Anglo-Saxon ancestry, middle class, baptized Christian, unmarried) contributed to Polacheck's ability, contradictorily, to assume positions of wife and mother within a Jewish and socialist community in Milwaukee. In sharp contrast to Hilda's mother, for whom economic survival demanded all her strength, energy, and time, Addams's multiple positionings—as host of Hull House, writer, organizer, teacher, leader, spokesperson for the poor, and friend—posited alternative gendered discourses as models for Polacheck. The traditional role for women as wife and mother circumscribed by the boundaries of the house could not serve Hilda, and the relative absence in the autobiographical narrative of the immigrant mother—an absence noted in Antin and many of the autobiographies—signified this condition. Jane Addams provided an alternative model for the female.

Thus, Autobiographical Polacheck occupies the space of the home and domestic arena as Antin does not, and the home becomes a site of adult Polacheck's happier years, a place that signifies her position in the gendered discourses of the patriarchy—though the space never wholly contains Autobiographical Polacheck. She discusses her courtship and marriage (events associated with the female in patriarchy and identified with the home), and unlike many immigrant women, she writes of childbearing. However, in writing about these female-identified events, Narrator Polacheck subsumes them under larger political and global events, in chapters entitled, "War," "Peace," "Woman's Suffrage," and "The Women's International League for Peace and Freedom." Autobiographical Polacheck also occupies spaces outside the home throughout the narrative, as political activist, as drama critic for *The Milwaukee Leader*, a socialist newspaper, and as hostess for political and intellectual guests who lectured in Milwaukee.

The attachment of Autobiographical Polacheck to Jane Addams is signified in the last chapter, "May 1935," focused on Addams's funeral, which also ends the narrative. In a sense Autobiographical Polacheck dies with Addams, since, though she is writing in the 1950s, Narrator Polacheck concludes her narrative with this event. The ideological power of Hull House reform discourses is signified in that narrative closure. Addams represented a struggle for justice and compassion, an alternative to the individualized narratives of Antin's schools or the monotony and exploitation Hilda found in the streets and factories of Chicago. Linked through spatial and temporal arenas of Hull House to spaces beyond, Historical Polacheck met a different vision of America—one that she embraced, one that sustained her and enabled her to transform gendered ideologies of domesticity and nationalistic ideologies of xenophobia into a meaningful life that incorporated a multiplicity of subjectivities.

Emma Goldman's two-volume autobiography *Living My Life* was begun in 1928 and first published in October 1931, while she lived in exile in St. Tropez, France.[13] Encouraged to write by friends and eventually receiving an advance from Alfred Knopf, Historical Goldman hoped the book would provide financial security for her remaining years and might gain her reentry to America when the injustice of her exile became evident.[14] Neither of these ends were achieved; nevertheless, the autobiography generally received favorable reviews and continues to remain in print.

In the opening of *Living My Life*, the Narrator positions Autobiographical Goldman at the moment of arrival in New York City from Rochester, New York, *not* from the old world: "It was the 15th of August, 1889, the day of my arrival in New York City. I was twenty years old. All that had happened in my life until that time was now left behind me, cast off like a worn-out garment" (p. 3). Although Historical Goldman had been in the United States for four years, married, and worked in Rochester, what provokes the rebirth is the imprisonment and execution on November 11, 1887, in Chicago of anarchists charged with murder in the Haymarket riot. Unlike Autobiographical Antin's rebirth as an American, which leaves her in adolescence, Autobiographical Goldman's rebirth as a political radical positions her as an adult—chronotopically, in New York at twenty, prepared to struggle against injustice in America. Narrator Goldman closes the autobiography in 1928 (the time of her writing), reflecting on efforts to release Sacco and Vanzetti, Italian anarchists also charged with murder, imprisoned (1921–1927) and executed (August 22, 1927). Although the Goldman Narrator covers the period from her birth in 1869 to the time she began to write the autobiography, she frames the life story with two events that dramatize American injustice—the Haymarket affair and the execution of Sacco and Vanzetti. The strategy of framing the autobiographical narrative with these events rather than with immigration to or deportation from the new world aligns the Autobiographical Goldman with a communal history and struggle against injustice rather than an individual history. This stimulates the reader to reflect on the injustices that Historical Goldman spent a lifetime fighting and serves to focus on the cause of justice rather than on a personal story.

The framework also subsumes Goldman's deportation from the United States in 1919 and self-exile with Alexander Berkman in 1921 from postrevolutionary Russia after the Kronstadt revolt and massacre. By situating these events in the middle of the narrative, the Autobiographical Goldman occupies the centers of Western capitalism (America and Western Europe) and Marxism (the Soviet Union), but she also leaves both. The effect not only diminishes their authority but implies a critique. Historical Goldman was exiled from both of these geographic and political arenas (involuntarily from the United States in 1919 and voluntarily from the Soviet Union in 1921); however, by foregrounding neither event in the autobiography, the Goldman Narrator calls attention to the struggle against injustice within both grand narratives and delegitimizes the power and authority of both systems. The effect is to align the Autobiographical Goldman with postmodern critiques of the grand narratives, whether capitalist or Marxist. Though the bulk of the autobiography is set in America, where Historical Goldman spent half her life (1885–1919), by framing the narrative with the executions of anarchists, Narrator Goldman foregrounds the injustices Historical Goldman struggled against rather than the personal life. The primary chronotopes signify that critique.

Autobiographical Goldman, primarily an adult, occupied spaces unimaginable to Autobiographical Antin—spaces generally closed to women. In late nineteenth century American discourses addressing gender, the ideology of separate spheres, prescribed appropriate spaces for males and females: males occupied public arenas, females the private arenas, namely the home, the spaces Autobiographical Polacheck occupies. Autobiographical Goldman's presence in the proscribed public spaces, particularly on the streets, challenges those ideologies. One moment early in the autobiography illustrates this pattern, a pattern repeated throughout the narrative. In 1891, radical German, Jewish, and Russian socialist groups in New York City decided to mark International Labor Day on May 1, secured Union Square for the celebration, and promised anarchists a platform to speak. When the platform was denied the anarchists, Emma Goldman was lifted onto a socialist truck. The Narrator writes: "I began to speak. The chairman left, but in a few minutes he returned with the owner of the wagon. I continued to speak. The man hitched his horse to the truck and started off at a trot. I still continued to speak. The crowd, failing to take in the situation, followed us out of the square for a couple of blocks while I was speaking" (vol. 1, p. 80).

The image of Historical Goldman speaking from the back of a wagon pulled down the street away from Union Square, followed by a receptive audience, signifies not only a woman occupying male/public spaces, but an anarchist female claiming the right to speak amidst radicals who would silence her. The image evokes the way in which Autobiographical Goldman throughout the autobiography occupies "forbidden spaces." The one site that most signifies the forbidden spaces, and the anarchist critique of dominant narratives, is the prison; prisons, wrote Goldman, had been her best school, an inversion of Autobiographical Antin's celebratory view of schools.

Historical Goldman was sentenced on October 18, 1893, to one year of imprisonment at Blackwell's Island Penitentiary, the first of three sentences she would serve in the United States. In Blackwell's, fellow inmates initially shunned the incomprehensible anarchist who refused to attend required church services. However, by defying prison authority (refusing to oversee workers in the sewing room, refusing to translate inmates' letters) Goldman won the hearts of her fellow prisoners. The Goldman Narrator writes that more than any other site, the prison "proved the best school. A more painful, but a more vital, school. Here I had been brought close to the depths and complexities of the human soul; here I had found ugliness and beauty, meanness and generosity" (vol. 1, p. 148). In granting her strength to stand alone, to live her life and fight for her ideals, she writes, "the State of New York could have rendered me no greater service than by sending me to Blackwell's Island Penitentiary" (vol. 1, p. 148). By occupying this forbidden space, Autobiographical Goldman not only inverts the prevailing ideology and allies herself with victims of injustice, but she gives dignity to those who share that space, not only in Blackwell's Penitentiary but in other prisons where she empathizes with victims of injustice. There, her conviction that crime is a result of poverty and the endless chain of injustice and inequality was reinforced. Historical Emma Goldman, one might argue, was deported precisely because she occupied forbidden spaces, ideologically, politically, and spatially—for women as well as for Americans. By occupying forbidden spaces, Autobiographical Goldman challenges prevailing representations of Americans, immigrant women and human beings.

These three autobiographies of immigrant women represent three significantly different kinds of ethnic and female subjectivities and three radically different responses to prevailing discourses surrounding Americanization and patriarchy, discourses in which immigrant women from the turn of the century were situated. Examining the temporal and spatial arenas in which these immigrant women are positioned in the autobiographies helps illuminate the relationships between the discursive formations and the autobiographical subject positions, revealing ideologies embedded in those discourses and subjectivities. The Autobiographical Antin, aligned with the discourses of Americanization, occupies primarily the spaces of the schoolroom in adolescence, meaning that the ideologies embedded in those discourses erase difference, including adulthood, femaleness, and ethnicity. Autobiographical Polacheck occupies the spaces of urban Chicago and Milwaukee, in the gendered and safe spaces of the settlement house and home, as a young adult and mature woman. The reform discourses of the settlement house movement enable Polacheck to take up adult positions in the patriarchy as wife and mother and to affirm American citizenship; however, the reform discourses also permit critiques of both patriarchal structures and American idealism, while they also enable Autobiographical Polacheck to occupy some public spaces in her efforts for peace and justice. Autobiographical Goldman, on the other hand, inverts prevailing ideologies, rejecting the grand discourses of Americanization, capitalism, and patriarchy, as she occupies forbidden spaces—both public arenas and prisons.

Mary Antin's autobiography, however, representing a chronotopic image of the immigrant in a childlike state, has been seen as the paradigmatic immigrant autobiography. Such representation clearly affects the reader, imaginatively locating the cultural Other in childhood/adolescence, in effect colonizing the immigrant in a childlike state. Ideologies operate by making what is said appear natural, masking constructedness. If we consider the speaking "I" of an immigrant autobiography to reveal naturally and transparently the historical subject, we fail to recognize the ideologies embedded in these narratives. Because autobiography functions as a powerful form to shape an image of the human being— and in the case of immigrant women's autobiographies, of the female, ethnic American—we require strategies for examining the subjectivities produced by different discourses and the meanings associated with these. The chronotopic analysis provides that strategy.

NOTES

1. Antin, *The Promised Land*, p. 364. For an elaboration of this discussion see Betty Bergland, "Reconstructing the 'Self' in America: Patterns in Immigrant Women's Autobiographies" (Ph.D. dissertation, University of Minnesota, 1990).

2. See, for example, Sophie Fergis, "Escape to a New Dawn," (unpublished manuscript, Greek Collection, Immigration History Research Center, St. Paul), which suggests a spatial metaphor in the flight and a temporal metaphor in the new beginning in America. For additional manuscript selections, see Rudolph Vecoli, ed., *American Immigrant Autobiographies, Part I: Manuscript Autobiographies from the Immigration History Research Center, University of Minnesota* (Frederick, Md.: University Publications of America). For bibliographic listings of published immigrant autobiographies, see Gabaccia, *Immigrant Women* and Francesco Cordasco, *The Immigrant Woman*. For more recent and general autobiographical titles, see Mary Louise Briscoe, ed., *American Autobiography, 1945–1980: A Bibliography* (Madison: University of Wisconsin Press, 1982).

3. Dearborn, *Pochahontas's Daughters*, p. 10.

4. Angela Mischke, untitled manuscript, (Polish Collection, Immigration History Research Center, St. Paul). The fact that Polacheck, *I Came a Stranger*, was written in the 1950s but not published until 1989 illustrates this renewed interest.

5. Richard Rodriguez, *Hunger of Memory: The Education of Richard Rodriguez* (New York: Bantam Books, 1982), and Kingston, *The Woman Warrior*.

6. The term ideology used here refers neither to false consciousness nor to a set of beliefs; rather it draws extensively on Louis Althusser's articulation of

the ideological interpellation of subjects; Antonio Gramsci's complex ideological formations, and Stuart Hall's rearticulation of ideology for the contemporary world. The concept of ideology elaborated by the post-Marxist Louis Althusser represents one of the most influential developments on ideology in the last two decades. While Gramsci's understanding of ideology affirms the constant struggle over hegemony, Althusser's theory of ideology emphasizes the way hegemonic powers—the "Ideological State Apparatuses"—interpellate subjects. See Louis Althusser in "Ideology and Ideological State Apparatuses (Notes toward an Investigation)" in *Lenin and Philosophy and Other Essays*, trans. Ben Brewster (New York and London: Monthly Review Press, 1971), pp. 127–186. Emphasizing the way power operates, Althusser argues that these institutions and the discourses they speak "hail" individuals. Thus, he posits the way ideology and power operate on historical subjects. Though the Althusserian model offers little room for resistance to ideological interpellation and ignores contradictory ideologies within a culture, Althusser's theory contributes to our understanding of how cultural ideologies affect consciousness. For Gramsci, "organic" ideology (as opposed to "arbitrary" ideology), is "a conception of the world that is implicitly manifest in art, in law, in economic activity and in all manifestations of individual and collective life." Ideology, however, functions as more than a set of beliefs: it inspires attitudes, provides orientations for action, and pervades the entire social arena in which one lives, thinks, and acts. Ideology becomes "the terrain on which men [*sic*] move, acquire consciousness of their position, struggle, etc." Antonio Gramsci, *Selections from the Prison Notebooks*, edited and trans., Quintin Hoare and Geoffrey Nowell Smith (New York: International Publishers, 1971), pp. 375–377; cited in Bottomore, *Dictionary*, p. 222. For Gramsci, ideology operates not simply on a theoretical plane but in the daily lives of men and women, shaping consciousness on at least four levels—philosophy, religion, common sense, and folklore. While the ruling class exercises hegemony over other classes through ideology, that hegemony is contested and challenged by competing ideologies; thus, power must constantly be reaffirmed.

Stuart Hall defines ideology as "the mental frameworks—the languages, the concepts, categories, imagery of thought and the systems of representation—which different classes and social groups deploy in order to make sense of, define, figure out and render intelligible the way society works" (Stuart Hall, "The Problem of Ideology—Marxism without Guarantees," in Betty Matthews, ed., *Marx: A Hundred Years On* [London: Lawrence & Wishart, 1983], pp. 57–86 here, 59). In other words, certain regimes of truth serve to reproduce prevailing power relations, while others are subordinated and do not serve the dominant forms of knowledge but function as plausible for subordinated subjects. Hall goes on to argue that ideology, therefore, concerns the ways in which different ideas grip the masses and consequently become a material force. Ideology has especially to do with the concepts and languages of practical thought that stabilize a particular form of power and domination or that reconcile and accommodate the mass of the people to their subordinate place in the social formation. It has also to do with the processes by which new forms of consciousness, new conceptions of the world, arise, conceptions that move the masses of the people into historical action against the prevailing system. These questions are at stake in a range of social struggles. It is to explain them, in order that we may better comprehend and master the terrain of ideological struggle, that we need not only a theory but a theory adequate to the complexities of what we are trying to explain (Hall, "Problem," p. 29). Rather than seeing one regime of truth, there are "different regimes of truth in the social formation"; and, Hall argues, these are not simply "plural" but form what he refers to as an "ideological field of force" (Stuart Hall, "On Postmodernism and Articulation: An Interview with Stuart Hall," *Journal of Communication Inquiry* 10, 2 [1986]: 48). Stuart Hall suggests that the object of ideological analysis should be the "differentiated terrain, of the different discursive currents, their points of juncture and break and the relations of power between them; in short, an ideological complex, an ensemble or discursive formation" (Stuart Hall, "Gramsci's Relevance for the Study of Race and Ethnicity," *Journal of Communication Inquiry* 10, 1 [1986]: 22).

7. Ideologies within ethnic discourses reinforce and challenge prevailing social practices; however, ideologies often remain invisible, meaning, for example, that by focusing on ethnic literatures, histories, or cultures and depoliticizing ethnic discourses, we ignore ideologies embedded in these narratives. In the works of two ethnic scholars—Werner Sollors and William Boelhower—both influential in defining the terms of discourse surrounding ethnicity and ethnic literatures, three critical issues surface: (1) how we understand the speaker in ethnic discourses and the meanings of experience, (2) the relationship between ethnic identity and the dominant culture, and (3) the meaning of gender within ethnic discourse.

Werner Sollors in *The Invention of Ethnicity* (New York: Oxford University Press, 1989) aims toward mediation between postmodern critiques of authentic experience and the ethnic scholar's effort to document ethnic experience. The value of Werner Sollors's work is that he challenges the concept of ethnic authenticity and recognizes the dynamic nature of ethnicity, culture, and language. The limitations of his approach are suggested in the metaphor of invention, in which he posits endless autonomous beings who seemingly choose ethnicity freely. So, for example, in this volume, Mary Dearborn in "Anzia Yezierska" (pp. 105–123) argues that Anzia Yezierska becomes a self-made ethnic, negotiating her identity by public relations. The concept of invention that Dearborn and Sollors employ, along with others in this volume, implies that autonomous individuals freely create themselves. This approach fails to demonstrate how the process of becoming ethnic occurs; in other words, how ideologies operate through discursive practices to produce ethnic subjects. Nor does the invention model address the real consequences of cultural constructions of ethnicity, historically, for groups imagined as less than human. Also, the question of gender is not posited here; presumably the ethnic is the universal male.

William Boelhower in *Through a Glass Darkly: Ethnic Semiosis in American Literature* (Venezia, Italia: Edizioni Helvetia, 1984) applies semiotics in a systematic way to suggest a strategy for thinking about how culture contributes to making ethnic subjects. There he defines ethnic semiotics as "nothing more nor less than the interpretive gaze of the subject whose strategy of seeing is determined by the very ethno-symbolic space of the possible world he [*sic*] inhabits" (pp. 86–87). This model of seeing is shaped by a dynamics of memory and project in which both belong to the same interpretive circle: without memory there can be no project, and without a project memory has no meaning. He suggests that in this process the subject "puts himself [*sic*] in contact with the foundational world of his [*sic*] ancestry" and then "reproduces himself [*sic*] within the ethnic community" and produces ethnic discourse (p. 87). Boelhower asserts that ethnic subjects inhabit a symbolic space, a space that is not constructed by discrete individuals, but one that they inherit; that by focusing on the dynamics and tensions between memory and project we can point to the link between cultural narrative and consciousness; and that the model of ethnic semiosis cannot be understood outside the context of the historical subject—the model exists only for the sake of identifying the "concrete spatio-temporal acts." In other words, all seeing, all knowing, is embodied, a concept that reinforces the chronotopic analysis. While Boelhower's model offers us significant insight into the ethnic subject, it also raises questions when we consider that the historical and embodied subject is necessarily gendered and therefore inhabits not only an "ethno-symbolic space" but also a "gendered-symbolic space." The interpretive gaze of the ethnic subject is also determined by one's position in the symbolic world of gender designating all persons as male/female, married/unmarried. When we apply the model to specific historical subjects, as Boelhower says we must, we inevitably confront the question of gender. While the male also exists within a gendered-symbolic space, generally gender surfaces as an issue only when we speak about women. The fact that Boelhower's system erases gender suggests the power of the dominant Western narrative to universalize the male subject. While the immigrant in Boelhower's discussion is the universalized male, this is generally the assumption regarding the immigrant, for if we wish to distinguish femaleness, we must add women to the term immigrant. Because the immigrant is considered primarily in the ethno-symbolic space, gendered systems frequently are erased in immigration studies. When women's experiences are named, they are invariably understood in terms of ethnic discourses, not gendered ones. (Such an erasure of gender has reflected generally the discussion of ethnicity: significantly, the *Journal of American Ethnic History* first devoted a special issue to Immigrant Women only in 1989.) We must also raise questions about the meaningfulness of traditional categories of old and new world, central to Boelhower's analysis, for understanding immigrant women. This is especially evident in *Rosa: The Life of an Italian Immigrant* (Minneapolis: University of Minnesota Press, 1970). Like many women, she followed her husband to the New World, but there she found (like many women) she lived under the same patriarchal conditions that operated in the Old World.

Sidonie Smith in *A Poetics of Woman's Autobiography: Marginality and the Fictions of Self Representation* (Bloomington and Indianapolis: University of Indiana Press, 1987), examines the way that patriarchal discourse has dominated the autobiographical form, which she asserts is androcentric and has "reproduced the patrolineage for the last five hundred years" (p. 26.) In addition, she argues, "autobiography has assumed a central position in the personal and literary life of the West precisely because it serves as one of those generic contracts that reproduces the patrilineage and its ideologies of gender" (p. 44). The notion of the "self" in Western civilization emerging both out of biblical and classical traditions (female as misbegotten male or inferior) is reproduced in the writing of autobiography; in other words, to write oneself into humanity has meant writing within those definitions of humanity. Thus, Smith argues, for a female to write autobiography was fraught with danger—one could either speak like a man, deny femaleness, and be heard, or speak like a female and risk being unread. This dilemma is illustrated, for example, in Maria Parrino's study of Italian immigrant women's autobiographies, "Breaking the Silence." Parrino demonstrates that these women often identified themselves with the fathers, substituting the father's story for their own and thereby denying their own experiences so they might be read. Parrino notes that identification with the father remains a common thread in three of the four autobiographies she discusses. She concludes: "Particularly striking is the relationship with the father, because of its unexpected connotation. What must have been in reality a much more complex and contrasting rapport is represented as an idyll. The Father is a friend, a confidant and sometimes even an ally against the mother" (p. 158). Rather than seeing this as a reflection of historical relations between fathers and daughters, we must consider this as ideological, as evidence of androcentric autobiographical discourse, as Sidonie Smith argues. If the immigrant daughters would achieve "legitimacy," in their stories they must speak through a male (the father's) voice. Unless we articulate the ideologies operating in such narratives, we tend to read them as reflecting presumed natural social relations.

8. M. M. Bakhtin, *The Dialogic Imagination*, ed. Michael Holquist, trans. Caryl Emerson and Michael Holquist (Austin: University of Texas Press, 1981), pp. 295–296.

9. The concept of the chronotope is derived from Bakhtin's discussion in *The Dialogic Imagination*. Literally, the term means time/space, and is used in both physics and mathematics. Bakhtin applies the terms to a discussion of the chronotopes found in Western fiction, arguing that our vision of the human is always chronotopic, always situated in concrete temporal and spatial arenas. Because autobiography has acquired particular power in American culture to provide images of the American or the ethnic, a chronotopic analysis of autobiography becomes meaningful to understand the image of the human represented in ethnic or immigrant autobiography.

10. Antin, *The Promised Land*; Polacheck, *I Came a Stranger*; and Emma Goldman, *Living My Life*.

11. Dena J. Polacheck Epstein, "Afterword" to *I Came a Stranger*.

12. Ibid.

13. Goldman, *Living My Life*.

14. Wexler, *Emma Goldman in Exile*, p. 132.

7

Picture Brides: Feminist Analysis of Life Histories of Hawai'i's Early Immigrant Women from Japan, Okinawa, and Korea

Alice Yun Chai

Hawai'i has the greatest ethnic diversity of Asian women in America and has received the greatest proportion of immigrants from Asian countries in both the early twentieth century and the recent wave of immigration since 1965. In 1985, Hawai'i commemorated the centennial of the arrival of Japanese immigrants. It was an opportune time for us to take a new look at the invisible, "forgotten" immigrant women as political strategists who demonstrated their strengths by patterns of resistance, protest, and creative adaptation.[1]

I was the Principal Humanities Scholar for a Hawai'i Committee for the Humanities grant to do a slide-tape project on "Hawai'i's Early Picture Brides from Japan, Okinawa, and Korea." The major objective of this research was to do feminist historical and anthropological analysis of life histories of the early Asian picture brides who immigrated to Hawai'i between 1908 and 1924. It focused on the elderly, working class, non-English-speaking immigrant women of color who have been multiply disadvantaged and who have left relatively few conventional records.

Many feminist historians and anthropologists today recognize the need for multidimensional analysis of women's experiences that would include economic forces, social organization, and ideology.[2] These feminist scholars propose that this multidimensional analysis should be applied to small-scale localized studies of a limited historical period with the assumption that women's experiences in society have to be seen from the dialectic relationship where women are both victims of oppression and active agents of change.[3]

Similarly, Rosaldo, a leading feminist anthropologist, argued that "gender relationships are a total social fact that takes its meaning and function from the wider cultural system of which it is a part, and needs to be studied in relation to class, religion, ethnicity, and race."[4] Hilda Smith, a pioneer feminist historian, also proposed in her recent writing a holistic approach to the study of women's lives on a local or regional level: "In turning to local or regional studies, we can deal with a unit sufficiently small to consider women's presence in a thorough manner. Rather than isolating one aspect of women's past... what is necessary, then, is to develop research questions, categories, and methods that illuminate the full range of women's lives, private and public, sexual and occupational, in kin groups and reform groups, across cultural boundaries and in the local community."[5] In taking a holistic approach, most of these feminists emphasize both the enduring character of women's oppression and the celebration of women's culture and strengths.

In this chapter, I would like to apply these feminist concepts and approaches to a comparative analysis of life histories of Hawai'i's early Asian picture brides from Japan, Okinawa, and Korea. By looking at the lives of early Asian picture brides in multidimensional historical, social, and cultural contexts, we would be able to show the dialectic relationship between the multiple oppressions of ethnicity, class, and race these women have undergone as well as their multiple adaptive strategies through female solidarity, religious faith, and memories of mothers' and grandmothers' strengths.

The life history method blends history and biography in order to explore the effects of social structures on women and to portray the ways in which women themselves create culture. It provides in-depth material about an individual woman's life over time and embodies two major concerns: a woman's life must be understood in its historical context, and women as a group "can shape their social position within a range of historically specific options."[6]

Twenty life history interviews (ten Korean, six Japanese, and four Okinawan picture brides) conducted in the women's native languages have been transcribed and translated into English, preserving their native flavor and meanings as much as possible. In selecting interviewees, a special effort was made to locate women with varied backgrounds in terms of regional origin, religious affiliation, and life experience. I selected equal numbers of Korean picture brides from the two oldest Korean Christian churches, since about 80 percent of Korean picture brides were Protestant Christians. Japanese and Okinawan women were selected from different prefectures and from different plantation towns of Oahu. Most Japanese and Okinawan women we interviewed were Buddhists, Japanese in Hongwanji temples and Okinawans in Jikoen temples. The life histories of these Asian picture brides will be analyzed in their historical, economic, social, and cultural contexts using feminist historical and anthropological conceptual frameworks.[7]

This chapter is organized around six themes and related questions: background (Why did these women come to Hawai'i?), domestic strategies (How did they respond to their subordinate status?), economic strategies (How did they survive?), social strategies (What did women do to support each other to achieve their goals?), mother-daughter relationships (How did they relate to their mothers?), and symbolic strategies (What was their female experience through the life cycle stages?).

BACKGROUND: WHY DID THEY COME?

The years 1885, 1900, and 1903 marked the first arrivals of immigrant laborers and their families to Hawai'i from Japan, Okinawa, and Korea respectively, but few women came prior to the picture bride period, resulting in a high sex ratio averaging ten men for every woman.

From the Gentlemen's Agreement of 1907–1908 until 1924 the Japanese government agreed not to issue passports to laborers to immigrate but allowed picture brides to enter the United States as wives of residents until 1921. The picture bride period, or *Yobiyose Jidai* (1908–1921), the period of summoning families and brides, was abruptly ended by the enactment of the Asian Exclusion Act of 1924. Due to the growing anti-Japanese public sentiment, which led to opposition against the traditional practice of picture marriage, considered "uncivilized," the Japanese government stopped issuing passports to picture brides in 1921. Between 1908 and 1920, 14,276 Japanese picture brides arrived in Hawai'i, resulting in significant demographic changes.[8]

The picture bride marriage was arranged through a mutual family friend or a relative of the prospective groom acting as a go-between, who would send the man's photograph to the bride or her parents. If the bride and her family were interested in the marriage, they would send the bride's photograph to the go-between to be considered by the prospective groom. This process of arranged marriage has been adopted by and similarly practiced by Koreans and Okinawans since the early twentieth century.

The Japanese and Okinawan brides usually came from the same home villages as the grooms, who were often their cousins. The majority of the Japanese and Okinawan picture brides came from poor farmers' families from overpopulated villages of the southwestern and central prefectures of Hiroshima, Yamaguchi, and Kumamoto, which comprised the origins of 60 percent of Japanese in Hawai'i in 1924. Okinawan brides were trying to escape from Japanese domination in addition to poverty and population increase.[9]

Approximately one thousand Korean women came as picture brides to Hawai'i between the Japanese annexation of Korea in 1910 and the time of the United States Asian Exclusion Act in 1924, more than doubling the number of women and transforming the nature of the Korean ethnic community in Hawai'i.[10] While the great majority of Korean immigrant men came from cities in the northwestern and central provinces of Pyongan and Hwanghae, most Korean women, who were between the ages of fifteen and twenty-five, "came from the farming communities of the more densely populated and poorer farming villages of southeastern provinces of Kyongsang."[11] This difference in geographical origins of Korean couples was partly due to natural disasters such as drought and flood in the north between 1898 and 1901 and in the south in 1910, and probably due to a chain migration of picture brides from same home villages promoted by Korean women matchmakers who had come to Hawai'i as picture brides earlier.[12] Many of them also hoped to free themselves from poverty, Confucian social and cultural constraints, and Japanese political and religious oppression.

Each woman had her own story, often based on individual desires and aspirations, about how she made her decision to become a picture bride, and each had idiosyncratic circumstances such as premarital pregnancy or being an old maid.[13] For most women, lack of other alternatives made marriage a means of achieving individual goals of adventure, social status enhancement, or a free and independent life. In fact, some women were so eager to come to Hawai'i that they arranged their own marriages.

Many Korean women came because of multiple reasons of economic deprivation and rejections of traditional marriage, religious persecution, and political oppression by the Japanese colonization. Other Korean Christian women, having been influenced by American women missionaries and by the Christian concept of freedom, dreamed of coming to Hawai'i for their political, religious, and personal freedom.[14]

Marriages in Japan and Okinawa arranged by a *nakodo* or *baishakunin* (a go-between) originated in the warrior class during the feudal period because daughters of the upper-class families led secluded lives and had no opportunity to meet eligible young men. Later, commoners adopted the practice of having a *nakodo*, and consequently, only an arranged marriage came to be considered proper.

Still regarded as necessary for solemnizing marriages today, the *nakodo* is depended upon by both families of the young couple to bring about a suitable match. In the past, when both parties lived in distant villages, the *nakodo* found it convenient to exchange photographs of both parties prior to the *miai* (arranged meeting). This is how the exchange of pictures of the prospective bride and groom originated. Exchange of photographs also saved embarrassment if either one of the parties was rejected.

The marriage was considered legal when the bride's name was entered into the *koseki* (family register) of the groom's family even if she had been married by proxy or in a groom's absentia.[15] Since the law required the picture brides who married in absentia to wait for six months after their names had been entered in the husband's *koseki*, they usually lived with their parents-in-law in Japan for six months until they joined their husbands. For the plantation bachelor in Hawai'i, this cultural practice provided a convenient and economical means of obtaining a wife. Thus the so-called picture bride marriage practiced across the Pacific Ocean was basically an extension of the traditional Japanese marriage custom.

Due to small sizes of home villages where people knew each other, Okinawan women's immigration was often more of an informal joint venture involving the cooperation of female relatives and friends in Hawai'i and the homeland.

In contrast, due to the customary norm of exogamy (marriage between bride and groom from different villages) and different sociohistorical situations of immigration, the majority of Korean picture brides who came from the southwestern provinces of Kyongsang married Korean bachelors from the northwestern provinces of Pyongan and Hwanghae. Their female relatives or home village women who had been living in Hawai'i introduced prospective grooms to prospective brides by sending pictures of the men in Hawai'i. Having decided to come to Hawai'i, most of the young brides were determined to have a new life in Hawai'i when they left their villages and families, but they were saddened by the possibility that they might never again see their families or homelands.[16]

The following experiences of arrivals and the first meetings between the brides and grooms were commonly shared by all three groups of women. When they arrived at Honolulu Harbor, the process of going through immigration inspection was frightening and strange. Brides and grooms had difficulties trying to match the photographs in their hands to their respective partners.[17] The brides were worried about their documents, their inability to communicate with officials who spoke a foreign language, and the possibility that they might be sent back home or be detained because of disease such as parasites, glaucoma, and tuberculosis.

DOMESTIC STRATEGIES: HOW DID THEY RESPOND TO THEIR SUBORDINATE STATUS?

When the brides disembarked, some of them faced grooms who were much older than expected, and sometimes the new country was not the dreamland they had anticipated.[18] Sometimes prospective bridegrooms had sent photographs of their youthful selves or sent that of a friend who was more attractive. Many of the picture brides cried bitterly and wished to return home, but the lack of funds, the shame that they would bring to their families and to themselves, and threats from the grooms made this almost impossible. Their matchmakers and ministers persuaded them to join their husbands, despite their disillusionment. In a Honolulu hotel where picture brides and grooms were staying, a Korean picture bride heard screaming, wrestling noises, and crying voices from many rooms in the hotel. Undoubtedly, a number of picture brides were sexually and physically abused by the grooms on the wedding night.

Because of initial disappointment in their husbands and later physical, sexual, and mental abuse, including wife selling to other men or as prostitutes, some women refused to marry or ran away from their husbands. Susannah Wesley Community Center, established in 1899 by the Women's Society of Harris Methodist Church in Honolulu, was called Fujin (women's) Home.[19] Many runaway picture brides sought refuge from husbands' violence against them perpetrated when the men learned of their wives' intentions to leave their marriages.

Due to loneliness, disappointment at not being able to make quick money to return, and mistreatment by the plantation managers, many Japanese immigrant men developed drinking, gambling, and prostitution businesses, and habits of sexual license that continued even after their marriage to picture brides.[20]

Compared to Japanese and Okinawan couples, Korean couples, due to differences in their home provinces and greater differences in age, seemed to have had more difficulties in marital adjustment. More fortunate women gradually adjusted to married life, and often grew close to their husbands.

ECONOMIC STRATEGIES: HOW DID THEY SURVIVE?

The economic strategies of multiple wage earners and multiple sources of income were the means by which picture brides met the demands of survival for themselves and for their families, their double burden. Because of their husbands' low wages (with ethnically discriminatory wage differentials, the Japanese received lower wages than the Portuguese and Puerto Rican workers) and the need to repay gambling debts and debts for passage to Hawai'i and to send remittances to family in the homeland, women found paid jobs as field workers or domestic servants soon after their arrival. Many of them provided domestic services to bachelor laborers and also sewed or raised vegetables and domestic animals to sell. Eventually there were economic contributions from their older children, who usually earned money by doing field work or domestic work starting as young as age thirteen.[21]

On pineapple and sugar plantations, women worked at planting, hoeing, weeding, cutting, gathering, and hauling.[22] The field work was both physically exhausting and interpersonally stressful due to language difficulties. Japanese women comprised a large percentage of the total female labor force on the sugar plantations. In May 1929, 84.6 percent of the women on the plantation payrolls were Japanese. Females on the plantations earned an average of $1.30 per day, while male laborers earned $1.84. By 1939, the population of Japanese women had dwindled to 56 percent of the total female population on the plantations.[23] Many other Japanese couples left the plantation camps to find higher-paid and easier work in the coffee industry or to become independent pineapple and vegetable growers, called *konpan*.[24]

Since Japanese and Okinawan women had been more accustomed to agricultural work and came from home villages with a larger population concentrated in separate plantation camps than Korean women, they continued working in the fields in Hawai'i longer than the Korean women. The most common nonagricultural service work for Japanese picture brides was domestic service. A stereotyped image of Japanese women—featuring cleanliness, docility, and patience—made employers consider them best suited for domestic work.[25]

Women who preferred self-employed work outside the formal sector cooked or did laundry in their own homes for bachelor field laborers, who were mostly Filipino men. Japanese women fetched and sold firewood and prepared water for the *furo* (Japanese-style outdoor bath). They also did babysitting, raised chickens and pigs, and prepared homemade food to sell. Those who peddled foods, vegetables, and meat were called *kaukau* women.

On a typical sugar plantation camp lived thirty or forty single men and three or four married men and their families. Most of the wives ran laundry services and kitchens called *kokusan* (a Japanese word for cook) for the single men. More than six thousand single Korean male laborers obtained most of their meals from these kitchens.[26] Some Korean women and their husbands did military tailoring or laundry work for higher pay. Work was neither less arduous nor shorter outside of the plantation. In the operation of family laundry businesses, however, women did most of the hard and strenuous physical work.

Okinawan and Korean women were known for their hard work, business ability, and ingenuity. Most Issei (first-generation, immigrant) Okinawan women, assisted by children, had a side business to supplement the family income, such as raising chickens to sell eggs, raising pigs, manufacturing and selling cooked food such as tofu, raising vegetables and fruits, or doing laundry for bachelors (while their husbands worked full-time on the plantations), or engaged in their independent family businesses as partners with their husbands.[27]

Many Korean couples, often urged by wives, moved to Honolulu earlier and more of them engaged in self-employed work with the exception of some Korean women and men who were employed by the United States Army during the Second World War years. In fact, Koreans stayed on the plantations shortest of all the thirty-three immigrant groups in Hawai'i. As a result, Koreans comprised only 4 percent of the total plantation workers in 1910, seven years after 1903 when the first wave of Korean immigration to Hawai'i started.[28]

As Japanese women were considered "enemy people" during the Second World War, the women were not hired by the United States Armed Forces Services. Japanese women could work only as private domestic workers for army officers and white civilian workers.

Family businesses occupied many women in grocery stores, restaurants, laundries, and dressmaking and tailor shops.[29] Japanese and Okinawan women started many family businesses, such as sugar farming; raising chickens, hogs, and dairy cattle; fishing, producing and cooking food; wholesaling; and retailing.[30] Some Japanese women opened barbershops with their husbands.

Tanomoshi, which is also called *mujin* in eastern and northern Japan and *moai* in Okinawan, is a folk tradition of mutual aid, long practiced in villages and small towns in Japan. In Hawai'i, it began because there were no lending institutions on plantations to serve immigrants who needed to borrow money for emergencies like sickness, injury, death, and birth. Later, after their contracts with the plantations expired, when they wanted some capital to start small stores or independent farms or to send money to bring their close kin or picture brides to Hawai'i, it was commonly utilized for borrowing money.[31]

Within many of the women's support networks, Korean women's *kye* groups were also formed, and picture brides gave each other financial support to pay for purchases of real estate and businesses and for visits to Korea. A *kye* group was made up of ten to twenty-four women from the same home village, province, or church who met monthly for fellowship and recreation as well as for economic cooperation. The main motive for participating in the *kye* was to have access, when needed, to a large sum of money. This was possible because many women, especially Korean women, were major economic providers for their families and managed their own incomes. For many Korean women, owning properties that brought income was and continues to be a dependable basis for economic security and social status mobility.[32]

When women worked outside the home, they were generally also responsible for the customary "women's work" for the family, and picture brides developed a number of strategies to handle this double burden. In addition to income-earning work, immigrant women cared for their large families without female kin support, which they would have expected in their home villages.[33] After a day's work for the plantation, women returned home to prepare the evening meal, wash the laundry for the family and the single men, tend a garden, and take care of children. Young children were left in the care of the older children, especially older daughters. Some mothers left young children home by themselves, while others worked on night shifts. Sometimes, however, the young children had to be taken to the fields by their mothers, and some were injured or died in accidents.

SOCIAL STRATEGIES: HOW DID THEY SUPPORT EACH OTHER TO ACHIEVE THEIR GOALS?

A female-defined concept of women's culture has been used by feminist historians to encompass the rich, meaningful, and empowering familial and friendship networks of relations among women who "define themselves first as women"; their affective ties and rituals are the basis of women's culture.[34] It has been found that strong bonds among women within the three ethnic groups considered here have produced a climate that induces mutual assistance and political activities and have become the basis of empowerment for the immigrant women.

Daily, close relationships with women were part of the cultural tradition derived from sexual segregation of activities that the Korean, Japanese, and Okinawan women brought to Hawai'i. By coming to Hawai'i, they lost close ties with their mothers, sisters, and grandmothers but replaced them with new friendships formed in Hawai'i. Bonds between women were stronger than conjugal bonds, since women had more contact with one another, such as in going daily to *furo* (a communal bath) together, than with their husbands, who preferred to socialize separately and often had little in common with their wives. Women created networks of friends at their workplaces, and some were reluctant to retire in their later years, as these friendships had been the most rewarding aspect of their work.

While Japanese men who came from the same prefectures joined together in community associations called *tokoromon*, Japanese and Okinawan women identified more closely with other women from the same home villages, cities, or towns for ancestral and religious ties, fellowship, mutual aid, and informal networks.[35]

Korean women, due to their smaller population and common provincial origins, established relationships with each other mostly based on residential locality and church membership. They took care of each other and each others' families as their own, shared each others' problems, and exchanged goods and services. In contrast to Japanese and Okinawan women, who addressed each other by first names or by married names, Korean women commonly called each other "sister," and the younger women addressed the older as *hyongnim*, meaning "my dear big sister."

By participating in Christian church activities, Korean women found options beyond the role of wife and mother. The Christian church became the training ground for community service work and leadership skills for political activities as well as an organizational base for the Korean independence movement against Japanese occupation. After the March 1919 nationwide Sam Il Mansei National Liberation Movement in Korea, when many Korean women were injured, imprisoned, or killed by the Japanese, Korean women in Hawai'i were overcome with emotion and formed the Korean Women's Relief Society. Dressed in traditional white, the members of the society marched in parades and sang Korean songs. Korean churchwomen in Hawai'i, empowered by their patriotism and female solidarity, became actively involved in the national liberation movement through fund-raising and political activities.[36] Due to language and cultural differences and ethnically segregated camp assignments, in addition to the nationalist feelings among Koreans and Japanese, the two groups had little chance to come in contact in everyday life.

One important political event, the Second World War, had both common and special effects on Japanese, Okinawan, and Korean women. All three ethnic groups of women suffered broken ties with their families and friends at home. They joined the war efforts for different reasons and with mixed motivations. In 1942, the International Institute of the YWCA organized over seven hundred women in twenty Japanese neighborhoods in Honolulu to work for the Red Cross and office of Civil Defense in service clubs. Japanese women felt conflicting loyalties between their home country and the newly adopted one for which their sons were fighting. A total of 370, including 6 women, were incarcerated in relocation camps for being religious and civic leaders of the Japanese community in Hawai'i; they included priests, intellectuals, and Japanese language school principals.[37]

During the Second World War, Japanese women faced a total blackout of their spiritual life because all communication with the Buddhist temple was halted by the war. They lost an important part of their lives that included socializing with their women friends. After the war, as the temples reopened, Japanese women and their women friends regained their spiritual life and purpose for living. The temple gave them happiness and the security of a proper burial by the Buddhist priest.[38]

Korean women worked hard in Red Cross and other war-effort volunteer organizations to help America win the war so that their homeland would be liberated from Japanese domination. On August 15, 1945, when Korean women heard about Japan's surrender, they made huge American and Korean flags and carried them up and down the streets of Oahu, tears of joy streaming down their faces.

Plantation women also supported sugar workers' efforts to organize labor unions for higher wages, better working conditions, and greater control over their lives. Japanese picture bride sugar workers played an important role in the 1920 strike involving 2,000 Filipino and 4,000 Japanese workers, a strike that lasted six months. About 3,000 plantation laborers, including many Japanese women workers dressed in *hoe-hana* (hoeing the ground) working clothes, marched in protest. In January 1921, 60 Japanese female *hapaiko* (cane loader) hands went on strike over heavy car loads and bullying by the *luna* (boss). They were granted a rate increase from 25¢ to 27¢ per ton load. Some of the earlier demands of the Japanese Higher Wage Association in the 1920s were allowance for childbirth and maternity leave for women in the work force.[39]

MOTHER-DAUGHTER RELATIONSHIPS: HOW DID THEY RELATE TO THEIR MOTHERS?

The female ties that integrate the world of women have much to do with shared suffering and longing for their mothers.[40] Whenever a woman looked sad, other women asked if she missed her mother, assuming that a woman's greatest hardship was her distance from her mother. Daughters tried their best to rush to their mothers' bedsides in crises such as illness. They were financed by women friends, who also took care of the children left behind in Hawai'i.

Very few Japanese and Okinawan women could visit their sick mothers at home because they had fewer financial resources and more children than Korean women; many of the Korean women were able to visit Korea because they joined all-women *kye* groups to finance their trips and had control over their own income.

Most of the Korean picture brides joined *kye* (in Korean) and *tanomoshi* (in Japanese) or collected funds from their friends to return home to see their sick mothers. Others took trips back home as soon as they were financially able to travel, which they had promised to do before they left home. However, unfortunately, many Japanese women could only visit Japan after the Second World War to pay respect to their mothers' graves (*hakamairi*) due to lack of funds and large numbers of children to be left behind in Hawai'i.

Many women said they persevered through their economic hardships and domestic difficulties by remembering their mothers' words and inner strength. One Japanese woman said that she remained married to her husband, who was an excessive drinker and a chronic gambler, because she remembered her mother's words that no matter how unsatisfactory married life might be, she should endure the fate of suffering.

SYMBOLIC STRATEGIES: WHAT WAS THE FEMALE EXPERIENCE THROUGH LIFE CYCLE STAGES?

Feminist historians have introduced the concept of the female life cycle, which provides a method of analyzing female behavior by separating women's lives into developmental stages and marital groupings, such as menarche, pregnancy, childbirth, motherhood, menopause, and widowhood.[41] Immigrant women helped each other through their female life cycle stages, such as pregnancy and childbirth, both of which seemed mysterious and fearful because they were so far away from home, and because giving birth was a serious medical hazard for which they lacked adequate knowledge.

The Japanese, Okinawan, and Korean women in Hawai'i had large families due to lack of knowledge about birth control and because children were considered to be economic assets, especially for Japanese and Okinawan women, who stayed in the plantation camps longer than Korean women. Similar to the case of other racial/ethnic immigrant women, to these women, children were a source of great personal satisfaction and self-esteem in the midst of social deprivation, loneliness, and hardships. Children also gave them a sense of achievement, meaning in life, and self-worth in the midst of social alienation and status deprivation.[42] In contrast to Japanese women, many Korean women did not have their countrywomen neighbors nearby to help them during pregnancy and childbirth due to the smaller size of Korean populations in Hawai'i and their dispersed settlement.

Women friends helped with information and assistance during pregnancy, childbirth, and the postpartum period. In households where the women also performed crucial economic functions, especially in plantation families with many children, a reasonable period of postnatal recuperation was considered a luxury that none could afford. Many women field-workers worked until the time their babies were born and returned to work shortly afterward.

Most of the women in all three ethnic groups either could not afford medical service, were living in isolated areas, or were afraid or too inhibited to be examined by white male doctors, so most of their babies were delivered by Japanese midwives, a customary practice in their home villages. Postnatal care, which would traditionally have come from the extended family, was also provided by neighbor women.

However, for the majority of picture brides, frequent pregnancies and large families left them in poor health and increased their economic problems. It was not uncommon for women to lose their children during infancy and early childhood or to become gravely ill themselves because health care was either difficult to get or too expensive.

Since most of the husbands were much older than their wives and many had drinking problems, widowhood and becoming household heads were common experiences. Almost all of the picture brides interviewed had been widowed for the last twenty years. Many women were young and had small children at the time of the husband's death. Since most of them did not remarry, they had to take what income-producing work they could.

A woman's widowhood was especially hard for her oldest daughter, who often assumed the household work her mother normally did. One of the women's most painful memories was the sacrifice that their oldest daughters made by dropping out of school as early as nine years old to care for younger siblings. Sometimes the daughters had to take on other work, including laundry for bachelor workers, domestic work for *haole* (Caucasian) families, or field or cannery work.

Despite many difficulties, some women viewed their widowhood and later years as a time of freedom, independence, and self-fulfillment. For the first time in their lives, these retired women enjoyed activities that they chose to do without having to serve their husbands or take on heavy household responsibilities in addition to their income-earning activities.

SUMMARY AND CONCLUSION

Throughout this chapter, I have emphasized, in looking at the women's lives across cultural boundaries, that it is important to consider both similarities and differences among Japanese, Okinawan, and Korean women's experiences. By analyzing both similarities and differences, we can begin to understand the contradictions that characterize women's lives. In looking at their lives in the context of multidimensional social reality, we have been able to show the dialectic relationship between the multiple oppressions of culture, class, and race these women have undergone and the adaptive strategies that they developed in Hawai'i through female solidarity, religious faith, and memories of mothers' and grandmothers' strengths.

Although history, culture, and politics differ and women vary in nationality, ethnicity, age, family, class background, and work experiences, we found many recurring themes due to the interviewees' common experiences as Asian immigrants in Hawai'i. The picture brides we interviewed felt positively about their lives and activities even under severe economic, racial, cultural, and sexual oppressions. Individual women's accounts of experiences reflect economic forces, cultural influences, and historical circumstances of women. Through analysis of their life histories, we can see the ways in which women's migration experiences have been both oppressive and liberating. The relationship between the reality of multiple oppressions and women's affirmative and often contradictory justification of experience can be explained by the dialectic relationship between economic and domestic oppressions and the celebration of a women's culture based on female friendship and women's groups.

The first commonality among all three groups of women was that after they realized that the conditions in Hawai'i were completely different from their anticipation, they justified their lives in Hawai'i with hopes of educating their children to become middle-class Americans and with the fact that they did not have to serve mothers-in-law.

The second commonality among them was that their life histories documented certain consistent patterns that challenged previous stereotypes and generalizations about gender roles in Asian immigrant communities. A strong disparity existed between the submissive female ideals and the women's actual behavior, as they have been active participants in creating their culture and social forms. In relation to men, the women were inferior, weaker, and powerless; however, by uniting with other women, they became active agents of change. When we asked general questions, many women stated their prescriptive roles, for example, "I was a perfect Japanese daughter, obedient wife, and sacrificing mother." However, when we asked more specific questions, their actual behavior differed from cultural norms. Some of the statements were: "I went against my parents' wishes and came to Hawai'i" and "I bought a property and started a business without the consent of my husband or the help of my children."

Other commonalities among them were female solidarity through very strong female friendship, autonomous women's groups, strong religious faith, and memories of their mothers' and grandmothers' inner strength. Women relied on each other to exchange goods and services in place of the extended familial ties that they had in their home villages in order to cope with economic hardships and domestic difficulties, and to go through the common female life cycle experiences of pregnancy, childbirth, child rearing, and widowhood.

Through the multilevel and multistage analysis of the women's lives, we hope to promote a better understanding and appreciation of their adaptive strategies and the valuable contributions they made to the larger society. These life histories reveal certain truths about the female human spirit—truths that remind us of what Audre Lorde, a black American feminist poet has called "the lessons of the black mothers in each of us," truths that we can also call the lessons of the Asian immigrant mothers in each of us.[43]

NOTES

1. This chapter is an enlarged and revised version of the slide-tape project entitled "Picture Brides: Lives of Hawai'i's Early Immigrant Women from Japan, Okinawa, and Korea" funded in part by the Hawai'i Committee for the Humanities and cosponsored by the Women's Studies Program of the University of Hawaii. We would like to acknowledge and express our deepest appreciation

to Susan M. Campbell and Jan Kobashigawa for their editorial assistance and to Esther Kwon Arinaga for interviewing Korean picture brides.

2. Ellen DuBois et al., *Feminist Scholarship: Kindling in the Grove of Academe* (Urbana: University of Illinois Press, 1985).

3. Nancy Schrom Dye, "Clio's American Daughters: Male History, Female Reality," in Julia A. Sherman and Evelyn Torton Beck, eds., *The Prism of Sex* (Madison: University of Wisconsin Press, 1978), pp. 9–32; Barbara Sicherman, ed., *Recent United States Scholarship on the History of Women* (Washington, D.C.: American Historical Association, 1980).

4. Michelle Zimbalist Rosaldo, "The Use and Abuse of Anthropology," *SIGNS* 5, 3 (Spring 1980): 389–417, here pp. 400–401.

5. Hilda Smith, "Female Bonds and the Family: Recent Directions in Women's History," in Paula A. Treichler, Chris Kamara, and Beth Stafford, eds., *For Alma Mater: Theory and Practice in Feminist Scholarship* (Urbana: University of Illinois Press, 1985), pp. 272–291, here p. 276.

6. Mary Sheridan and Janet W. Salaff, "Introduction" in Mary Sheridan and Janet W. Salaff, eds., *Lives: Chinese Working Women* (Bloomington: Indiana University Press), pp. 272–291, here p. 276.

7. Susan N. G. Geiger, "Women's Life Histories: Method and Content," *SIGNS: Journal of Women in Culture and Society* 11, 2 (1982): 334–351; Gerda Lerner, *Teaching Women's History* (Washington, D.C.: American Historical Association, 1981), pp. 67–68.

8. Romanzo Adams, *Japanese in Hawaii* (New York: National Committee on American Japanese Relations, 1924), p. 16; "A Survey of Education in Hawai'i," *Bulletin of the Bureau of Education* 16 (1920): 28; Ichihashi Yamato, *Japanese in the United States* (Stanford, Calif.: Stanford University Press, 1932), p. 71.

9. Yukiko Kimura, *Issei: Japanese Immigrants in Hawaii* (Honolulu: University of Hawaii Press, 1988), pp. 4, 22.

10. Chai, "Korean Women in Hawaii," p. 332.

11. Chai, "Korean Women in Hawaii," p. 332. Wayne Patterson, *The Korean Frontier in America, Immigration to Hawaii, 1896–1910* (Honolulu: University of Hawaii Press, 1988), pp. 103–111.

12. Warren W. Kim, *Koreans in America* (Seoul: Po Chin Chal, 1971), p. 10.

13. Noriko Sawada, "Papa Takes a Bride," *Harper's* 261, 1567 (December 1980): 58–64.

14. Margaret Pai, *The Dreams of Two Yi-min* (Honolulu: University of Hawaii Press, 1989).

15. Ezra Vogel, "The Go-Between in a Developing Society: The Case of Japanese Marriage Arrangers," in George K. Yamamoto and Kiyoshi Ishida, eds., *Selected Readings on Modern Japanese Society* (Berkeley: McCutchan, 1971), pp. 1–13, here pp. 2–3.

16. Dennis Ogawa, *Jan Ken Po* (Honolulu: University of Hawaii Press, 1973), pp. 28–31; Gee, "Issei," p. 11.

17. Gee, "Issei," pp. 11–12.

18. Ibid., p. 11.

19. *Susannah Wesley Community Center Newsletter* 1, 1 (1980): 1.

20. Raku Morimoto, "The Interpreter," *Oral History Recorder, Quarterly News-*

letters of the Oral History Project, Social Science Research Institute, University of Hawai'i at Manoa, (Winter 1985): 5; Kimura, *Issei*, pp. 6–8, 44.

21. Saiki, *Japanese Women*, pp. 63–79; Mari H. Clark, "Woman-headed Households and Poverty: Insights from Kenya," *SIGNS* 10, 2 (Winter 1984): 338–354, here pp. 348–349; Kimura, *Issei*, pp. 6–9, 44.

22. Mary Cooke, "Hoe Hana Women," *Paradise of the Pacific* 72 (1960): 42–44; Margaret N. Harada, "The Sun Shines on the Immigrant," in Dennis M. Ogawa, ed., *Kodomo no tame ni: For the Sake of the Children* (Honolulu: The University Press of Hawaii, 1978), pp. 27–35.

23. Nomura, "Issei Working Women"; Laura Hirayama, "Labor and American Japanese Women," *The Hawaii Herald* 3, 6 (March 1982): 10–11.

24. Kimura, *Issei*, pp. 6–8, 90, 100–101.

25. Lind, "Changing Position of Domestic Service"; Glenn, *Issei, Nisei, War Bride*.

26. Chai, "Korean Women in Hawaii"; Alice R. Appenzeller, "A Generation of Koreans in Hawaii," *Paradise of the Pacific* 56, 12 (1944): 81–83.

27. Kimura, *Issei*, p. 62.

28. Patterson, *Korean Frontier*, pp. 121–122, 173.

29. Ronald Takaki, *Pau Hana: Plantation Life and Labor in Hawaii, 1835–1920* (Honolulu: University of Hawaii Press, 1983), p. 114.

30. Gayle Sueda, "Plantation Lifestyles: The Hamakua Coast Yesterday and Today," *Social Process in Hawaii* 28 (1980–1981): 162–168; Yukiko Kimura, "Okinawans and Hog Industry in Hawaii," in Ethnic Studies Oral History Project, *Uchinanchu: A History of Okinawans in Hawaii* (Honolulu: University of Hawaii and United Okinawan Association of Hawaii, 1981), pp. 217–222, here p. 220.

31. Kimura, *Issei*.

32. Pai, *Dreams of Two Yi-min*.

33. Seller, *Immigrant Women*, pp. 115–116.

34. Carroll Smith-Rosenberg, Gerda Lerner, and Ellen DuBois, "Politics and Culture in Women's History," *Feminist Studies* 6, 1 (Spring 1980): 26–64, here p. 62.

35. Kimura, *Issei*, p. 84.

36. Chai, "Korean Women in Hawaii," p. 340.

37. Kimura, *Issei*, p. 229.

38. Margaret Mikki, "Mother and Her Temple," *Social Process in Hawaii* 12 (1948): 18–22.

39. Yukiko Kimura, "Psychological Aspects of Japanese Immigration," *Social Process in Hawaii* 6 (1940): 10–22; Miyasaki, "Contributions of Japanese Women," p. 10.

40. Lila Abu-Lughod, "A Community of Secrets: The Separate World of Bedouin Women," *SIGNS* 10, 4 (Summer 1985): 637–657, here p. 651.

41. Gerda Lerner, *The Female Experience: An American Documentary* (Indianapolis: Bobbs-Merrill Educational Publishing, 1977).

42. Seller, *Immigrant Women*, p. 7.

43. Audre Lorde and Adrienne Rich, "An Interview with Audre Lorde," *SIGNS* 6, 4 (Summer 1981): 713–736, here p. 728.

Part III

Immigrant Women Since 1920

8

The Flapper and the Chaperone:
Historical Memory among
Mexican-American Women

Vicki L. Ruiz

Imagine a gathering in a barrio hall, a group of young people dressed "to the nines" trying their best to replicate the dance steps of Fred Astaire and Ginger Rogers. This convivial heterosocial scene was a typical one in the lives of teenagers during the interwar period. But along the walls, a sharp difference was apparent in the barrios. Mothers, fathers, and older relatives chatted with one another as they kept one eye trained on the dance floor. They were the chaperones—the ubiquitous companions of unmarried Mexican-American women. Indeed, the presence of *la dueña* was the prerequisite for attendance at a dance, a movie, or even church-related events. "When we would go to town, I would want to say something to a guy. I couldn't because my mother was always there," remembered Maria Ybarra. "She would always stick to us girls like glue. . . . She never let us out of her sight."[1]

Chaperonage was a traditional instrument of social control. This chapter examines the ways in which young Mexican women in the United States between the wars rationalized, resisted, and evaded parental supervision. It offers a glimpse into generational conflict that goes beyond the more general differences in acculturation between immigrants and their children. Chaperonage existed for centuries on both sides of the political border separating Mexico and the United States. While conjuring images of patriarchal domination, chaperonage is best understood as a manifestation of familial oligarchy whereby elders attempted to dictate the activities of youth for the sake of family honor. A family's standing in the community depended, in part, on women's purity. Loss of virginity tainted the reputation not only of an individual, but of her kin as well. For Mexicano immigrants living in a new, bewildering environment filled with temptations, the enforcement of chaperonage assumed a particular urgency.[2]

In 1910, 100,000 Mexicans lived in small towns and cities throughout the Southwest. Their numbers increased tenfold as over one million Mexicanos migrated northward. Escaping the devastation of the Mexican Revolution and lured by the prospect of jobs in U.S. agriculture and industry, they settled into the existing barrios and created new communities in both the Southwest and the Midwest. Los Angeles, for example, in 1900 had three to five thousand Mexican residents; by 1930 approximately 150,000 persons of Mexican birth or heritage had settled into the city's expanding barrios. Mexican immigrants resided side by side with those whose parents had arrived from Mexico a generation earlier and with others whose roots went back three centuries.[3] With this background in mind, I use the term Mexicano(-a) as signifying someone of Mexican birth residing in the United States (either temporarily or permanently), while Mexican-American denotes a person born in the United States with at least second-generation status. Mexican is an umbrella word for both groups. I refer to Chicano(-a) only for the contemporary period, as most of the older women whose oral interviews appear in this study do not identify as Chicanas. Latino(-a) indicates someone of Latin American birth or descent.

Whether first or seventh generation, Mexicans have been stratified into low-paying, low-status jobs with little opportunity for social or economic advancement. Amid poverty and segregation, they developed a rich community life, one that embodied elements as diverse as celebrating Cinco de Mayo and applying Max Factor cosmetics. Thus, Mexican-American youth had to negotiate across multiple terrains of gender, culture, class, and generation.

Historians Donna Gabaccia and Sydney Stahl Weinberg have urged immigration historians to notice the subtle ways women shaped and reshaped their environments, especially within the family. In addition, path-breaking works by Elizabeth Ewen, Andrew Heinze, and Susan Glenn examined the impact of U.S. consumer culture on European immigrants. Taking into account a buffet of cultural choices emanating from Japanese communities and U.S. society at large, Valerie Matsumoto's study of Nisei women teenagers before the Second World War elegantly outlined the social construction of the Nisei world. Matsumoto emphasized the agency of adolescents in creating and nurturing their own youth culture.[4] For Mexican-Americans, second-generation women have received scant scholarly attention. Among Chicano historians and writers, there appears a fascination with the sons of immigrants, especially as *pachucos*.[5] Young women, however, may have experienced deeper generational tensions, as they blended elements of Americanization with Mexican expectations and values. In tandem with Matsumoto,

I am intrigued by the shifting interplay of gender, cultures, class, ethnicity, and youth and the ways in which women negotiate across specific cultural contexts.

In grappling with ethnic women's consciousness and agency, both Matsumoto and I rely on oral interviews. Oral history offers a venue for exploring teenage expectations and for preserving a historical memory of attitudes and feelings. The recollections of fourteen women serve as the basis for my reconstruction of adolescent aspirations and experiences (or dreams and routines). First, I would like to introduce these women by grouping them geographically. María Fierro, Rose Escheverria Mulligan, Adele Hernández Milligan, Beatrice Morales Clifton, Mary Luna, Alicia Mendeola Shelit, Carmen Bernal Escobar, Belen Martínez Mason, and Julia Luna Mount grew up in Los Angeles. Lucy Agosta and Erminia Ruiz came of age in El Paso and Denver, respectively. Representing the rural experience are María Arredondo (California), María Ybarra (Texas), and Ruby Estrada (Arizona).[6]

The women themselves are fairly homogeneous in terms of nativity, class, residence, and family structure. With one exception, they are U.S. citizens by birth and attended southwestern schools. All of the interviewees were born between 1910 and 1926.[7] Although two came from families once considered middle-class in Mexico, most can be considered working class in the United States. Their fathers' typical occupations included farm worker, miner, day laborer, and railroad hand. The most economically privileged woman in the sample, Ruby Estrada, helped out in her family-owned hardware and furniture store. She is also the only interviewee who attended college.[8] These women usually characterized their mothers as homemakers, although several remembered that their mothers took seasonal jobs in area factories and fields. Most families were nuclear, rather than extended, although kin usually (but not always) resided nearby. It should be noted that over one-half of the informants married Anglos. Though intermarriage was uncommon, these oral histories give us insight into the lives of those who negotiated across cultures in a deeply personal way and who felt the impact of acculturation most keenly. Rich in emotion and detail, these interviews reveal women's conscious decision making in the production of culture. In creating their own cultural spaces, the interwar generation challenged the trappings of familial oligarchy.

Within families, young women, perhaps more than their brothers, were expected to uphold certain standards. Indeed, Chicano social scientists have generally portrayed women as "the 'glue' that keeps the Chicano family together" as well as the guardians of traditional culture.[9] Parents, therefore, often assumed what they perceived as their unquestionable prerogative to regulate the actions and attitudes of their adolescent daughters. Teenagers, on the other hand, did not always acquiesce in the boundaries set down for them by their elders. Inter-generational tension flared along several fronts.

Like U.S. teenagers, in general, the first area of disagreement between an adolescent and her family was over her personal appearance. As reflected in F. Scott Fitzgerald's "Bernice Bobs Her Hair," the length of a young woman's tresses was a hot issue spanning class, region, and ethnic lines. During the 1920s, a woman's decision "to bob or not bob" her hair assumed classic proportions within Mexican families. After considerable pleading, Belen Martínez Mason was permitted to cut her hair, though she soon regretted the decision: "Oh, I cried for a month."[10] Differing opinions over fashions often caused ill feelings. One Mexican-American woman recalled that as a young girl, her mother dressed her "like a nun" and she could wear "no make-up, no cream, no nothing" on her face. Swimwear, bloomers, and short skirts also became sources of controversy. Some teenagers left home in one outfit and changed into another at school. Once María Fierro arrived home in her bloomers. Her father inquired, "Where have you been dressed like that, like a clown?" "I told him the truth," Fierro explained. "He whipped me any-way.... So from then on whenever I went to the track meet, I used to change my bloomers so that he wouldn't see that I had gone again."[11] The impact of flapper styles on the Mexican community was clearly expressed in the following verse taken from a *corrido* appropriately entitled, "Las Pelonas" (The bobbed-haired girls):

> Red Bananas [*sic*]
> I detest,
> And now the flappers
> Use them for their dress.
> The girls of San Antonio
> Are lazy at the *metate*.
> They want to walk out bobbed-haired,
> With straw hats on.
> The harvesting is finished,
> So is the cotton;
> The flappers stroll out now
> For a good time.[12]

With similar sarcasm, another popular ballad chastised Mexican women for applying makeup so heavily as to resemble a piñata.[13]

The use of cosmetics, however, cannot be blamed entirely on Madison Avenue ad campaigns. The Spanish-language press can take plenty of credit for promoting acculturation through consumer culture. The society pages of the Los Angeles–based *La Opinión*, for example, featured advice columns, horoscopes, and celebrity gossip. Advertisements for makeup, clothing, even feminine hygiene products reminded teenagers of an awaiting world of consumption.[14] What role did a Spanish-language newspaper play in filtering to its readers the messages of U.S. popular culture and, by inference, its perceptions of gender relations within that culture?

In her essay "City Lights: Immigrant Women and the Rise of the Movies," historian Elizabeth Ewen has argued that "the social authority of the media of mass culture replaced older forms of family authority and behavior." Ewen further explained that the "authority of this new culture organized itself around the premise of freedom from customary bonds as a way of turning people's attention to the consumer market place as a source of self-definition."[15] Mexican-American women teenagers also positioned themselves within the cultural messages they gleaned from English- and Spanish-language publications, afternoon matinees, and popular radio programs. Their shifting conceptions of acceptable heterosocial behavior, including their desire "to date," heightened existing generational tensions between parents and daughters.

Obviously, the most serious point of contention between an adolescent daughter and her Mexican parents regarded her behavior toward young men. In both cities and rural towns, close chaperonage was a way of life. Recalling the supervisory role played by her "old maid" aunt, María Fierro laughingly explained, "She'd check up on us all the time. I used to get so mad at her." Ruby Estrada recalled that in her small southern Arizona community, "all the mothers" escorted their daughters to the local dances. Estrada's mother was no exception when it came to chaperoning her daughters. "She went especially for us. She just sit there and take care of our coats and watch us." Even talking to male peers in broad daylight could be grounds for discipline.[16] Adele Hernández Milligan, a resident of Los Angeles for over fifty years, elaborated: "I remember the first time that I walked home with a boy from school. Anyway, my mother saw me and she was mad. I must have been sixteen or seventeen. She slapped my face because I was walking home with a boy."[17] Describing this familial protectiveness, one social scientist remarked that the "supervision of the Mexican parent is so strict as to be obnoxious."[18]

Faced with this type of situation, young women had three options: they could accept the rules set down for them, they could rebel, or they could find ways to compromise or circumvent traditional standards. "I was *never* allowed to go out by myself in the evening; it just was not done," related Carmen Bernal Escobar. In rural communities, where restrictions were perhaps even more stringent, "nice" teenagers could not even swim with male peers. According to Ruby Estrada, "We were ladies and wouldn't go swimming out there with a bunch of boys." Yet many seemed to accept these limits with equanimity. Remembering her mother as her chaperone, Lucy Acosta insisted, "I could [not] care less as long as I danced." "It wasn't devastating at all," echoed Ruby Estrada. "We took it in stride. We never thought of it as cruel or mean. . . . It was taken for granted that that's the way it was."[19] In Sonora, Arizona, as in other small towns, relatives and neighbors kept close watch over adolescent women and quickly reported any suspected indiscretions. "They were always spying on you," Estrada remarked. Women in cities had a distinct advantage over their rural peers in that they could venture miles from their neighborhood into the anonymity of dance halls, amusement parks, and other forms of commercialized leisure. With carnival rides and the Cinderella Ballroom, the Nu-Pike amusement park of Long Beach proved a popular hangout for Mexican youth in Los Angeles.[20] It was more difficult to abide by traditional norms when excitement loomed just on the other side of the street car line.

Some women openly rebelled. They moved out of their family homes and into apartments. Considering themselves free-wheeling single women, they could go out with men unsupervised, as was the practice among their Anglo peers. Others challenged parental and cultural standards even further by living with their boyfriends. In his field notes, University of California economist Paul S. Taylor recorded an incident in which a young woman had moved in with her Anglo boyfriend after he had convinced her that such arrangements were common among Americans. "This terrible freedom in the United States," one Mexicana lamented. "I do not have to worry because I have no daughters, but the poor *señoras* with many girls, they worry."[21]

Those teenagers who did not wish to defy their parents openly would sneak out of the house in order to meet their dates or to attend dances with female friends. Whether meeting someone at a drug store, roller rink, or theater, this practice involved the invention of elaborate stories to mask traditionally inappropriate behavior.[22] In his study of Tuscon's Mexican community, Thomas Sheridan related the following saga of Jacinta Pérez de Valdez:

As she and her sisters grew older, they used to sneak out of the house to go to the Riverside Ball Room. One time a friend of their father saw them there and said "Listen, Felipe, don't you know your daughters are hanging around the Riverside?" Furious, their father threw a coat over his longjohns and stormed into the dance hall, not even stopping to tie his shoes . . . Doña Jacinta recalled. "He entered by one door and we left by another. We had to walk back home along the railroad tracks in our high heels. I think we left those heels on the rails." She added that when their father returned, "We were all lying in bed like little angels."[23]

A more subtle form of rebellion was early marriage. By marrying at fifteen or sixteen, these women sought to escape parental supervision; yet it could be argued that for many of these child brides, they exchanged one form of supervision for another in addition to the responsibilities of child rearing.[24] In her 1933 ethnography, Clara Smith related the gripping testimony of one teenage bride:

You see, my father and mother wouldn't let us get married. . . . Mother made me stay with her all the time. She always goes to church every morning at seven-thirty as she did in Mexico. I said I was sick. She went with my brothers and we just ran away and got married at the court. . . . They were strict with my sister, too. That's why she took poison and died.[25]

One can only speculate on the psychic pressures and external circumstances that would drive a young woman to take her own life.

Elopement occurred frequently, as many parents believed that no one was good enough for their daughters. "I didn't want to elope . . . so this was the next best thing to a wedding," recalled María Ybarra as she described how the justice of the peace performed the ceremony in her parents' home. "Neither my Dad or my Mom liked my husband. Nobody liked him," she continued. "My husband used to run around a lot. After we got married, he did settle down, but my parents didn't know that then."[26]

If quiet acquiescence, apartment living, early marriage, or elopement were out of the question, what other tactics did teenagers devise? The third alternative sometimes involved quite a bit of creativity on the part of young women as they sought to circumvent traditional chaperonage. Alicia Mendeola Shelit recalled that one of her older brothers would accompany her to dances ostensibly as a chaperone. "But then my oldest brother would always have a blind date for me." Carmen Bernal Escobar was permitted to entertain her boyfriends at home but only under the supervision of her brother or mother. The practice of "going out with the girls," though not accepted until the 1940s, was fairly common. Several Mexican-American women, often relatives, would escort one another to an event (such as a dance), socialize with the men in attendance, and then walk home together. In the sample of fourteen interviews, daughters negotiated their activities with their parents. Older siblings and extended kin appeared in the background as either chaperones or accomplices. Although unwed teenage mothers were not unknown in Mexican barrios, families expected adolescent women to conform to strict standards of behavior.[27]

Chaperonage exacerbated conflict not only between generations but within individuals as well. In gaily recounting tales of ditching the *dueña* or sneaking down the stairwell, the laughter of the interviewees fails to hide the painful memories of breaking away from familial expectations. Their words resonate with the dilemma of reconciling their search for autonomy with their desire for parental affirmation. It is important to note that every informant who challenged or circumvented chaperonage held a full-time job at the time, as either a factory or a service worker. In contrast, most women who accepted constant supervision did not work for wages. Perhaps because they labored for long hours, for little pay, and frequently under hazardous conditions, factory and service workers were determined to exercise some control over their leisure time. Indeed, Douglas Monroy has argued that outside employment "facilitated greater freedom of activity and more assertiveness in the family for Mexicanas."[28]

Of the employed teenagers, none had attended high school. They had entered the labor market directly after or even before the completion of the eighth grade. Like many female factory workers in the United States, most Mexican operatives were young, unmarried daughters whose wage labor was essential to the economic survival of their families. As members of a "family wage economy," they relinquished all or part of their wages to their elders. According to a 1933 University of California study, of the Mexican families surveyed with working children, the children's monetary contributions comprised 35 percent of total household income.[29] Cognizant of their earning power, they resented the lack of personal autonomy.

Delicate negotiations ensued as both parents and daughters struggled over questions of leisure activities and discretionary income. Could a young woman retain a portion of her wages for her own use? If elders demanded every penny, daughters might be more inclined to splurge on a new outfit or other personal item on their way home from work or, even more extreme, they might choose to move out, taking their paychecks with them. Recognizing their dependence on their children's income, some parents compromised. Their concessions, however, generally took the form of allocating spending money rather than relaxing traditional supervision. Still, women's earning power could be an important bargaining chip.[30]

On one level, many teenagers were devoted to their parents as evident (at least, in part) by their employment in hazardous, low-paying jobs. For example, Julia Luna Mount recalled her first day at a Los Angeles cannery:

I didn't have money for gloves so I peeled chiles all day long by hand. After work, my hands were red, swollen, and I was on fire! On the streetcar going home, I could hardly hold on my hands hurt so much. The minute I got home, I soaked my hands in a pan of cold water. My father saw how I was suffering and he said, "*Mi hija*, you don't have to go back there tomorrow," and I didn't.[31]

On the other hand, adolescents rebelled against what they justifiably perceived as an embarrassingly old-fashioned intrusion into their private lives. They wanted the right to choose their own companions and to use their own judgment.

Chaperonage triggered deep-seated tensions over autonomy and self-determination. "Whose life is it anyway?" was a recurring question with no satisfactory answer. Many women wanted their parents to consider them dutiful daughters, but they also wanted degrees of freedom. While ethnographies provide scintillating tales of teenage rebellion, the voices of the interviewees do not. Their stories reflect the experiences of those adolescents who struggled with boundaries. How could one retain one's good name while experiencing the joys of youth? How could one be both a good daughter and an independent woman?

To be fair, we also have to consider the perspective of parents. Mexican immigrants encountered a youth culture very different from their generation's. For them, courtship had occurred in the plaza; young women and men promenaded under the watchful eyes of town elders, an atmosphere in which an exchange of meaningful glances could well portend engagement. One can understand their consternation as they watched their daughters apply cosmetics and adopt the apparel advertised in fashion magazines. In other words, they wondered, If she dresses like a flapper, will she then act like one? Seeds of suspicion reaffirmed the penchant for traditional supervision.

While parents could not completely cloister their children from the temptations of modern society, chaperonage provided a way to monitor their activities. It was an attempt to mold young women into sheltered young matrons. But one cannot regard the presence of *la dueña* as simply an old world tradition on a collision course with twentieth-century life. The regulation of daughters involved more than a conflict between peasant ways and modern ideas. Chaperonage was both an actual and a symbolic assertion of familial oligarchy. A family's reputation was linked to the purity of women. As reiterated in a Catholic catechism, if a young woman became a "faded lily," she and her family would suffer dire consequences.[32] Since family honor rested, to some degree, on the preservation of family chastity (or *vergüenza*), women were to be controlled for the collective good, with older relatives assuming unquestioned responsibility in this regard. Mexican women coming of age during the 1920s and 1930s were not the first to challenge the authority of elders. Ramón Gutiérrez, in his path-breaking study of colonial New Mexico, uncovered numerous instances of women who tried to exercise some autonomy over their sexuality.[33] The Mexican-American generation, however, had a potent ally unavailable to their foremothers—consumer culture.

U.S. consumerism did not bring about the disintegration of familial oligarchy, but it did serve as a catalyst for change. The ideology of control was shaken by consumer culture and the heterosocial world of urban youth. As previously indicated, chaperonage proved much easier to enforce in a small town. Ruby Estrada described how a young woman would "get the third degree" if caught with a potential boyfriend alone. "And they [the elders] would say what are [you] doing there all alone. . . . Yeah, what were you up to or if you weren't up to no good, why should you be talking to that boy?"[34]

In contrast, parents in the barrios of major cities fought a losing battle against urban anonymity and commercialized leisure. The Catholic church was quick to point out the "dangerous amusement" inherent in dancing, theatergoing, dressing fashionably, and reading pulp fiction. Under the section "The Enemy in the Ballroom," a Catholic advice book warned of the hidden temptations of dance. "I know that some persons can indulge in it without harm; but sometimes even the coldest temperaments are heated by it."[35] Therefore, the author offered the following rules:

(1) If you know nothing at all . . . about dancing do not trouble yourself to learn. (2) Be watchful . . . and see that your pleasure in dancing does not grow into a passion. . . . (3) Never frequent fairs, picnics, carnivals, or public dancing halls where Heaven only knows what sorts of people congregate. (4) Dance only at private parties where your father or mother is present.[36]

Pious pronouncements such as these had little impact on those adolescents who cherished the opportunity to look and act like vamps and flappers.

Protestant teens also yearned for more freedom of movement. As a manifestation of familial oligarchy, chaperonage crossed denominational lines. "I was beginning to think that the Baptist church was a little too Mexican. Too much restriction," remembered Rose Escheverria Mulligan. Indeed, she longed to join her Catholic peers who regularly attended church-sponsored dances because "I noticed they were having a good time."[37]

As mentioned earlier, popular culture offered an alternative vision to parental and church expectations complete with its own aura of legitimacy. While going out with a man alone violated Mexican community norms, such behavior seemed perfectly appropriate outside the barrio. Certainly Mexican-American women noticed the less confined life-styles of their Anglo co-workers who did not live at home and who went out on dates unchaperoned. Some wage-earning teenagers rented apartments, at times even moving in with Anglo peers. Both English- and Spanish-language media promoted a freer heterosocial environment. Radios, magazines, and movies held out images of neckers and petters, hedonistic flappers bent on a good time. From Middletown to East Los Angeles, teenagers across classes and ethnic groups sought to emulate the fun-seeking icons of a burgeoning consumer society.[38]

Even the Spanish-language press fanned youthful passions. On May

9, 1927, *La Opinion* ran an article entitled, "How Do You Kiss?" Informing readers that "el beso no es un arte sino una ciencia" (kissing is not an art but rather a science), this short piece outlined the three components of a kiss: quality, quantity, and topography. The modern kiss, furthermore, should last three minutes.[39] Though certainly shocking older Mexicanos, such titillating fare catered to a youth market. *La Opinion*, in many respects, reflected the coalescence of Mexican and American cultures. While promoting pride in Latino theater and music, its society pages also celebrated the icons of Americanization and mass consumption.

Coming of age during the interwar period, young women sought to reconcile parental expectations with the excitement of experimentation. Popular culture affirmed women's desires for greater autonomy, and in hearing its messages, they acted. Chaperones had to go.

Mexican-American women were not caught between two worlds. They navigated across multiple terrains at home, at work, and at play. They engaged in what I have termed cultural coalescence. The Mexican-American generation selected, retained, borrowed, and created their own cultural forms. There is not a hermetic Mexican or Mexican-American culture, but rather *cultures* rooted in generation, gender, region, class, and personal experience. These children of immigrants may have been captivated by consumerism, but few would attain its promises of affluence. Racism, economic segmentation, and sexism constrained the possibilities of choice.[40]

Indeed, what seems most striking is that the struggle over chaperonage occurred at a time when Mexicans were routinely rounded up and deported. Between 1931 and 1934 an estimated one-third of the Mexican population in the United States (over 500,000 people) were either deported or repatriated to Mexico, even though many were native U.S. citizens.[41] By 1935 the deportation campaigns had diminished, but prejudice and segregation remained. According to historian Albert Camarillo, by 1946 80 percent of Los Angeles–area municipalities had restrictive real estate covenants prohibiting Mexicans and other people of color from purchasing residences in certain neighborhoods. Throughout California and the Southwest, many restaurants, theaters, and public swimming pools discriminated against their Mexican clientele.[42]

Mexican-American adolescents felt the lure of Hollywood and the threat of deportation. In dealing with all the contradictions in their lives, many young women focused their attention on chaperonage, an area where they could make decisions. The inner conflicts expressed in the oral histories reveal that such decisions were not taken impetuously. Hard as it was for young heterosexual women to carve out their own sexual boundaries, imagine the greater difficulty for lesbians coming of age in the barrios of the Southwest. Chicano history has a distinctly heterosexist bias—not a single monograph, to date, addresses the experiences of gays and lesbians. Their lives must be included in any comprehensive study of Mexicans in the United States.

Although only one facet in the realm of sexual politics, chaperonage was a significant issue for teenagers coming of age during the interwar period. The oral interviews on which I relied represented the experiences of those who were neither deported nor repatriated. Future studies of chaperonage should examine the experiences of those adolescents whose families returned to Mexico. This physical uprooting, no doubt, further complicated the ways in which they negotiated across shifting cultural terrains. For example, in Mexico were young women expected to tolerate even more stringent supervision? Did they, in essence, return to the ways of their mothers, or did they adopt distinctive patterns of behavior depending on which side of the political border they found themselves?

Future research should also look more closely at the worlds of Mexican mothers. Were they, in fact, the tradition-tied Mexicans who longed for a golden age of filial obedience, or did they too hear the siren song of consumption? Recent studies on European immigrants by Susan Glenn and Andrew Heinze suggest that U.S. popular culture made inroads among mothers as well as daughters. Based on my previous work, I would argue that employment outside the home would accelerate the process of acculturation among immigrant women.[43] Interestingly, several Mexican actors attributed the decline of Spanish-language theater in the Southwest during the Great Depression to financial hard times, to repatriation drives, *and* to the Americanized tastes of Mexican audiences.[44]

In studying the interwar generation, a pattern emerges regarding the presence of *la dueña*. Although still practiced in some areas, chaperonage appeared less frequently after World War II. By the 1950s chaperonage had become more a generational marker. Typically only the daughters of recent immigrants had to contend with constant supervision. Mexican-Americans relegated chaperonage to their own past, a custom that they as parents chose not to inflict upon their children. Family honor also became less intertwined with female virginity, but the preservation of one's reputation was still a major concern.[45] Some Mexican-American women found themselves invoking the threats of their mothers. María de las Nieves Moya de Ruiz warned her daughter Erminia that if she ever got into trouble and disgraced the family, she would be sent packing to a Florence Crittenden home for unwed mothers. During the 1960s and 1970s, Erminia repeated the exact same words to her teenage daughters. Chaperonage may have been discarded, but familial oligarchy remained.[46]

In challenging chaperonage, Mexican-American teenagers did not attack the foundation of familial oligarchy—only its more obvious manifestation. (It would take later generations of Chicana feminists to take on this task.) Chaperonage, however, could no longer be used as a method of social control, as an instrument for harnessing women's personal autonomy and sexuality. Through open resistance and clever evasion, daring young women broke free from its constraints. Their actions represent a significant step in the sexual liberation of Mexican-American women.

NOTES

1. Interview with María Ybarra, December 1, 1990, conducted by David Pérez. With grateful thanks to Valerie Matsumoto, Howard Shorr, and Donna Gabaccia for their support and encouragement.

2. For colonial New Mexico, Ramón Gutiérrez convincingly demonstrates how family honor was tied, in part, to women's *vergüenza* (literally, shame or virginity). See Gutiérrez, "Honor, Ideology, and Class Gender Domination." I contend that since mothers and elder female relatives played major roles in enforcing chaperonage, strict supervision of daughters related more to what I term "familial oligarchy" than to patriarchal control.

3. For more information on twentieth-century Mexican-American history, see Albert Camarillo, *Chicanos in California* (San Francisco: Boyd and Frazer, 1984); Mario T. García, *Desert Immigrants* (New Haven: Yale University Press, 1980); Mario T. García, *Mexican-Americans* (New Haven: Yale University Press, 1989); David Montejano, *Anglos and Mexicans in the Making of Texas*, (Austin: University of Texas Press, 1988); Ricardo Romo, *East Los Angeles* (Austin: University of Texas Press, 1983); and Ruiz, *Cannery Women, Cannery Lives*. Population statistics are taken from Romo, *East Los Angeles*, p. 61, and Albert Camarillo, *Chicanos in a Changing Society* (Cambridge, Mass.: Harvard University Press, 1979), pp. 200–201.

4. Donna R. Gabaccia, *From Sicily to Elizabeth Street*; Weinberg, "The Treatment of Women" (this volume); Stuart Ewen and Elizabeth Ewen, *Channels of Desire* (New York: McGraw-Hill, 1982); Ewen, *Immigrant Women*; Andrew Heinze, *Adapting to Abundance* (New York: Columbia University Press, 1990); Glenn, *Daughters of the Shtetl*; Valerie Matsumoto, "Desperately Seeking 'Deirdre': Gender Roles, Multicultural Relations, and Nisei Women Writers of the 1930s," *Frontiers: A Journal of Women's Studies* 12 (1991): 19–32.

5. Mauricio Mazón's *The Zoot Suit Riots* (Austin: University of Texas Press, 1984) and the Luis Valdez play and feature film *Zoot Suit* provide examples of the literature on *pachucos*.

6. Of the fourteen full-blown life histories, nine are housed in university archives, seven as part of the *Rosie the Riveter* collection at California State University, Long Beach. I became familiar with most of these interviews during the course of my research for *Cannery Women, Cannery Lives*, and two surfaced as student oral history projects. I personally interviewed three women. I appreciate the generosity and long-standing support of Sherna Gluck, who has given me permission to use excerpts from the *Rosie* interviews.

7. The age breakdown for the fourteen interviewees is as follows: seven were born between 1910 and 1919 and seven between 1920 and 1926.

8. Interview with Ruby Estrada, August 4, 1981, conducted by María Hernández, "The Lives of Arizona Women" Oral History Project, transcript, Special Collections, Hayden Library, Arizona State University, Tempe, Arizona, pp. 2, 15, 17, 19. I gratefully acknowledge ASU librarian Christine Marin for providing me with this interview.

9. George Sanchez, " 'Go After the Women': Americanization and the Mexican Immigrant Woman, 1915–1929," in DuBois and Ruiz, eds. *Unequal Sisters*, pp. 250–263, here p. 251.

10. F. Scott Fitzgerald, *Flappers and Philosophers* (London: W. Collins Sons and Co., Ltd., 1922), pp. 209–246; Emory S. Bogardus, *The Mexican in the United States* (Los Angeles: University of Southern California Press, 1934), p. 741; Interview with Belen Martínez Mason, Volume 23 of Sherna Berger Gluck, ed. *Rosie the Riveter Revisited: Women and the World War II Work Experience* (Long Beach: CSULB Foundation, 1983), p. 44. During the 1920s, Mexican parents were not atypical in voicing their concerns over the attitudes and appearance of their "flapper adolescents." A general atmosphere of tension between youth and their elders existed—a generation gap that cut across class, race, ethnicity, and region. See Paula Fass, *The Damned and the Beautiful* (New York: Oxford University Press, 1977).

11. Interview with Alicia Mendeola Shelit, Volume 37 of Gluck, *Rosie the Riveter*, p. 18; Paul S. Taylor, *Mexican Labor in the United States, Volume II* (Berkeley: University of California Press, 1932), pp. 199–200; Interview with María Fierro, Volume 12 of Gluck, *Rosie the Riveter*, p. 10.

12. Manuel Gamio, *Mexican Immigration to the United States* (Chicago: University of Chicago Press, 1930; repr., New York: Arno Press, 1969), p. 89. The verse taken from "Las Pelonas" in the original Spanish follows:

>Los paños colorados
>   Los tengo aborrecidos
>Ya hora las pelonas
>   Los usan de vestidos.
>Las muchachas de S. Antonio
>   Son flojas pa'l metate
>Quieren andar pelonas
>   Con sombreros de petate.
>Se acabaron las pizcas,
>   Se acabó el algodón
>Ya andan las pelonas
>   De puro vacilón.

13. Taylor, *Mexican Labor, Vol. II*, pp. vi–vii.

14. For examples, see *La Opinion*, September 26, 1926; *La Opinion*, May 14, 1927; *La Opinion*, June 5, 1927; *La Opinion*, January 15, 1933; *La Opinion*, January 29, 1938.

15. Ewen and Ewen, *Channels of Desire*, pp. 95–96.

16. Martínez Mason interview, pp. 29–30; Ybarra interview; interview with Carmen Bernal Escobar, June 15, 1986, conducted by the author; Fierro interview, p. 15; Estrada interview, pp. 11–12; interview with Erminia Ruiz, July 30,

1990, conducted by the author. Chaperonage was also common in Italian immigrant communities. Indeed, many of the same conflicts between parents and daughters had surfaced a generation earlier among Italian families on the East Coast, although in some communities chaperonage persisted into the 1920s. See Peiss, *Cheap Amusements*, pp. 69–70, 152.

17. Interview with Adele Hernández Milligan, Volume 26 of Gluck, *Rosie the Riveter*, p. 17.

18. Evangeline Hymer, *A Study of the Social Attitudes of Adult Mexican Immigrants in Los Angeles and Vicinity: 1923* (San Francisco: R and E Research Associates, 1971), pp. 24–25. Other ethnographies that deal with intergenerational tension include Helen Douglas, "The Conflict of Cultures in First-Generation Mexicans in Santa Ana, California" (M.A. thesis, University of Southern California, 1928), and Clara Gertrude Smith, "The Development of the Mexican People in the Community of Watts" (M.A. thesis, University of Southern California, 1933).

19. Escobar interview; Estrada interview, pp. 11, 13; Interview with Lucy Acosta conducted by Mario T. García, October 28, 1982, transcript, Institute of Oral History, University of Texas, El Paso, p. 17. I wish to thank Emma Pérez, coordinator of the Institute of Oral History, for permission to use excerpts from the Acosta interview.

20. Estrada interview, p. 12; Shelit interview, p. 9; Antonio Ríos-Bustamante and Pedro Castillo, *An Illustrated History of Mexican Los Angeles, 1781–1985* (Los Angeles: Chicano Studies Research Center, UCLA, 1986), p. 153.

21. Quoted material in Paul S. Taylor, "Women in Industry," field notes for his book *Mexican Labor in the United States, 1927–1930*, Bancroft Library, University of California, Berkeley, 1 box; Richard G. Thurston, "Urbanization and Sociocultural Change in a Mexican-American Enclave" (Ph.D. dissertation, University of California, Los Angeles, 1957; San Francisco: R and E Research Associates, 1974), p. 118; Bogardus, *The Mexican*, pp. 28–29, 57–58. Note: Paul S. Taylor's two-volume study, *Mexican Labor in the United States*, is considered the classic ethnography on Mexican-Americans during the interwar period. A synthesis of his field notes, "Women in Industry," has been published. See Taylor, "Mexican Women in Los Angeles Industry."

22. Martínez Mason interview; Ruiz interview; Thomas Sheridan, *Los Tucsonenses* (Tucson: University of Arizona Press, 1986), pp. 131–132.

23. Sheridan, *Los Tucsonenses*, loc. cit.

24. Interview with Beatrice Morales Clifton, Volume 8 of Gluck, *Rosie the Riveter*, pp. 14–15.

25. Smith, "The Development of the Mexican People," p. 47.

26. Ybarra interview. Ethnographies by Smith, Thurston, and Douglas refer to elopement as a manifestation of generational tension.

27. Shelit interview, pp. 9, 24, 30; Ruiz interview; Escobar interview; Martínez Mason interview; Hernández Milligan interview, pp. 27–28; interview with María Arredondo, March 19, 1986, conducted by Carolyn Arredondo; Taylor notes.

28. Douglas Monroy, "An Essay on Understanding the Work Experiences of Mexicans in Southern California, 1900–1939," *Aztlán* 12 (Spring 1981): 70. Note: Feminist historians have also documented this push for autonomy among the

daughters of European immigrants. In particular, see Peiss, *Cheap Amusements*, Glenn, *Daughters of the Shtetl*, and Ewen, *Immigrant Women*.

29. Heller Committee for Research in Social Economics of the University of California and Constantine Panunzio, *How Mexicans Earn and Live*, University of California Publications in Economics, XIII, No. 1 Cost of Living Studies V (Berkeley: University of California Press, 1933), pp. 11, 14, 17; Taylor notes; interview with Julia Luna Mount, November 17, 1983, by the author; Ruiz interview; Shelit interview, p. 9. For further delineation of the family wage economy, see Louise A. Tilly and Joan W. Scott, *Women, Work, and Family* (New York: Holt, Rinehart, and Winston, 1978).

30. These observations are drawn from my reading of the fourteen oral interviews and the literature on European immigrant women. For excellent accounts of generational conflict over women's wages and leisure, see Peiss, *Cheap Amusements*, and Glenn, *Daughters of the Shtetl*.

31. Luna Mount interview.

32. Rev. F. X. Lasance, *The Catholic Girl's Guide and Sunday Missal* (New York: Benziger Brothers, 1905); Esther Pérez Papers, Cassiano-Pérez Collection, Daughters of the Republic of Texas Library at the Alamo, San Antonio, Texas, pp. 279–280. I have a 1946 reprint edition passed down to me by my older sister, who had received it from our mother.

33. Gutiérrez, "Honor, Ideology," pp. 88–93, 95–98.

34. Estrada interview, p. 12. Focusing on the daughters of European immigrants, Elizabeth Ewen has written that "the appropriation of an urban adolescent culture" served as "a wedge against patriarchal forms of social control." (See Ewen and Ewen, *Channels of Desire*, p. 95.) This holds true, to some degree, for the women profiled here. But for Mexican-Americans, the underlying ideological assumption was familial oligarchy rather than patriarchy.

35. Lasance, *Catholic Girl's Guide*, pp. 249–275, here p. 270.

36. Ibid., p. 271.

37. Interview with Rose Escheverria Mulligan, Volume 27 of Gluck, *Rosie the Riveter*, p. 24.

38. Taylor notes; Monroy, "An Essay on Understanding," p. 70; Gonzalez, "Chicanas and Mexican Immigrant Families," p. 72; Ruiz, *Cannery Women*, pp. 10–12, 17–18; Ruiz interview; Estelle B. Freedman and John D'Emilio, *Intimate Matters* (New York: Harper and Row, 1988), pp. 233–235, 239–241. Note: *Intimate Matters* provides a thought-provoking analysis of sexual liberalism during the interwar period.

39. *La Opinion*, May 9, 1927.

40. I develop the concept of cultural coalescence to a greater degree in "Dead Ends or Gold Mines: Using Missionary Records in Mexican-American Women's History," *Frontiers: A Journal of Women's Studies* 12 (1991): 33–56.

41. Rodolfo Acuña, *Occupied America*, 2nd ed. (New York: Harper and Row, 1981), pp. 138, 140–141; Camarillo, *Chicanos in California*, pp. 48–49; Abraham Hoffman, *Unwanted Mexican-Americans in the Great Depression* (Tucson: University of Arizona Press, 1974), pp. 43–64; Francisco Balderrama, *In Defense of La Raza* (Tucson: University of Arizona Press, 1982), pp. 16–20.

42. Albert Camarillo, "Mexican-American Urban History in Comparative Ethnic Perspective," Distinguished Speakers Series, University of California, Davis,

January 26, 1987; Acuña, *Occupied America*, pp. 310, 318, 323, 330–331; Shelit interview, p. 15; Arredondo interview; Ruiz interview.

43. Ruiz, *Cannery Women*, pp. 18–19, 35–36; Glenn, *Daughters of the Shtetl*; Heinze, *Adapting to Abundance*.

44. Nicolás Kanellos, *A History of Hispanic Theatre in the United States* (Austin: University of Texas Press, 1990), pp. 39, 42–43. As María Teresa Montoya explained, " 'nuestros compatriotas no son ni mexicanos ya, ni americanos . . . ' "

45. Acosta interview; Ruth D. Tuck, *Not with the Fist, Mexican-Americans in a Southwest City* (New York: Harcourt, Brace, 1946), pp. 126–127; Thurston, "Urbanization," pp. 109, 117–119; Ruiz interview.

46. Ruiz interview.

9

Understanding U.S. Immigration: Why Some Countries Send Women and Others Send Men

Katharine M. Donato

Late in the 1970s migration researchers took notice of an interesting demographic fact. Since 1930, women comprised a substantial presence among immigrants to the United States, and by 1979, women numbered over one million of all U.S. immigrants.[1] Their substantial presence continued during the 1980s, when women's representation among legal immigrants was about equal to men's.

Female migration to the United States is part of a worldwide trend of more women crossing international borders than ever in recorded history. While women predominated among immigrants in just three countries—Argentina, Israel, and the United States—in the recent past, data available on migration flows elsewhere show that women constitute an increasing share of migrants in West Africa, the Persian Gulf States, and the twenty-four nations that are members of the Organization for Economic Cooperation and Development.[2] Men dominate international migration from other countries, however. Brettell described the emigration of single and married Portuguese men to Spain and Brazil,[3] whereas Keyder and Aksu-Koç showed that men outnumbered women among Turkish migrants moving to Western Europe prior to 1974 and to the oil-rich Arab nations more recently.[4]

Sex composition variability across immigrants' countries of birth is an interesting feature of contemporary migration. As Table 9.1 shows, some countries send mostly men and others send primarily women as immigrants to the United States. Men are overrepresented as immigrants from countries that send relatively few immigrants, for example, Africa and Islamic nations, and from Mexico, which is the largest source of legal and undocumented migrants to the United States. Women, how-

Table 9.1

Sex Composition of U.S. Immigrants by Country of Birth, For Those 20 Years and Older, Who Immigrated between 1975 and 1980*

Male-Sending Countries (Less than 45% Female)		Percent Female	N
Africa	Nigeria	27.9%	3,489
	Ghana	34.6	2,182
	Ethiopia	39.2	1,682
America	St. Lucia	43.5	1,579
Asia	Bangladesh	38.8	2,079
	Iran	40.7	18,469
	Cambodia	40.8	3,377
	Jordan	42.3	8,563
	Pakistan	42.4	12,013
	Lebanon	42.6	12,134
	Israel	44.5	9,267
	Iraq	44.8	8,157
Europe	Greece	43.5	25,475

Gender-Neutral-Sending Countries (45 to 55% Female)			
Africa	Morocco	45.6	1,791
	Egypt	46.2	9,245
	Uganda	46.9	1,122
	Rep. South Africa	49.3	4,636
	Tanzania	50.2	1,184
	Cape Verde	50.3	2,216
	Kenya	51.1	1,845
America	Canada	48.1	42,884
	Mexico	48.5	175,085
	Dominica	49.8	1,634
	Argentina	50.3	9,616
	Uruguay	50.8	3,116
	Antigua	51.3	2,345
	St. Kitts	52.4	2,462
	St. Vincent	52.4	1,737
	Haiti	52.6	18,614
	Chile	52.7	7,498
	Bahamas	52.9	1,058
	Dominican Republic	52.9	43,697
	Guyana	53.3	15,534
	Peru	53.9	13,481
	Jamaica	53.8	38,508
	Bolivia	54.5	2,562
	Venezuela	54.8	1,904

Gender-Neutral-Sending Countries (45 to 55% Female)		Percent Female	N
Asia	Cyprus	45.3%	1,896
	Syria	46.4	5,163
	India	46.5	68,641
	Laos	46.8	3,915
	Vietnam	47.4	68,686
	Sri Lanka	50.3	1,408
	China	52.6	66,718
	Burma	53.2	3,394
Europe	Portugal	47.8	28,831
	Italy	48.7	25,470
	Romania	48.7	6,893
	Hungary	50.2	3,604
	Czechoslovakia	50.7	2,617

Table 9.1 (continued)

		Percent Female	N
	Turkey	50.7	6,650
	Yugoslavia	51.2	9,333
	Switzerland	52.5	2,303
	Spain	52.9	8,616
	U.S.S.R.	53.2	20,000
	Norway	53.3	1,374
Oceania	Tonga	45.1	1,728
	Fiji	48.6	2,109
	Samoa	48.7	1,383

Female-Sending Countries (Greater than 55% Female)

America	Ecuador	55.2	15,800
	Barbados	55.4	7,304
	Trinidad & Tobago	56.5	15,789
	Cuba	57.0	122,703
	Guatemala	57.8	9,552
	Grenada	59.2	3,214
	Colombia	59.9	26,423
	Belize	60.3	2,534
	Costa Rica	62.7	4,171
	El Salvador	63.6	12,429
	Honduras	65.0	6,144
	Brazil	65.2	4,633
	Nicaragua	65.2	4,730
	Panama	69.7	7,461
Asia	Indonesia	55.0	2,507
	Taiwan	55.7	14,413
	Hong Kong	58.7	10,027
	Malaysia	59.0	1,776
	Philippines	63.5	131,633
	Korea	64.7	83,124
	Japan	66.0	16,645
	Thailand	68.0	14,319

Female-Sending Countries (Greater than 55% Female)

		Percent Female	N
Europe	Ireland	55.2%	4,647
	Austria	55.3	1,599
	Netherlands	55.6	3,898
	United Kingdom	55.7	39,881
	Poland	56.1	16,560
	Denmark	57.8	1,589
	France	59.7	5,890
	Sweden	62.5	2,249
	Belgium	64.4	1,395
	Finland	71.7	1,204
	Germany	77.5	19,574
Oceania	New Zealand	57.2	1,898
	Australia	59.6	4,619
	Samoa	48.7	1,383
Total, All Countries		54.0	1,454,431

Source: Unpublished tabulations of immigrants admitted in 1975-1980, by country or region of birth and age, from the Immigration and Naturalization Service.

*Because data by sex are not available beginning in October of 1979, data refer to immigrants entering the U.S. during the period, January 1975 through September 1979.

ever, are the clear majority among U.S. immigrants from nations in Central and South America, the Caribbean, Southeast Asia, and Europe.

Explanations for international migration usually rely on a variety of economic and social characteristics in sending and receiving countries. In this chapter, I examine the extent to which sex-specific conditions in sending countries explain why some countries send female immigrants while others send men. To set the context for this analysis, I describe how U.S. law governing immigration influenced the type of migrant admitted to the United States, and then review previous research to identify components of an explanation for cross-national variability in the sex composition of U.S. immigrants. In the section that follows, using a country data set, I estimate determinants of the variability in women's representation among immigrants admitted to the United States under a variety of admission statuses in 1986.

Although few studies address this particular issue, Jasso and Rosenzweig investigated the country-specific determinants of the proportion female among spouses admitted in 1971.[5] The present chapter extends previous literature by examining differences between immediate-family-relative immigrants who enter regardless of numerical limits and immigrants who enter under numerically limited admission preferences. The analysis also enlarges the set of explanatory variables originally identified by Jasso and Rosenzweig by focusing on the different experiences of men and women in their countries of origin. Finally, by analyzing data on 1986 migrants, I elaborate on female immigration for a period of recent U.S. immigration (fifteen years later than 1971).

U.S. IMMIGRATION LAW

With the exception of the Immigration Reform and Control Act of 1986, which was designed to reduce undocumented migration, the laws governing U.S. immigration affected the type of legal immigrant admitted to the United States.[6] Prior to the twentieth century, immigration to the United States was not restricted.[7] Gradually, however, public concern about this open-door policy grew in direct proportion to the increase and diversity of immigrants. By the 1920s, xenophobia was rampant and exclusionary laws were the norm and not the exception. As a result, the 1921 and 1924 quota laws were designed to substantially reduce the numbers of immigrants entering the United States by allocating visas based on the national origin composition of immigrants in 1890. As shown in Figure 9.1, this decline was accompanied by a change in the sex distribution of immigrants. After 1910, women's presence among immigrants began to grow and twenty years later women outnumbered men. Thus, while national quota legislation limited the absolute number of immigrants, it clearly curbed female immigration less.

Figure 9.1
Sex Composition of U.S. Immigrants

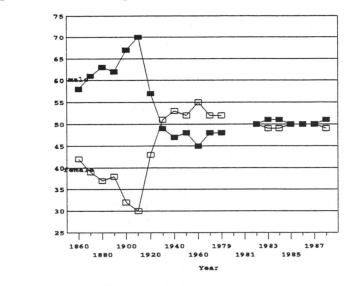

Source: Houstoun, et al., "Female Predominance,"
Appendix Table A-1.   U.S. Department of Justice, Annual
Report of the Immigration and Naturalization Service
(Washington, D.C.:   Department of Justice, 1988).

Notes: For 1860, the percents male and female are
based on the total number of alien passengers who
arrived in t he United States.   For 1870, 1880, and
1890, the percents are based on the total number of
immigrant aliens who arrived in the United States.   For
1900 to the present, the percents are based on the
total number of immigrant aliens admitted to the United
States.

From 1860 to 1970, data are for years ending June 30.
For 1979, data refer to the year beginning October 1,
1978, and ending September 30, 1979.

Data are not presented for 1980 and 1981 because data
by sex are not available from INS for those years.

During the second half of the twentieth century, immigrant laws were
substantially revised. The 1952 Immigration and Nationality Act (INA)
reaffirmed national-origin quotas and established an admission preference system in which preference was given *for the first time* to immigrants
who were relatives of U.S. citizens and permanent residents. Children
and spouses of U.S. citizens were exempted from numerical quotas,

permitting the immigration of many Asian wives and children of American servicemen above the small quotas set on Asian nations.[8]

In 1965, the national-origin quota system was abolished.[9] A new visa-allocation system continued to favor immigrants with close relatives in the United States, with at most 20 percent of visas awarded to immigrants with occupational skills deemed to be in short supply by the U.S. Department of Labor.[10] Countries from the Eastern Hemisphere were restricted to sending 20,000 immigrants each, with a total annual ceiling of 170,000. In addition, immigrants admitted as parents of U.S. citizens were added to the spouses already exempt from numerical limits. Three years later, immigrants from Western Hemisphere countries were also capped at 120,000; and in 1976, the 20,000-per-country limit and the new preference system was extended to the Western Hemisphere. By 1978, a single worldwide ceiling was set; no more than 270,000 immigrants were permitted to enter the United States each year.

Once these changes were implemented, legal immigrants generally entered the United States in two ways. A spouse or parent of a U.S. citizen was admitted exempt from current numerical limitations, whereas all other immigrants entered under one of the numerically limited admission categories if they met familial or occupational criteria (e.g., being a brother or sister of a U.S. citizen or having occupational skills in short supply in the U.S. labor market).[11] Thus, changes in U.S. immigration policy made family ties important for legal immigration. Since 1965, most visas have been allocated to relatives of persons already resident in the United States.

DETERMINANTS OF THE SEX COMPOSITION OF IMMIGRANTS

It is clear that the legal admission categories that permit migrants to obtain permanent residency do not explain why persons seek to migrate to the United States. Admission categories are the mechanisms through which persons become legal immigrants, whereas the decision to migrate is a matter that usually precedes legal entry. Although people now recognize that selectivities reflected in the initial decision to migrate link to behaviors following immigration, such as emigration, naturalization, and earnings attainment,[12] less is known about the larger social structures within which these decisions are made.[13] In this section, I suggest that the decision to migrate is shaped by the different experiences that women and men face in their countries of birth. These specific experiences derive from conditions in sending nations and are important for understanding why women immigrate from some countries and men from others.

Recent research shows that the decision to migrate is determined by factors relating to conditions in sending and receiving countries, a prospective immigrant's information about these conditions, the direct costs of moving, and the migrant's own personal characteristics.[14] For example, Massey argued that international migration is a natural consequence of economic development, which substitutes capital for labor, sets boundaries around rural property, and creates new markets.[15] These changes integrate rural villages and weaken ties to land and tradition, thus creating conditions ripe for emigration. Findley also emphasized the structural determinants of migration by documenting how the contexts of Filipino communities affected migration decisions in households.[16] Social networks also play an important role; as Massey and associates have repeatedly stressed, they fuel the migration process by passing on information that lowers the costs of migration and encourages new and recurrent immigration to the United States from Mexico.[17]

Choosing appropriate indicators of these factors comprises a key challenge in empirical work on immigration. To understand how marriage relates to female immigration, Jasso and Rosenzweig chose a set of explanatory variables that included economic indicators, such as GNP (gross national product) per capita and whether nations have a centrally planned economy; social indicators, such as literacy rates and whether nations have U.S. military bases or English as their official language; and measures that pertain to geography, specifically whether nations are in the Western Hemisphere and how distant countries are from the United States.[18] The authors found that distance is a good indicator of the direct costs of moving to the United States, and that variables such as having English spoken and English-language print, radio, and television in sending countries measures information about life in the United States.

Data limitations further complicate the task of choosing appropriate indicators. The Immigration and Naturalization Service (INS), for example, does not link data about immigrants to characteristics of the petitioners who sponsor them. Without this information, we are unable to assess the composition and magnitude of immigration flows or how social networks operate and encourage legal migration to the United States.[19] We are also unable to set accurate immigration levels because no data exist on the emigration of persons leaving the country. And finally, studies on the effects of immigration are hampered by a lack of longitudinal data, which would permit analyses of the gains and losses of immigration over time. Often the best we can do is to analyze repeated cross-sectional data sets, which are no doubt informative but not superior to following immigrants throughout the life cycle.

Our task of deriving appropriate indicators and testable hypotheses to help explain female predominance among immigrants is thus a formidable one. I begin by examining women's prospects for marriage at home and the strength of marriage as an institution. It is more than coincidental that many of the nations with U.S. military installations send mostly women as immigrants. Having a military presence results in an excess supply of single military men available to marry resident women in the countries of their birth. Indeed, Jasso and Rosenzweig report that having a military base in a sending country is a powerful predictor of the number of foreign wives admitted to the United States in fiscal year 1971.[20] In addition, women who live in nations that espouse nonlegal unions may not face the legal responsibilities incurred by marriage and may be freer than women from other countries to cross international borders. Hence, where consensual marriage is sanctioned and the U.S. military is resident, women may have opportunities to leave and migrate to the United States.

A certain amount of gender equality may also be necessary for women to be able to migrate across international borders independently of men. To this end, one indicator seems particularly appropriate: the educational opportunities of women. Sex differences in school enrollment by cohorts indicate the extent to which women have access to good positions in the modern sector of a country's economy, occupations that give women some of the economic resources necessary for them to cross borders. This may affect the sex composition of immigrants by either offering women an opportunity to migrate to the United States or by allowing women to have the same desire as men to stay and succeed in the countries of their birth.

In addition to the different environments of men and women in their home countries, perceived differences in the worlds of men and women in the United States are likely to attract prospective female immigrants. Countries may be sending female immigrants in part because women are able to work for pay in service occupations in the United States, creating desire on the part of potential migrants to move. These occupations have been accessible to immigrant women, with proportionately more foreign-born than native-born persons working in service jobs in 1980 (16 versus 13 percent, respectively).[21]

Data and Variables

The data set I use was constructed from a variety of sources; the variables are defined in Table 9.2. The unit of analysis is the country. Inclusion of countries was based on the availability of data and the need to have sufficient immigrants to compute a reasonable sex composition estimate. My sample includes 91 countries that reported at least 1,000 persons immigrating to the United States between 1975 and 1980.[22]

As already mentioned, immigrants who obtain permanent residency in the United States may enter in one of two ways: as an immediate

Table 9.2
List of Variables

DEPENDENT VARIABLES

Proportion Female Among Exempt-Immediate Relative
Immigrants in 1986[1]
 Logit transformation of the proportions female
 among immigrants who entered as spouses and
 parents of U.S. citizens (and hence exempt from
 numerical limitations) in 1986 by national origin.

Proportion Female Among Numerically Limited Immigrant
New Arrivals in 1986[1]
 Logit transformation of the proportions female
 among immigrants admitted under sex admission
 preferences:
 1) unmarried adult children of U.S. citizens;
 2) spouses and unmarried sons and daughters of
 permanent resident aliens;
 3) professionals or persons of exceptional ability
 in the arts or sciences and their spouses;
 4) married children of U.S. citizens and their
 spouses;
 5) brothers and sisters of adult U.S. citizens and
 their spouses;
 6) skilled and unskilled workers in short supply
 in the U.S. and their spouses.

INDEPENDENT VARIABLES

Relative Prevalence of Widowhood[2]
 Ratio of the life expectancy of men at age 55
 divided by the life expectancy of women at age 55.

Institutional Strength of Marriage in Sending
Countries: Consensual Marriage[3]
 0,1 dummy variable (1 = reports consensual
 marriage; 0 = else). The countries coded as
 reporting consensual marriage are South Africa,
 Antigua, Argentina, Bahamas, Brazil, Colombia,
 Costa Rica, Cuba, Chile, Dominican Republic,
 Ecuador, El Salvador, Guatemala, Haiti, Honduras,
 Jamaica, Mexico, Panama, Peru, Uruguay, Venezuela,
 Sri Lanka, Poland, and Portugal.

Presence of U.S. Military in Sending Countries[4]
 The number of U.S. military personnel divided by
 the number of single women aged 15-39 in sending
 country.

Table 9.2 (continued)

Gender Inequality in Sending Countries: Educational Inequality[5]

    Ratio of female enrollment ratios to total school enrollment ratios for the second level of education.

Potential Employment Demand in the United States: U.S. Immigrant Women in Service Occupations[6]
    Percent of foreign-born women who are service workers in the United States by country of birth.

Composition of Previous Immigrant Flows by Country of Birth[7]

    Spouses: Average number of immigrants admitted in 1978 as spouses of U.S. citizens, permanent residents, professional and skilled workers, needed skilled and unskilled workers, brothers or sisters of U.S. citizens, married sons or daughters of U.S. citizens, and ministers and employees of the U.S. government abroad.

    Parents: Average number of immigrants admitted in 1978 as parents of U.S. citizens.

    Sons and Daughters: Average number of immigrants admitted in 1978 as sons/daughters of unmarried sons and of U.S. citizens and permanent residents, and of married sons and daughters of U.S. citizens.

    Brothers and Sisters: Average number of immigrants admitted in 1978 as brothers and sisters of U.S. citizens.

    Workers: Average number of immigrants admitted in 1978 under occupational preferences, and includes professional, skilled and unskilled workers.

Maturity of Migration Stream: Years Since Migration Flow Began[8]
    The difference between the year U.S. immigration begins from a particular country began and 1975. I defined the first year that migration began as the year that immigrants to the United States totalled 1,000 and remained at that level for at least five years.

Wealth of Sending Countries: GNP per Capita[9]
    Gross national product (GNP) for each nation.

Table 9.2 (continued)

Costs of Migration: Kilometers from the United States[10]
   Distance between sending country and nearest port
   of entry in the United States in kilometers.

Information about the United States: English Spoken[11]
   0, 1 dummy variable (1 = some English spoken in
   the country).

Sources:

1. U.S. Department of Justice, Unpublished Tabulations,
   1972, 1978, and 1986.

2. United Nations, Demographic Yearbook 1980.

3. United Nations, Demographic Yearbook 1980, Table
   40; United Nations, Demographic Yearbook 1976,
   Table 41.

4. U.S. Department of Defense, Unpublished
   Tabulations, 1978; U.S. Department of Defense,
   Worldwide Manpower Distribution by Geographical
   Area (Washington, D.C.: Department of Defense,
   1986).

5. UNESCO, Statistical Yearbook (England: UNESCO,
   1980); UNESCO, Statistical Yearbook (England:
   UNESCO, 1988).

6. U.S. Bureau of the Census, "Foreign-Born Population
   in the United States," Microfiche prepared by the
   Bureau of the Census. (Washington, D.C.: Bureau
   of the Census, 1988).

7. U.S. Department of Justice, "Unpublished
   Tabulations in 1972, 1978, and 1986."

8. U.S. Department of Justice, "Unpublished
   Tabulations in 1982-1987."

9. The World Bank, World Tables, 2nd ed. (The World
   Bank: Oxford University Press, 1980); The World
   Bank, World Development Report (1986).

10. George Fitzpatrick and Marilyn Modlin, Direct-line
    Distances (Metuchen: Scarecrow Press, 1989).

11. Michael Kidron and Ronald Segal, The New State of
    the World Atlas (New York: Simon and Schuster,
    1984).

relative of a U.S. citizen exempt from numerical limitations, or as a relative or worker admitted under a numerically limited admission preference. The distinction is not trivial; explanations that link conditions in sending countries to the sex composition of immigrants are likely to differ by the type of immigrants admitted. Conditions that directly link U.S. natives to particular countries are more likely to explain variability in the sex composition of immediate-relative immigrants than other features of sending nations.

Differences between the types of legal immigrants are captured in two dependent variables. The first is the proportion female among exempt immediate-relative immigrants admitted to the United States by country of birth in 1986, whereas the second is the proportion female among immigrants admitted in a numerically limited category. Data for the variables came from unpublished tabulations of U.S. immigrants admitted in 1986, by admission status, country of birth, and sex.[23] To derive the proportion of female immigrants, I divided the number of female immigrants by the total number of immigrants admitted to the United States for each country.

To measure how strong marriage is as an institution in sending countries, I include a dummy variable to refer to nations that report consensual or not legally sanctioned unions.[24] We expect that countries reporting consensual marriage offer women greater opportunities than other nations to leave and migrate to the United States. I also estimate presence of the U.S. military relative to the supply of never-married women in these nations, and expect that the greater the proportion of U.S. military men to never-married women in home countries, the greater the opportunities for women to leave.

To measure the educational opportunities of women in their countries of birth, I include data on the secondary level of education because it provides the basic skills necessary to work in any country. Although enrollment ratios are only a partial measure of differential access to school,[25] where women are approximately as likely as men to get educational skills, they may be faced with opportunities to migrate. I also measure the extent to which foreign-born women work in low-status service occupations in the United States, and suspect that one reason some countries are sending female immigrants is that these women are attracted by such labor opportunities.

Because women live longer than men, I include a measure of the relative prevalence of widowhood. Our measure is based on the standard definition of life expectancy; it estimates the average number of years of life of men relative to women at age 55, assuming their mortality experience at age 55 was extended throughout the remaining years of life.[26] Since women's life expectancy is greater than that for men, I expect the average ratio for all nations to be less than one, and that the desire and opportunity to migrate will increase as the discrepancy between the sexes increases (and the ratio gets smaller).

To measure migrant networks already established in the United States, I include the average number of immigrants who entered in 1978 as spouses, parents, siblings, adult children, and workers. Because these measures are statistically dependent, we enter each separately in these models (see Table 9.4). Each represents immigrants who entered the United States in particular admission categories in the recent past. In an early study of the housing arrangements of immigrants in Chicago, Hunt suggested that women enter the United States as spouses to adjust a sex ratio imbalance created by the prior entry of men as unskilled, salaried workers.[27] In the present study, I also include a control for the length of time countries have sent immigrants to the United States. Maturation of a nation's migration stream refers to the number of years since migration to the United States began, which I defined as the difference between the year that immigrants totalled at least 1,000 for five years or more and 1975.[28] I expect that the composition and maturation of previous migration flows attract new female immigrants because migrant networks in the United States often support large-scale migration.[29]

Other characteristics included as controls are country wealth, estimates of the direct costs of migration, and the ability to speak English. To investigate the relationship between the wealth of a nation and immigration, I include GNP per capita; this was obtained by dividing the gross national product, which is a measure of the total domestic and foreign output claimed by residents (at market prices in U.S. dollars), by the midyear population.[30] Finally, to reveal effects of the direct costs of migration and information about life in the United States, I use a measure of the distance (in kilometers) between capitals of sending countries and the nearest major U.S. port of entry, and whether some English is spoken in these sending countries. Few direct costs and knowledge of English are likely to encourage U.S. immigration.

Methods and Estimation

The analysis focuses on how country-of-origin conditions link to the choices that *adults* make about establishing permanent residency in the United States.[31] I employed ordinary least squares (OLS) regression methods to estimate these models. Before doing so, however, I transformed each dependent variable (proportion) into a logit to satisfy the boundary constraints associated with grouping underlying continuous dependent variables into categorical ones.[32]

Working with aggregate data requires that some caveat be made about missing data. In the analyses that follow, I dealt with this problem by deleting missing data pairwise. This means that the regression coefficients in Table 9.4 are based on a correlation matrix, which is computed by using for each pair of variables as many cases as have values for both variables. When data are missing for either variable for a country, the pair is excluded from the least squares computation. Because different correlation coefficients are not based on the same countries or the same number of countries, estimates of statistical inference may not be as sturdy as if the maximum number of cases had been maintained throughout the analysis.[33] Thus, I approach my results conservatively and refer to effects as significant only when a t-statistic equals at least three.

One problem with handling missing data in this way is that it assumes data are missing randomly.[34] If they are missing selectively, the absence of values on an independent variable may be related to the dependent variable or other variables in the model. I tested for this assumption by regressing each dependent variable on five missing data dummy variables, scoring countries missing data as one and those with values as zero. When my findings suggested some data were nonrandomly missing, I reran the equations in Table 9.4 adding in the dummies that significantly affected the dependent variable. The results do not differ from those reported here and are available upon request.[35]

Findings

Table 9.3 provides a summary of the characteristics of the nations in this sample. We see that women's life expectancy exceeds that of men's, whereas the ratio of U.S. military personnel to never-married women is on average very small. The former describes a simple demographic fact worldwide; the latter is expected, given that there are 328 U.S. military installations in just 16 nations in this sample. One obvious consequence of a densely concentrated military presence is an excess supply of single military men available to marry resident women, and hence, foreign brides as spouses of U.S. citizens.

The relative equality in educational attainment found on average in these countries suggests that both women and men are equipped with the educational prerequisites necessary to pursue the economic opportunities that international migration promises. Women from these countries were only slightly underrepresented relative to total enrollment in secondary school, where the basic skills necessary to work in any country are transferred. The extent to which female immigrants work in low-status service occupations in the United States is illustrated by the 27 percent of immigrant women who work on average in these jobs. Note, however, that service work varies widely by the national origin of immigrants. For example, just 9 percent of female immigrants from Cyprus work in service occupations, compared to 67 percent of female immi-

Table 9.3
Means, Medians, and Standard Deviations

	Mean	Median	Standard Deviation	N
Prevalence of Widowhood	.848	.835	.061	45
Institutional Strength of Marriage	.258	0	.440	91
Presence of U.S. Military	.002	.000	.007	58
Gender Inequality in Sending Countries	.969	1.01	.142	76
Potential Employment Demand in the United States	26.6	24.0	13.0	91
Composition of Previous Immigrants:				
Spouses (in 00s)	16.0	5.60	30.5	91
Parents (in 00s)	2.80	.583	7.77	91
Siblings (in 00s)	3.17	.957	5.50	91
Children (in 00s)	4.98	1.49	10.0	91
Workers (in 00s)	1.91	.617	4.27	91
Maturity of Migration Stream	60.0	47.8	.550	55
Country Wealth (in 00s)	3.74	1.85	4.27	68
Direct Costs of Migration	69.1	68.2	40.8	91
Country Speaks Some English	.312	0	.466	91
Sex Composition of Exempt-Immediate Relative Immigrants in 1986	.557	.562	.109	91
Sex Composition of Numerically Limited Immigrants in 1986	.412	.408	.126	91

grants from Western Samoa. With respect to the composition of previous immigrants in the United States, we see that 1,600 spouses, 280 parents, 317 siblings, and 498 adult children were admitted on average in 1978.

The countries in this sample have been sending immigrants to the United States for 60 years. Vietnam is the youngest sender of immigrants sending at least 1,000 immigrants only since 1970 (five years), whereas the United Kingdom is the oldest sender of immigrants (155 years). Moreover, these nations lie on average 6,910 kilometers from the United States. Finally, note the rather large difference in the proportion female between immediate-family-relative immigrants and numerically limited immigrants; women comprised approximately 56 percent and 41 percent, respectively.

Table 9.4 reports estimates from an analysis of the variability in the sex composition of immediate relatives and numerically limited immigrants admitted in 1986 by national origin. Consistent with Jasso and Rosenzweig, explanatory variables account for at least 50 percent of the variance in women's representation.[36] In general, the models are better predictors of the sex composition of immediate relatives than that of numerically limited immigrants, but several features of countries differentially affect the sex composition of these two types of immigrants.

An examination of the standardized coefficients in Panels 1–5 reveals differences between the two types of immigrants. For immediate relatives of U.S. citizens, having a U.S. military presence is the most important factor facilitating female immigration; country wealth and distance from the United States are the next best predictors. In contrast, country wealth (with a negative effect) is the best predictor of the proportion female among numerically limited immigrants, followed by gender equality in educational opportunities and having information about life in the United States.

The importance of the U.S. military for the sex composition of exempt immediate relatives is consistent with expectations and previous research. In fiscal year 1971, having a U.S. military base in sending countries added approximately 1,500 immigrants admitted as wives of U.S. citizens.[37] Country wealth exhibits the expected result, with relatively wealthy nations sending women as immediate-relative immigrants of U.S. citizens. The strong positive effect for distance suggests that countries distant from the United States encourage women's entry among immediate relatives. Apparently, for these immigrants, having a U.S. citizen sponsor offsets the direct costs that distance usually plays in immigration. In fact as Jasso and Rosenzweig suggest, the U.S. government will often absorb the expenses that incur from the transportation of military spouses.[38]

With respect to models predicting the sex composition of numerically limited immigrants, the biggest surprise is the strong, negative effect for country wealth. Relatively poor nations sent female immigrants who entered under one of the admission preferences, a finding that suggests that women (with or without spouses) migrate in search of economic opportunities in the United States. The positive, significant effects of education in these equations suggest that nations where women are relatively equal to men—where their status assures them schooling com-

Table 9.4
Coefficients from OLS Regressions of the Proportions Female Among Exempt-Immediate Relatives and Numerically Limited Immigrants in 1986

	Exempt–Immediate Relative Immigrants		Numerically Limited Immigrants	
Panel 1: With Spouses				
Prevalence of Widowhood	-2.01	(-.256)	.560	(.060)
Institutional Strength of Marriage	.227	(.208)	-.224	(-.174)
Presence of U.S. Military	29.5	(.448)**	-.408	(-.005)
Gender Inequality	.917	(.270)	1.22	(.306)*
Potential Employment Demand in U.S.	.008	(.211)	.005	(.117)
Composition Prev. Immigrant Flows: Spouses (in 00s)	.001	(.089)	.001	(.022)
Maturity of Migration Stream	-.036	(-.078)	-.134	(-.249)
Wealth	.037	(.325)*	-.057	(-.428)**
Cost of Moving	.005	(.389)**	-.002	(-.160)
Information about Life in U.S.	-.151	(-.146)	.379	(.311)**
Intercept	.420		-1.39	
R_2	.560		.500	
F Statistic	10.2		8.00	
N	91		91	

Table 9.4 (continued)

	Exempt-Immediate Relative Immigrants		Numerically Limited Immigrants	
Panel 2: Parents				
Prevalence of Widowhood	-2.28	(-.290)*	.586	(.063)
Institutional Strength of Marriage	.279	(.255)	-.220	(-.171)
Presence of U.S. Military	28.9	(.439)**	-.340	(-.004)
Gender Inequality	.758	(.223)	1.22	(.304)*
Potential Employment Demand in U.S.	.009	(.240)*	.005	(.114)
Composition Prev. Immigrant Flows: Parents (in 00s)	.014	(.228)*	.001	(.018)
Maturity of Migration Stream	-.050	(-.109)	-.134	(-.248)
Wealth	.045	(.399)**	-.056	(-.425)*
Cost of Moving	.004	(.369)**	-.002	(-.164)
Information about Life in U.S.	-.181	(-.175)	.379	(.311)**
Intercept	.792		-1.40	
R_2	.597		.500	
F Statistic	11.8		8.00	
N	91		91	

176

Table 9.4 (continued)

	Exempt-Immediate Relative Immigrants		Numerically Limited Immigrants	
Panel 3: Siblings				
Prevalence of Widowhood	-1.85	(-.235)	.662	(.067)
Institutional Strength of Marriage	.247	(.225)	-.222	(-.172)
Presence of U.S. Military	29.4	(.446)**	-.333	(-.004)
Gender Inequality	.965	(.284)*	1.24	(.309)*
Potential Employment Demand in U.S.	.008	(.230)	.005	(.115)
Composition Prev. Immigrant Flows: Siblings (in 00s)	.010	(.114)	.001	(.013)
Maturity of Migration Stream	-.027	(-.059)	-.131	(-.244)
Wealth	.039	(.350)*	-.057	(-.427)**
Cost of Moving	.005	(.398)**	-.002	(-.161)
Information about Life in U.S.	-.148	(-.143)	.382	(.313)**
Intercept	.155		-1.46	
R_2	.564		.500	
F Statistic	10.4		8.00	
N	91		91	

Table 9.4 (continued)

	Exempt-Immediate Relative Immigrants		Numerically Limited Immigrants	
Panel 4: Children				
Prevalence of Widowhood	-2.23	(-.283)*	.559	(.060)
Institutional Strength of Marriage	.254	(.232)	-.220	(-.171)
Presence of U.S. Military	29.6	(.449)**	-.318	(-.004)
Gender Inequality	.776	(.228)	1.21	(.301)*
Potential Employment Demand in U.S.	.009	(.254)	.005	(.120)
Composition Prev. Immigrant Flows: Adult Children (in 00s)	.009	(.192)	.001	(.026)
Maturity of Migration Stream	-.034	(-.074)	-.133	(-.146)
Wealth	.043	(.383)*	.056	(-.422)*
Cost of Moving	.005	(.415)**	-.002	(-.158)
Information about Life in U.S.	-.185	(-.179)	.375	(.308)**
Intercept	.626		-1.38	
R_2	.582		.500	
F Statistic	11.2		8.01	
N	91		91	

178

Table 9.4 (continued)

	Exempt- Immediate Relative Immigrants	Numerically Limited Immigrants
Panel 5: Workers		
Prevalence of Widowhood	-2.18 (-.277)*	.754 (.081)
Institutional Strength of Marriage	.272 (.249)	-.239 (-.186)
Presence of U.S. Military	27.8 (.421)**	.454 (.066)
Gender Inequality	.843 (.248)	1.27 (.317)*
Potential Employment Demand in U.S.	.009 (.248)*	.004 (.095)
Composition Prev. Immigrant Flows: Workers (in 00s)	.028 (.248)*	-.008 (-.059)
Maturity of Migration Stream	-.042 (-.092)	-.127 (-.235)
Wealth	-.042 (.359)*	-.059 (-.444)**
Cost of Moving	.004 (.358)**	-.002 (-.159)
Information about Life in U.S.	-.207 (-.200)	-.401 (.330)**
Intercept	.608	-1.57
R_2	.605	.503
F Statistic	12.2	8.08
N	91	91

Note: Standard coefficients are in parenthesis
** p<.001
*   p<.01

pared to that of men—send female immigrants. Information about the United States is also significant, and English appears to be the mechanism by which information is transferred. From countries where some English is spoken, women are likely to immigrate under a numerically limited preference. Finally, although not significant, how long a nation has been sending immigrants to the United States depresses women's representation. Countries with relatively newer immigrant flows sent more women, suggesting that contemporary female migrants may not always follow the footsteps of their male counterparts who migrated earlier.

Not all effects are consistent in these models, however. For example, there is some evidence that the prevalence of widowhood affects the sex composition, but only among immediate relatives. Thus, a relative surplus of males over females at age fifty-five depressed women's representation among these immigrants. In addition, the presence of parents and workers among recent immigrants appears to lower the costs of women's entry among immediate relatives. Countries which sent parents and workers as immigrants in 1978 encouraged the entry of women as immediate relatives in 1986, whereas spouses, siblings, and adult children had no discernible impact on the sex composition. Finally, an effect for the service labor that female immigrants supply is evident in having an abundance of service jobs in the United States without claimants, but this appears only in nets of parents and workers admitted in 1978 (see Panels 2 and 5). Thus, there is some evidence that demand for immigrant women in service jobs encouraged foreign-born women who are immediate relatives of U.S. citizens to obtain permanent residency.

˙In sum, poor economic conditions, gender equality, and access to information about the United States encourage women to obtain permanent residency through a numerically limited admission preference. In contrast, countries with a U.S. military presence, a strong economy, and those distant from the United States promote the immigration of female immediate-relative immigrants.

DISCUSSION

The present analysis attempts to explain variability in the sex composition of U.S. immigrants by national origin. It helps us understand not only the motivations and desires of the women who immigrate to the United States, but conditions in their home countries that account for womens' decisions to migrate. In general, sex-specific features of sending countries help explain variability in the sex composition of immigrants, but these effects are different for immediate relatives and numerically limited immigrants.

For immediate relatives of U.S. citizens, the importance of marriage for female immigrants appears in part to be a variability of a demand for husbands at home, evident in the supply of prospective American husbands living as military personnel. Countries with a large supply of U.S. native men spur the entry of female immigrants as immediate relatives. Although these women often reside in relatively wealthy nations distant from the United States, the usual high travel costs associated with migration from far-away places are often subsidized for these relatives by the U.S. military, which lowers the overall costs for this type of female immigration.

Countries send women who enter the United States under numerically limited preferences because these nations offer women opportunities to develop human capital. Whether in the form of English language ability or because of relative equality in educational opportunities, a certain amount of human capital is essential for women to be represented among numerically limited immigrants. Once obtained, these investments combine with relatively few opportunities in sending countries to encourage female immigration to the United States.

My findings suggest that female immigration is also linked to the formation of migrant networks in the United States, and that once parents became legal immigrants in the 1970s, they were likely to sponsor their daughters and other immediate relatives in the 1980s. Immigrants admitted as workers also promoted female migration, a finding consistent with the growing demand for nurses during the decade and the increasingly uneven supply of nurses from a handful of nations, such as the Philippines and Jamaica. Women's representation among immigrants is thus a consequence of conditions in their countries of birth, especially those related to marriage and the development of human capital and to conditions in the United States.

Whether women will continue to migrate in large numbers is open to question, but recent changes in immigration policy suggest this is a strong possibility. Since the mid-1980s, three significant pieces of legislation have been signed into law. In 1986, the Immigration Reform and Control Act (IRCA) was designed to reduce undocumented migration by offering amnesty to over three million migrants already in the United States, sanctioning employers who knowingly hire undocumented migrants, and increasing enforcement of its borders. Although its effects are currently being debated by migration researchers, studies found little evidence that IRCA deterred female or male undocumented migrants from entering the United States.[39] Furthermore, the passage of the Immigration Nurses Act in 1989 virtually ensures at least a short-term increase in women's representation among legal immigrants since it offered thousands of foreign nurses who lived and worked in the United States in the recent past permanent residency. And the new Immigration Act of 1990 may further encourage female immigration through its provisions to increase the visas allocated for employment-based immigrants.

Although women's increasing presence may be a consequence of U.S. immigration policy, it is also likely to reflect changes in sending nations. As Massey has argued elsewhere, promoting economic growth in sending nations increases the likelihood of migration at least in the short run.[40] Women's greater role in U.S. immigration is thus likely to result from the economic transformations now taking place in many countries, as rural small-scale societies shift into urban industrial ones. How women in these nations become incorporated into the migration process is an essential topic for future research.

Perhaps the most important implication of this study is that understanding recent U.S. immigration implies understanding female migration. I found that national-origin variability in the sex composition of immigrants differs by the type of legal immigrant admitted and that specific conditions in both sending nations and the United States are important facilitators of female immigration. Additional studies of larger data sets that follow immigrants over time will be required in the future to explore more fully what appears to be significant variations in the migration of women to the United States.

NOTES

1. I gratefully acknowledge Nancy Denton, Douglas Massey, Tom Mroz, Joachim Singelmann, Marta Tienda, Andrea Tyree, and Insan Tunali for their helpful comments. An earlier version of this chapter was presented at the 1990 annual meeting of the Population Association of America in Toronto. On female majorities, see Houstoun, Kramer, and Barrett, "Female Predominance."

2. Organization for Economic Cooperation and Development, *The Integration of Women into the Economy* (Paris: OECD, 1985); Andrea Tyree and Katharine M. Donato, "A Demographic Overview of the International Migration of Women," in Simon and Brettell, *International Migration*, pp. 21–42.

3. Brettell, *Men who Migrate.*

4. Caglar Keyder and Ayhan Aksu-Koç, *External Labor Migration from Turkey and Its Impact: An Evaluation of the Literature* (Ottawa: The International Development Research Centre, 1988).

5. Guillermina Jasso and Mark R. Rosenzweig, *The New Chosen People: Immigrants in the United States* (New York: Russell Sage Foundation, 1990).

6. Jasso and Rosenzweig, *The New Chosen People.*

7. Daniel B. Levine, Kenneth Hill, and Robert Warren, eds., *Immigration Statistics: A Story of Neglect* (Washington, D.C.: National Academy Press, 1985).

8. Houstoun, Kramer, and Barrett, "Female Predominance."

9. Levine, Hill, and Warren, eds., *Immigration Statistics.*

10. A large proportion of these are given to family members of workers and *not* the workers themselves. George J. Borjas, *Friends or Strangers: The Impact of Immigrants on the U.S. Economy* (New York: Basic Books, 1990), p. 31.

11. The 270,000 numerically limited visas are awarded to immigrants who are unmarried adult children of U.S. citizens and their children, spouses and

unmarried children of permanent residents and their children, professional or highly skilled workers and their spouses and children, married children of U.S. citizens and their spouses and children, siblings of adult U.S. citizens and their spouses and children, needed skilled and unskilled workers and their spouses and children, and nonpreference immigrants. Levine, Hill, and Warren, eds., *Immigration Statistics*.

12. See, for example, M. J. Greenwood and J. M. McDowell, "The Factor Market Consequences of U.S. Immigration," *Journal of Economic Literature* 24 (1986): 1738–1772.

13. Pedraza-Bailey, "Immigration Research."

14. Jasso and Rosenzweig, *The New Chosen People*.

15. Massey, "Economic Development and International Migration."

16. Sally E. Findley, "An Interactive Contextual Model of Migration in Ilocos Norte, the Philippines," *Demography* 24, 2 (1987): 163–190.

17. Massey et al., *Return to Aztlan*.

18. Jasso and Rosenzweig, *The New Chosen People*.

19. Guillermina Jasso and Mark R. Rosenzweig, "Using National Recording Systems for the Measurement and Analysis of Immigration to the United States," *International Migration Review* 21, 4 (1987): 1212–1244.

20. Jasso and Rosenzweig, *The New Chosen People*.

21. U.S. Bureau of the Census, "Foreign-Born Population in the United States, Microfiche Prepared by the Bureau of the Census" (Washington, D.C.: Bureau of the Census, 1984).

22. U.S. Department of Justice, Immigration and Naturalization Service, "Unpublished Tabulations of Immigrants Admitted by Country of Birth and Age, 1975–1980" (Washington, D.C.: Immigration and Naturalization Service, 1986).

23. U.S. Department of Justice, Immigration and Naturalization Service, "Unpublished Tabulations of Immigrants Admitted in 1972, 1978, and 1986, by Admission Preference, Country or Region of Birth, and Sex."

24. United Nations, *Demographic Yearbook 1980* (New York: United Nations, 1982), table 40; United Nations, *Demographic Yearbook* (New York: United Nations, 1976), table 41.

25. United Nations, *Compiling Social Indicators on the Situation of Women* (New York: United Nations, 1984).

26. United Nations, *Demographic Yearbook 1980*.

27. Milton B. Hunt, "The Housing of Non-family Groups of Men in Chicago," *American Journal of Sociology* 16, 2 (1910): 145–170.

28. U.S. Department of Justice, Immigration and Naturalization Service, "Unpublished Tabulations of Immigrants Admitted in 1970–1987, by Country of Birth" (Washington, D.C.: Immigration and Naturalization Service, 1988).

29. Massey et al., *Return to Aztlan*; Tienda, "Familism and Structural Assimilation."

30. The World Bank, *World Development Report 1986* (New York: Oxford University Press, 1986).

31. Children are excluded from this analysis because few migrate to the United States independently of their families. In 1985, for example, approximately one-quarter of the children of immediate relatives were adoptive children.

U.S. Department of Justice, *Statistical Yearbook* (Washington, D.C.: Immigration and Naturalization Service, 1985).

32. Eric A. Hanushek and John E. Jackson, *Statistical Methods for Social Scientists* (New York: Academic Press, 1977), p. 201.

33. Jacob Cohen and Patricia Cohen, *Applied Multiple Regression/Correlation Analysis for the Behavioral Sciences* (Hillsdale, N.J.: Lawrence Erlbaum Associates, 1975).

34. Ibid., p. 268.

35. A final sensitivity test estimated regression coefficients using listwise deletion and substituted means of the nonmissing values of the variable for the missing data. Again the effects were consistent with those in Table 9.4.

36. Jasso and Rosenzweig, *The New Chosen People*.

37. Jasso and Rosenzweig, "Using National Recording Systems," Table 4.4.

38. Jasso and Rosenzweig, *The New Chosen People*.

39. For evidence of the law's effect on the deterrence of undocumented migration, see Donato, Massey, and Durand, "Stemming the Tide?" Regarding trends of female migration from Mexico, see Donato, "Current Trends and Patterns of Female Migration: Evidence from Mexico."

40. Massey, "Economic Development and International Migration."

10

Cuban Women in New Jersey: Gender Relations and Change

Yolanda Prieto

How have Cuban migrant women viewed changes in their lives as a result of migration? This chapter discusses women's perceptions of gender relations and gender ideologies, focusing on work, family, and sexuality.

This chapter is based on research conducted among 107 Cuban immigrant women in Hudson County, New Jersey, during the period 1979–1980, and on 18 recent in-depth interviews with eight women, their daughters and their Cuban husbands or boyfriends in the towns of Union City, West New York, and North Bergen in the same New Jersey county.[1]

My initial interest was in the high level of labor force participation among Cuban women in the United States. Female participation in paid production differs among the three major Hispanic groups in the country. In 1980, Cuban women's labor force participation rate (55.4 percent) exceeded that of Mexican-American females (49 percent) as well as that of Puerto Rican women (40.1 percent). When we look at specific regions, the proportion of Cuban women in production is even higher than the national percentage. For example, the official figure for Cuban women's labor force incorporation in the state of New Jersey in 1980 was 60 percent.[2]

The first study in Hudson County revealed that the strongest reason behind the intense economic activity of Cuban women was their commitment to help the family regain its lost economic status as a result of migration, or to fulfill their aspirations to move to a middle-class position here. Moreover, a combination of middle-class values or aspirations, a rejection of socialism as a system, and positive attitudes about the U.S.

political and economic systems were translated into a powerful work ethic and aspirations for social mobility.

Ten years have passed since the data for this research were collected. Since then, the literature on women's work has posed very important questions about the relationship between wage labor and the status of women in society. Women may be working outside the home in great numbers and still not getting the recognition they deserve as full human beings at work or at home.[3] Similarly, women may continue to be traditional in other areas of their lives even when they are part of the labor force.

Thus, this part of my study focuses on the place of gender ideology in the lives of Cuban migrant women, their daughters, and men. When socially constructed ideas about gender confront a totally different environment (as happens with migration), migrant men and women may resist, change, or adapt their old beliefs to the new situation. My most recent interviewing focuses on the results of this confrontation. I conducted long interviews (3 to 3½ hours) with as many of the women from my original study as I could find. I also interviewed their daughters and husbands (if applicable) as well as some relatives or friends who fit the purposes of the study.[4]

WORK AND THE DOMESTIC-PUBLIC DICHOTOMY

In prerevolutionary Cuba, there was strong disapproval of women working outside the home. Leaving the home to work for pay in the homeland was viewed as risky and, unless absolutely necessary, only done by "bad" women. These beliefs had a sexual basis. At issue here was the control of female sexuality; it was believed that the public sphere of society jeopardized female virginity and virtue.[5] This gender ideology sustained the structural inability of the Cuban economy to provide jobs for women since colonial times.

The notion that good women stayed home (*la casa*) and bad women worked outside (*la calle*) had polarizing effects in Cuban society and became central to the conception of social status and social mobility. Most upper- and middle-class women did not take part in public life in Cuba. Their fathers or husbands could support them comfortably. For them the ideology was a reality. Their place was at home ensuring the status of the family. On the other hand, very poor white and black women could not afford the luxury of staying home. For example, black women, since the abolition of slavery, constituted a cheap supply of labor for the Cuban upper classes. In 1889, the Cuban Census reported 74.4 percent of all women working as black; most worked as servants and laundresses.[6] However, even before independence, some poor white women were also incorporated into the labor force, often in the tobacco industry.[7]

For black and poor white women, who were forced to work outside the home and who had internalized the definition of bad women for doing so, the only way to ensure the status of their families and to move up socially was, as suggested before, by protecting their virginity, a fundamental element of their family's respectability and a necessary token for a good, honorable marriage.[8]

In the 1950s, the number of women in the labor force in Cuba increased. More women, many of them from the lower ranks of the middle class, worked as elementary teachers, typists, stenographers, and in other white-collar jobs. White-collar occupations became available as a result of the economic boom of the 1950s. The increase in the corporate, bureaucratic structures (especially in the banking and finance sectors) was due to an expanding phase of U.S. investments, predominantly in utilities, communications, oil refining, and tourism. Also, the growing state bureaucracy provided employment opportunities for women with the required education.[9] But even after these changes, in 1959 the labor force participation rate for women was 13 percent, the lowest in Latin America.[10]

The sudden change in work behavior among middle-class Cuban women and men as a consequence of migration provides an interesting example of the opposition of domestic and public in a changing context. Upon arrival in the United States, Cuban men and women took blue-collar jobs. Cuban men no longer derived social status from the public sphere, and women now entered the same realm. How did these individuals adjust their old ideologies to the new reality? For one thing, it was much more common for women in the United States to work outside the home, especially for immigrant women. Also, historically and at present, economic need in the adopted land has made it "natural" for all members of the immigrant family to work. For Cuban women and men, as for other immigrants, female work outside the home responded primarily to the economic need of the family. Work became very instrumental, not a conscious step toward the emancipation of women.

When I interviewed Cuban women in Hudson County in 1979–1980, an additional element was present in their explanations of why they worked. Most women said they worked hard to help the family regain what it had lost in Cuba as a result of the revolution, and for that end, any type of work became acceptable. Former class positions or class aspirations became central influences motivating women's behavior. Thus, female employment outside the home was seen as vital not only for survival, but also for the upward mobility of the family. For example, an elementary school teacher in the original Hudson County sample told me:

I am an elementary school teacher. Even though my husband has a business now I want to continue working. I think it would be inconsiderate on my part to stay home while he works. Life is very expensive and we Cubans are used to living comfortably.... No wonder most Cuban women have jobs here. Cuban women have been forced to help their families recuperate in only a few years the standard of living they had achieved in Cuba before communism took over. (Married white woman, 40 years old, middle-class with university education in Cuba, from Las Villas.[11])

Have the discourses of Cuban women regarding work changed between 1980 and 1990? Have other issues—other than helping the family regain its lost status—surfaced as reasons to work outside the home among these women? Before examining these questions, let us look at the characteristics of the eight women recently interviewed in Hudson County, New Jersey.

In examining Table 10.1, we see that, contrary to what the norms said, five out of eight respondents had worked for pay in Cuba. Given the previous discussion about ideology on female work in Cuba, it is necessary to clarify certain points. If we look at the age range of these women, and we take notice that in almost all cases they had white-collar jobs, we can place them in the late 1950s' expansive economic period which employed women from the middle class and the lower segments of the middle-class to work in the many bureaucratic jobs opening up at the time. That is, in the late 1940s and 1950s it was more common to see women working, at least in urban areas, especially in these more respectable middle-class jobs. Also, the average years in the United States for these women is about twenty-two years, which means that they came in the late 1960s. This suggests that many of them worked (perhaps for the first time) under the revolution, even if they were planning to leave the country. Gradually, it seems that the ideology of *la casa* and *la calle* was beginning to fade away for some of these women even before they left Cuba.[12]

Looking back at Table 10.1, we see that six out of eight women have an occupation in the United States at present. Even the two who described themselves as housewives or as not working outside the home are still engaged in paid labor; they babysit or take care of older children after school until their mothers pick them up after work.

One striking difference is that, for most women today, work has acquired an intrinsic value. Although the economic needs of the family were still mentioned, the 1990 interviewees feel that work is good in and of itself and that it makes people, especially women, feel positive and fulfilled.

"I love to work," said Eva, 47, widow, who owns a hairdressing salon. "Work makes me feel satisfied, genuine. Work is central to my life."[13]

Marina, 59, divorced and the Spanish-language editor of a publishing house in New York City, conveyed similar feelings:

Table 10.1
Characteristics of Interviewees

	Age	Education	Years in U.S.	Occupation in Cuba	in U.S.
Rosa*	69	8 years	18	White-Collar Office	Retired
Marta*	56	7	19	Seamstress	Sales
Ana*	53	12	20	White-Collar Office	Garment Examiner
Berta	51	12	25	White-Collar Office	Garment Sample Maker
Eva	47	12	20	Housewife	Small Business Owner
Marina	59	16	28	Elementary School Teacher	Editor Publishing House
Maria de los Angeles	57	8	21	Housewife	Housewife
Pura*	56	9	26	Housewife	Factory Operator

*Members of original survey study.

Note: With the exception of one woman respondent who was Mulatto, all other interviewees were white.

You know, work gives color to life. In Cuba, it was not common that women worked, although I was a teacher myself. But things have changed here. Most Cuban women work and are very active. I am not saying all these nice things about work because I have a nice job. I worked in a factory many years ago when I came to the United States and I still would say that work, no matter what kind, is good for human beings.[14]

Work is seen as good for women's minds. Eva commented: "It is good for women to work. They keep their minds occupied [at the same time that they earn money]. Besides, idleness is bad company. It is better for a marriage if the woman has a job, because an idle woman at home is no good."[15]

Others emphasized what work confers: self-respect, family and community recognition, money. "A woman needs to work," Marta told me. "She feels better and more in control of herself. She doesn't have to ask her husband for money. It seems to me that if a woman has a job, she is given more respect by her husband and her children."[16]

Other interviewees confirm Marta's statements. For example, Marina, reflecting about these issues, told me, "Women who don't work feel useless."[17]

If Cuban women now consider working outside the home a respectable activity for themselves, how do these women's daughters feel about these issues? I would propose that the second generation of Cuban women and men suffered many difficult changes growing up, as children of all immigrants do.[18] Even more than their parents, they had to live in two worlds. But the second generation, for the most part, did not face the painful consequences of deeply rooted, old beliefs that clashed with those of their new society. They never saw recovering their family status in Cuba as their main motive to work or to choose a career in the United States. Most were too young. Daughters expected that they would work outside the home. Moreover, they never questioned that they would have a career. Let us now look at some of their characteristics in Table 10.2.

All the daughters have high levels of education. Older ones are professionals; younger ones are in school pursuing careers. In other words, all the daughters assume that women should work and have careers. And even more than their mothers they emphasized self-actualization as the main goal when working or pursuing a career.

Graciela, one daughter, holds a degree in mathematics with a minor in physics from the New Jersey Institute of Technology (NJIT). After graduation she worked at various places, ranging from an insurance company to an office in New Jersey Bell. It was at New Jersey Bell that she learned the computer. By that time, Graciela had a strategy:

I wanted to learn a skill that would help me become independent because I had realized that what I wanted to do was to write and if I became an independent computer consultant at home that would give me enough money to contribute to the household and great flexibility with my time. And I am doing it! I get enough jobs while I can write my poems, my plays. I just finished a play on the Cuban family![19]

Table 10.2
Characteristics of Daughters

	Age	Education	Occupation	Birthplace	Years in U.S.
Martica	18	13 years	college	Spain	17
Graciela	35	16	Free-lance Computer Consultant and Writer	Cuba	28
Susy	16	10	High School	U.S.	
Evelyn	36	18	Lawyer	Cuba	29
Mariela	19	14	College	U.S.	
Adriana	26	16	Accountant Legal Firm	U.S.	

Susy, who is in high school now, wants to be a pharmacist. She has worked as a cashier at a pharmacy during summers and other vacations. What does work or a career mean to her? "I love to work," she reported. "I feel independent. It is not so much the money that I care about, you know. It is the pleasure that I get out of it."[20]

How did the men in these women's lives feel about these issues? First, let us look at Table 10.3 to see who these men are.

One, Roberto, is of the younger, U.S.-raised generation; the others are of the first generation. Most have high levels of educational attainment, and all except for one are professionals or business owners. Since most came from Cuba during the first or second wave of migration after 1959, we can see that they fit the type of middle-class or middle-class-aspiring Cuban refugee who came to the United States at the time.

Men were significantly more reserved than the women in expressing their opinions. Perhaps the fact that the interviewer was a woman explains their caution.

José, a small business owner from West New York, summarized how he feels about women working outside the home in the United States:

I think that women should like the home. But I recognize that they have to work here. They have to help the family financially, so there is no choice. That's why men have to accept that helping women with the chores at home is not only

Table 10.3
Characteristics of Men

	Age	Education	Years in U.S.	Occupation	
				in Cuba	in U.S.
Roberto (Mariela's boyfriend)	24	16 years	22		Electrical Engineer
José (Eva's boyfriend)	49	16	28	Student	Small Business Owner
Evelio (Pura's husband)	59	12	26	Sales	Small Business Owner
Pedro (Maria de los Angeles' husband)	59	8	21	Barber	Factory Foreman

good, but necessary, because women also work outside. To help each other is good. We have to put yesterday's "machismo" behind.[21]

Pedro, a factory foreman, prefers to have his wife do only housework while he goes out, earns a living, and provides for all:

I don't think it's a question of being "macho." It is the traditions we grew up with. I think that if I can keep my wife home, if she does not have to work, I am ensuring her dignity as a woman. If there comes a time when we really need it and my wife has to get a job, she'll have to do it, but not while I can provide for the family.[22]

Roberto, much younger than the other men, predictably said that he "has no problems with women working and having their careers."[23] Even though he considers women's participation in public life to be natural, there is part of him that still sees women at home as "natural." When asked a general question about the contributions of Cuban women's work to family and community, he replied:

About Cuban women? Oh yes, they work a lot. The work of Cuban women is very important for the community. The Cuban economic success is, in part, due to female work. My mother has always worked. Every woman in my family works. I expect my wife to work. But I would like my wife to cook for me. I'd like to find her home when I come home from work.[24]

It seems that men are gradually accepting women's new roles, especially as workers, because they have no choice. This is more apparent among the older men. What is interesting is that, even in the case of the second-generation Cuban male, men feel strongly about the primacy of the domestic role for women. There is no doubt that Cuban women are changing at a much faster pace than men! It may take longer for Cuban men to disregard the distinction between *la calle* and *la casa*, the public and the domestic spheres.

Obviously, in this tension between the domestic and the public, the historical power struggle between the sexes continues to take place. As men perceive themselves losing control over women and as women become more conscious and assertive about their actions, conflict between males and females will continue. What we can hope for is that in the process, this conflict will lead to a less gender-conscious society.

WOMEN AND THE FAMILY

In reviewing the literature about Cubans in the United States, the Cuban-American family emerges as a cohesive unit. Some argue that its cohesiveness has contributed to Cubans' relative economic success because the Cuban family is organized around realizing aspirations for economic achievement.[25] Everyone pools resources for the benefit of all in the family.

Recent studies have proposed that the three-generation family is a distinctive feature of the Cuban-American community.[26] This family form includes parents, children and grandparents, since there is resistance among Cubans to placing the elderly in nursing homes. The alternative is that the elderly are kept home while they also contribute economically, mainly with the care of the grandchildren.

Nevertheless, the Cuban family in the United States is small. According to the 1980 U.S. Census, Cuban-American households (2.96 persons per residence) are significantly smaller than other Hispanic households (3.48), and are almost comparable to average households in the United States (2.75). This fact is partly explained by the very low level of fertility among Cuban women.[27]

Cuban women had low fertility levels even in prerevolutionary Cuba, especially among the urban middle class. The fact that the postrevolutionary migration to the United States had an overrepresentation of individuals and families from the middle classes may explain the continuity of that trend among Cuban women in the United States.

Cubans also have fewer female-headed households than do other Hispanic groups. The percentage of families headed by women (14.9 percent), is lower than that for Mexican-Americans (16.4 percent) or for Puerto Ricans (35.3 percent), and it is comparable to the figure for the total U.S. population (14.3 percent).[28]

My earlier Hudson County study (1979–1980) confirmed the predominance of the small, mainly nuclear family type among members of the sample. The majority of the women were married and living with their spouses (73.8 percent). The mean number of children among women in the sample was only 2.0, while the mean number of persons per household was 3.2. Only half of the children were living at home with their parents. Most others were living elsewhere, generally after they were married.

Perhaps the intergenerational household mentioned before occurs more commonly in the Miami area, where Cuban cultural norms are more easily preserved and where spatial conditions permit the housing of more individuals per dwelling than in Hudson County. However, my recent interviews suggest that the Cuban family is changing in Hudson County as well. Specific reasons may predominate in different Cuban settlements. Divorce, as it happens with other groups, is an important factor behind structural family change. Widowhood also breaks the conjugal unit, and it generally creates other problems for the surviving partner and his or her offspring regarding care of the elderly. The nuclear unit is giving way to other forms of family arrangements.

Of eight women interviewed, only three were married, living with their spouses and unmarried children. Among the rest of the women we find three older women who never married, a widow who lives with her daughter and is dating one of the male interviewees (who is divorced himself), and a divorcee living with her daughter and two sisters.

Still, the family is viewed as very important, even essential by all respondents, regardless of gender or age. These feelings could be typical of any other Latin American group, since the institution of the family is the single most important social unit in Latin societies. Idealization of the family, especially of the postindustrial, nuclear type, is a widespread phenomenon. While the traditional nuclear family is becoming a minority in the United States, it continues to be a powerful cultural symbol, the ideal.

Even though some of the interviewees had experienced disruptions in their family lives such as divorce or the death of a young spouse or parent, the image of family that always surfaced was the married couple with two children at most. This was clearly expressed by the daughters who, regardless of their commitment to pursue careers, universally stated their intentions of getting married and having a family (two daughters were already married and also expressed these views).

Conflict is also part of family life. Do the respondents acknowledge the existence of conflict in their families? Here, the economics of the family provides an illustration. Economic cooperation in Cuban families is usually seen as one of the reasons for their relative economic success. Most respondents told me that the economics of the family should be based on a common interest, and that resources should be pooled. It was not clear, however, who would make the decisions about those resources. Most suggested that both husbands and wives made important economic decisions. The ideology of equal input into decisions on household economics was the strongest theme. As Roberto, the 24-year-old, second-generation Cuban, said: "Pooling together all resources for one purpose, that's what the economics of marriage and the family mean to me."[29]

But there were also dissenting voices. When asked if a married couple should have separate banking accounts, Marina, who is divorced, replied, "Of course. Dependency does not yield anything good. Married individuals should maintain independent finances. Especially in this country. It wasn't like that in Cuba. Women were dependent on men."[30] Responding to the same question, Graciela, a second-generation daughter who is married, said, "Yes, my husband and I have separate checking accounts. This arrangement allows us to keep our individuality. That's the main reason we did it."[31]

Increasing rates of divorce may influence ideas about family economics. Ana, who had participated in my earlier study, noted:

Many marriages stay together, but many are breaking up. There is no doubt that divorce is on the rise. In some cases, men start making separate financial arrangements when they are getting ready to make a move. For example, many leave their wives of many years for younger women. But Cuban women are very alert, and when they smell something they prepare themselves. Women are also keeping their financial resources separate [mainly savings, checking accounts]. As soon as they realize that something is going on, women protect their interests. I have a friend in that situation right now.[32]

I would like to briefly discuss a last point in this section: the relationship between mothers and daughters among the respondents. A common trait among the daughters is their admiration for their mothers, whom they view as strong individuals. Some daughters recalled how important their mothers were to the family when they were growing up and how hard they worked. In some instances these memories referred to the beginning years in the United States, after migrating from Cuba. Mothers were also pleased with the daughters' lives, their relationships to the family and the seriousness with which they approached their education. The mothers were concerned about other issues, too, mainly having to do with sexuality.

Expressing admiration for their mothers did not prevent some daughters from being critical of them. Evelyn is an example: "My mother is an exceptional person. She has devoted herself to her children. My mother has been a driving force. I admire her a lot. She always encouraged my brother and me to get a profession. But she is very strong willed and controlling. She can be suffocating."[33]

Adriana, also an admirer of her mother, does not think she should put her on a pedestal: "I think a great deal of my mother and I have a great relationship with her. However, I look at my mother as a human being, with her good qualities and her weaknesses. I think that admitting that is better than trying to put her on an altar. I don't like altars."[34]

WOMEN'S ROLES AND SEXUALITY

The cultural norms governing sexuality in Cuba, as in the rest of Latin America, had their origins in Spanish culture. Since Cuba remained a Spanish colony until 1899, some authors argue that the Spanish legacy on this point was strongest in Cuba.[35]

Except for slaves and prostitutes, women were expected to be pure, chaste, respectful, innocent, and well behaved and to serve as good housekeepers and model daughters, wives, and mothers. Men, on the other hand, were expected to become sexually active before marriage and could have sexual relations with any women they wanted after they married. Sexual prowess was an essential component of the definition of manhood.[36] But these norms implied that there had to be two kinds of women in society, the virgins or future wives, and the bad ones, those with whom men could have sex when they wanted to.

Spanish patriarchal values emphasized the importance of honor and shame, cultural codes that regarded female virginity and virtue as the main components of the family's status and ultimately of the male's dignity. The concepts of honor and shame are present in all Mediterranean countries, the Middle East, and Northern Africa.[37]

In Cuba, this sexual culture survived colonial rule, depending on race, social class, and social status of women and men. Confinement in the home of those women who were expected to be "good" became a requirement for the preservation of the family's honor. As Nelson P. Valdes has cogently summarized:

Spanish Colonial framework did not believe women capable of resisting male sexual advances, because they were by definition intellectually inferior and morally too backward. That is why the lives of females were controlled in a strict fashion, with *rules proscribing most activities outside the home* [emphasis mine]. This cultural standard, of course, could not be found throughout the entire society. This kind of family structure was viable only among the middle and upper strata of the society where the women did not have to face the harsh economic conditions endured by agricultural laborers and peasants.[38]

The topic of sexuality emerged through two basic themes in the Hudson County interviews: the *la casa* (domestic) and *la calle* (public) distinction, and changes due to contact with American society and with the women's liberation movement.

Though views on sexuality have changed drastically in Cuba and among Cubans outside of Cuba, the cultural legacy of placing women in the home to protect them from the "dangers of the street" still resonates. This fact becomes evident in indirect comments made by some respondents, especially males. "A woman should like the *home* [emphasis mine]," said one man. And the young male who had "no problem with women pursuing careers," said that when he married he "would like to find his wife *home* [emphasis mine]" when he "comes back from work." Even if there is acceptance of the inevitability of women's work outside, maximizing their time at home is symbolic of male sexual control, even when no one admitted openly that this issue had anything to do with sexuality.

The second theme that appeared regarding sexuality was the impact that contact with American society and changes in women's roles had on the migrants' adjustment to a new life. Both first-generation females and males admitted that work outside the home for a woman became more agreeable to them after realizing that it was common for so many women in this country to work for pay.

The influence of U.S. society and of the women's liberation movement was discussed in relation to the second generation of women and to female sexual liberation. The issue of virginity was of great importance to most of the first generation. Mothers were accepting, resigned and convinced that living in the United States meant adjusting to new ways of life. They did not expect their daughters to be virgins until marriage. Almost all mothers said that they try to talk to their daughters and to exchange views about sex sometimes. They asked them to be careful about who they go out with.

Many mothers are not only resigned but are willing to change. When I asked Maria de los Angeles if she would have preferred to raise her daughter in Cuba rather than in New Jersey, she replied, "Yes, but she would have had to have been born hundreds of years ago, because the change is happening all over. The sexual revolution is not a question of Cuba or the U.S., it is a question of these times. I am the one who has to change."[39]

The daughters were very candid about expressing their views. "What do I think about virginity? It is an old concept! If you are a virgin you are a nerd, you are an oddity. The first-generation Cubans still hold to the old views. It is very hard for them to deal with this issue."[40]

The different treatment of male and female children by parents concerning sexuality annoys Mariela. "One day I overheard my mother reminding my brother as he was going out, 'Please do not forget to take condoms in these days of AIDS.' Why doesn't she ask me?"[41]

There seems to be growing communication between mothers and daughters (but not fathers and daughters) about sex. Susy told me, "My mother and I talk about sex. She understands the gap between the ages. My mother and I don't always agree, but we try to resolve our conflicts by talking to each other."[42] An interesting summary of the gap between the generations regarding sexuality was given by young Roberto: "The older generation has had no choice but to accept premarital sexual relationships. I think there is a silent agreement where the younger Cubans do what they have to do, have premarital sex, and the parents pretend not to know anything."[43]

On several occasions, the subject of homosexuality was introduced by the interviewees, usually the daughters. They complained about the degree of homophobia existing in the Cuban community. In one particular case, a daughter shared her concern because her boyfriend was very homophobic and she did not think that was right. On the other hand, the only mention of homosexuality among men was by one who expressed some anxiety that homosexuality had risen significantly in the Cuban community. This is an issue that deserves further attention, and I will expand on this topic as my research continues.

CONCLUSION

This chapter has explored changes in gender relations and gender ideologies among Cuban women and their families in Hudson County, New Jersey. Using an open-ended, qualitative mode of analysis, I examined the ideas and feelings of the interviewees in three principal areas related to women: work, family, and sexuality. My goal was to elicit the meanings of these concepts for the interviewees.

Work for the women interviewed is no longer a solely instrumental activity. All women referred to the intrinsic value of work and the benefits that it confers: recognition of women by the family and the community, improved self-esteem, and economic and other forms of value. Daughters, it is obvious, never questioned whether they should work or not or pursue careers.

Men seemed to accept that women in this country have to help the family economically and work outside the home. Some believed men should "help" women with "their" housework. But one of the men said that he will keep his wife home as long as he is able to provide for the family.

The family remained very important for all the respondents, male or female, young or old. Even when they were very committed to their careers and professional lives, the daughters said the family came first. But the family is changing. The typical nuclear family seems to be giving rise to other forms of family among Cubans in New Jersey. Divorce, widowhood, and rearrangements into extended family situations are all introducing a diversity in family structure in the Cuban community in the United States.

Mothers and daughters appeared to have good relationships. Admiration for their mothers was a general sentiment among the daughters. Mothers were perceived to be strong individuals. Satisfaction with their daughters was a constant when interviewing the mothers.

The area of sexuality seems the most conflictual. Explicitly or not, all the men interviewed expressed their wishes that women stay home or spend more time at home. Clearly, the domestic terrain is still the place where men can exert their sexual power, be it real or symbolic. Also, having women at home has always signified having maids around. Missing women's services may be, consciously or unconsciously, behind men's answers.

The most striking finding in this area is the acceptance by parents and daughters of new views of virginity, a highly regarded virtue in Cuba. Parents (especially mothers) accept that as a result of growing up or coming to the United States as a child, daughters have been influenced by the surrounding culture and the new attitudes on women's sexuality. There seem to be good efforts at communication between mothers and daughters about the issue of sexuality. Still, views of premarital sexual relations and homosexuality at times indicate that on the subject of sexuality, the generational gap among Cubans is greater than has been generally accepted.

NOTES

1. I am grateful to Professor Christopher Mitchell and Professor Constance Sutton for their support while working on the most recent part of this research as a Scholar-in-Residence at New York University's Faculty Resource Network's program in the spring of 1990. I am indebted to Barbara Schroder for her helpful comments on this manuscript. I want to thank all the women and men interviewed here who gave so generously of their time.

2. U.S. Bureau of the Census, *General Population Characteristics*, and U.S. Bureau of the Census, *General Social and Economic Characteristics, New Jersey* (Washington, D.C.: GPO, 1980). Also, the rate of labor force participation in the study sample described above was 68 percent.

3. See Moore, *Feminism and Anthropology*.

4. A few words on methodology: in order to maximize continuity in looking at change, I have made great efforts to locate the sample members from my initial study. So far, out of eight women interviewed here, four had participated in the original study.

Daughters are included in the study because I am interested in the differences between the first and second generations of Cuban women in this country. I also want to assess how men react to the changes in women's lives.

Since I am interested primarily in the study of ideology and culture and how they are affected by change, I am relying on qualitative methods. Sociologists have recently been rediscovering the value of retrospective analysis in the in-depth interview, which some authors have called life-story. Like the historian's oral history, the life story is based on the free self-expression of the informants. They organize their stories their own way. The sociologist "listens beyond" the words of the person to make sense of a social culture, of specific ideologies (Isabelle Bertaux-Wiame, "The Life-History Approach to the Study of Internal Migration," in Daniel Bertaux, 249–266, *Biography and Society* [Beverly Hills: Sage Publications, 1981]). Open-ended means of analysis, many agree, allows for a "better-grounded" sociology through building theory step-by-step with the discovery of facts (Paul Thompson, "Life Histories and the Analysis of Social Change" in Bertaux, 289–306, *Biography and Society*).

When I interview, I ask only an initial question for each theme. I let the respondents answer spontaneously for as long as they want. Usually they talk extensively and very openly (the women more than the men). On occasion I probe to get more information about a specific topic. For a good collection of articles on the use of this methodology in sociology see Bertaux, *Biography and Society*.

5. These beliefs were not unique to Cuba. Since they were part of Spanish culture, these values spread throughout Latin America. There will be a more detailed discussion of these issues in the section on sexuality.

6. JUCEPLAN, *Aspectos Demograficos de la Fuerza Laboral Femenina en Cuba* (Havana: Direccion Nacional de Estadisticas, 1975), p. 5.

7. Ibid., pp. 5–6.

8. On this topic see Verena Martinez Alier, *Marriage, Class and Colour in Nineteenth-Century Cuba* (Cambridge: Cambridge University Press, 1974), and Nelson P. Valdes, "Women and Sexual Relations in Cuba: Family, Consensual Unions, Divorce and Prostitution before 1959" (Paper presented at the conference "Women and Change," Boston University, Boston, 1977).

9. Lourdes Casal, "Images of Cuban Society among Pre- and Post-Revolutionary Novelists" (Ph.D. dissertation, the New School for Social Research, New York, 1975), and James O'Connor, *The Origin of Socialism in Cuba*, (Ithaca: Cornell University Press, 1970).

10. Oficina Nacional de los Censos Demografico y Electoral, *Censos de Poblacion, Viviendas y Electoral*, Informe General, 1953 (Havana: P. Fernandez y Cia, S. en C., 1955) and Union Panamericana, *America en Cifras* (Washington, D.C.: Instituto Interamericano de Estadistica, 1960), pp. 39–40. Percentages computed by Marifeli Pérez-Stable.

11. Prieto, "Cuban Women in the U.S. Labor Force."

12. The justifications given for working outside, especially among the lower

middle class, was the economic need of the family. This is similar to what the women in the Hudson County study revealed ten years ago.

13. Interview with Eva, Union City, N.J., October 1, 1990.

14. Interview with Marina, North Bergen, N.J., September 30, 1990.

15. Interview with Eva, Union City, N.J., October 1, 1990.

16. Interview with Marta, Union City, N.J., August 14, 1990.

17. Interview with Marina, North Bergen, N.J., September 30, 1990.

18. By second generation I am referring to the daughters of the migrants, whether they were born in Cuba or in the United States.

19. Interview with Graciela, Union City, N.J., September 15, 1990.

20. Interview with Susy, Union City, N.J., October 1, 1990.

21. Interview with José, Union City, N.J., October 6, 1990.

22. Interview with Pedro, West New York, N.J., October 5, 1990.

23. Interview with Roberto, West New York, N.J., October 1, 1990.

24. Ibid.

25. Lisandro Perez, "Immigrant Economic Adjustment and Family Organization: The Cuban Success Story Reexamined," *International Migration Review* 20 (Spring 1986): 17.

26. Ibid., p. 14.

27. Ibid., p. 13, and U.S. Bureau of the Census, *General Population Characteristics*.

28. U.S. Bureau of the Census, *General Population Characteristics*.

29. Interview with Roberto, West New York, N.J., October 5, 1990.

30. Interview with Marina, North Bergen, N.J., September 30, 1990.

31. Interview with Graciela, Union City, N.J., September 15, 1990.

32. Interview with Ana, West New York, N.J., October 5, 1990.

33. Interview with Evelyn, North Bergen, N.J., September 30, 1990.

34. Interview with Ariana, North Bergen, N.J., August 27, 1990.

35. Susan Kaufman-Purcell, "Modernizing Women for a Modern Society: The Cuban Case," in Ann Pescatello, ed., *Female and Male in Latin America* (Pittsburgh: University of Pittsburgh Press, 1970).

36. Nelson P. Valdes, "The Historical Context of the Cuban Family," (Unpublished manuscript, n.d.).

37. Ibid., p. 4.

38. Ibid., p. 15.

39. Interview with Maria de los Angeles, West New York, N.J., October 7, 1990.

40. Interview with Susy, Union City, N.J., October 1, 1990.

41. Interview with Mariela, West New York, N.J., October 5, 1990.

42. Interview with Susy, Union City, N.J., October 1, 1990.

43. Interview with Roberto, West New York, N.J., October 5, 1990.

11

A Study of Asian Immigrant Women Undergoing Postpartum Depression

Young I. Song

In starting new lives in a Western country, Asian immigrant women are confronted with Western culture, but to a great degree, they retain their own traditions. Focusing on Asian immigrant womanhood's transition will help to promote understanding of postpartum depression in Asian immigrant women.

China, Japan, Korea, and Vietnam are countries of strict morals, ethics, and conventions. Although each country has a distinctive language and culture, in general Confucianism has played the leading role in defining women's status in most Asian countries. The function of the woman within the teaching of traditional thought is simple and clear. Throughout the history of most Asian countries, a woman's obedience has been unquestionable and absolute regarding her duties and obligations.

In traditional Asian society a woman's normative role has been difficult to satisfy because it has been based on unrealistic expectations and overwhelming tasks, and few questions are allowed. Asian women married and continue to marry "commanders" rather than men. Even in China, Japan, and Korea today, the husband and his family have rights and privileges, while the wife has the duties and obligations.

The purpose of this study was to investigate to what extent Asian immigrant women suffer from postpartum depression: how they cope, how this strength is acquired, and what impact depression has on women and their families.

The myth of the quiet Asian-American tends to hide postpartum depression in Asian immigrant families. Furthermore, as the following folktale illustrates, being an Asian woman means that one has no voice, no other option but to tolerate hardships silently during marriage.

ce upon a time a man said to his daughter when she was setting out to go to
er wedding, "A woman's life is very hard. She must pretend that she does not
see the things that are to be seen, that she does not hear the words spoken
around her, and she must speak as little as possible." So for three years after
her marriage, the woman never spoke a word.[1]

Thus a virtuous woman should silently weather the hardships, tribulations, and pains of married life. She should be passive and quiet.

To what extent does this tradition affect Asian women in the United
States? Despite the revolutionary changes that have marked almost every
aspect of the lives of immigrants to the United States, especially in the
present century, immigrants feel an abiding and deep sense of identity
with their cultural past and make a conscious effort to perpetuate it.
Such cultural persistence is especially strong in the institution of
marriage.

As marriage partners, women have been socially tangential to men
and also have had to continually validate their duties in order to retain
their marital status. In traditional Asian societies, women have always
served primarily as childbearers and child rearers. Women, within the
teachings of Confucianism, have been bound by strict rules and duties
in traditional Asian society. If a woman violated any of the taboos, she
could face unconditional divorce. One of the taboos was the failure to
produce children, particularly male children.[2]

The idea of male preference at birth still prevails. According to the
Research Institute of Behavior Science, 50 percent of all Korean women
in maternity said in a survey that if they could not bear a son, they would
even try to get a son for their husbands through a second wife of the
man. Son describes two psychological reasons for this kind of answer: a
mother does not want to have a daughter to whom the heritage of
suffering and insult will be transferred; a mother deserves human treatment only when she bears a son.[3]

Until she gives birth to a son, a wife feels as if she is "sitting on a
cushion of needles." With the birth of a son, her duty is fulfilled in
perpetuating the ancestral lineage, and she finds protection and security
in the future of her son. Even treatment during the childbearing period
exemplifies the different values attributed to the sexes. After giving birth
to a son, the young mother is encouraged to lie quietly in bed for two
or three weeks. However, if the mother bears a girl and lies in bed for
more than one week, she is put to shame and suffers insults. In Kyongsang Province, noted as the stronghold of Confucianism, it is customary
for a mother-in-law to prepare a feast for the birth of a grandson. If,
however, a girl is born, the mother-in-law immediately leaves the house
and does not return for a week as an expression of regret and disap-

pointment about the birth. This disappointment is sometimes transm̲‍
ted to the female child by the way she is named—"Soun̲‍
(disappointment), "Sop-sop" (pity), or "Yukam" (regret).[4]

By the time a girl reaches puberty, she is expected to believe that (1)
women are inferior to men; (2) women must expect and acquiesce to
the preferential treatment accorded to males; (3) women are subject to
spatial constraints in movements; (4) women must maintain proper social
distance from men in their household and practice social avoidance with
unrelated men; (5) women must conceal emotions that are incompatible
with their role requirements; (6) women must cultivate covert strategies
for goal realization, that is, learn to "work the system"; (7) women are
married into strange households where their reception is uncertain; (8)
women uphold cultural values by their conformity and commitment to
their female roles. Since, almost by definition of their role, traditional
Korean women have been perpetually caught in restricted and una-
voidable situations, their adequate and appropriate socialization has involved learning to survive through womanhood without interfering with
cultural norms.[5]

For women to improvise or deviate in their role beyond the culturally
permissible range has been tantamount to placing one's individuality
above one's social utility and accountability to the entire ethnic group.
Suppression of self-expression has been a key socialization task for Asian
women. In such a cultural context, it is inconceivable to admit postpartum depression because it directly conflicts with the image of a virtuous
Asian woman.

The complete lack of research on Asian immigrant women in the
postpartum period does not indicate that they do not have serious problems, but rather suggests that existing problems have not yet been examined. Studies on Asian-American women have been severely limited
in the United States by the limited nature of existing data. In the case
of the postpartum period in Asian immigrant women, there has been
no study conducted to date. This population has received no attention
in social research literature, nor has it received the social services provided for minority women.

As the population of Asian women in America increases and becomes
more visible, family problems and service needs also increase. During
the period of cultural adjustment, Asian immigrant women experience
a heightened sense of vulnerability as they suffer from both the deep-
rooted, traditional cultural biases against women and the strains caused
by cultural barriers as well as unfamiliarity with the use of social resources.

Unfortunately, the postpartum experience does occur in this context.
Problems experienced by Asian women might have been overlooked in

e past either because of their relatively small numbers or the mysti-
ication that Asian-Americans "take care of their own" and "rarely become social problems."[6]

The problems faced by Asian immigrant women are further complicated by the fact that many postpartum women are ignorant of available
services or are reluctant to seek help due to cultural conflict. Their
problems go untreated and become liabilities to the community as a
whole. Consequently, these postpartum Asian immigrant women will
continue to be isolated, and their problems with child rearing will
increase.

THE TRANSITION TO MOTHERHOOD

Having a child is not only a biological but also a cultural act. Human
childbirth is accomplished in and shaped by culture, both in a general
sense and in the particular sense of the varying definitions of reproduction offered by different cultures. How a society defines childbirth
is closely linked with its articulation of women's position; the connections
between female citizenship and the procreative role are social, not biological.[7] Therefore, childbirth stands uncomfortably at the junction of
the two worlds of nature and culture. Women's experience of childbirth
has been seen as a unique catastrophe for women in its physiological
and psychological impact.[8]

Asian immigrant women are no exception. The components of nature
and culture are more potently and ambiguously mixed in the case of
childbirth than in any other physiological state. Having babies must be
deeply natural. Yet at the same time, childbirth creates far-reaching
consequences for the mother and for the life of society. Though the
months after the birth of a child may be one of the most joyful times in
a woman's life, this is also among the most stressful periods.

The birth of a child, the beginning of a new life, is generally regarded
as a welcome event, paradoxically bringing with it increased risks of
emotional turmoil to the mother. The transition to motherhood—pregnancy, delivery, and then the postpartum period—constitutes a serious
and irrevocable event in the life cycle of women.

Postpartum depression is viewed as the most common of the serious
depressions among women. During the first months postpartum, women
are at the highest risk in their entire lives of suffering psychiatric illness.
The high incidence of postpartum depression raises concern regarding
the emotional health and well-being of the baby, the new mother, and
the family.[9]

The relative past neglect of the postpartum depression experienced
by Asian immigrant women in research and practice is a by-product of
the Asian emphasis on women's fulfillment of their destiny through

reproduction and the cultural reluctance to believe that this could in a way be less than an ideal experience for women.

Most important, women also considered acceptance and adherence to their sex role the highest virtue. It may be true that Asia has gone through tremendous social changes in recent years, marked by the incorporation of Western ideology; however, even today, the situation of women regarding the performance of what is considered to be their primary (and biologically determined) role remains largely unchanged in Asian society. In such a cultural context, women are inhibited from expressing negative experiences during the postpartum period.

Given these considerations, the objective of this study was to investigate the psychological and social aspects as well as the contribution of cultural factors in the development of postpartum depressive episodes. This study attempts to broaden and deepen our understanding of women's postpartum experiences by means of depth interviews in which women talk at length about their personal experiences. I employed an interview schedule outlining research goals and specifying the particular areas I intended to investigate.

METHOD

Subjects consisted of forty Asian immigrant married women. All those interviewed lived in the San Francisco Bay area, and their length of residence in the United States was less than ten years. They were recruited through three private obstetricians (one Chinese, one Japanese, one Korean).

Initially advised of the project by the obstetrician who delivered the child within the previous five to seven months, each woman who was interested in participating in this study was scheduled for an interview. Each woman was given an interpretation of the purpose and nature of the project and was told what would be required if she decided to participate. During the first phase of data collection, initial contacts were made with each obstetrician. After the introductory letters were mailed out, visitations and meetings with each obstetrician were made in order to facilitate their cooperation in the study.

During the second phase, structured interviews were administered by the bilingual interviewers at various designated locations, including churches, shops, and restaurants.

During the final phase, home visit interviews were administered after telephone contact with the women. This approach was purposefully used in order to include women who stay at home most of the time.

Subjects were advised that the data would be made available only to the interviewers for use in the study, and that they would be protected from any disclosure of personal identifying information. The interview each woman by the author lasted approximately one and a half hours. The interviews allowed the women to talk at length about their personal experience.

The social composition of the sample was as follows: 13 Chinese, 7 Japanese, 16 Korean, 4 Vietnamese. The average age was 27; two thirds of the subjects had some college education. These women ranged from working class to upper middle class. Most of the marriages were relatively traditional in that the wife was primarily responsible for child care regardless of her employment status: 8 were professionals; 19, nonprofessionals; 3, students; and 10, unemployed. Approximately half of the women had boys and half had girls.

Difficulties in obtaining a study population with regard to Asian immigrants have been reported by many researchers.[10] There are also limitations in the design of this study, which must be considered in evaluating the results and generalizations from the findings:

1. All of the women who participated were volunteers who must have felt somewhat uncomfortable talking of personal experiences. The cultural reluctance among these women must be considered in interpreting the findings.

2. It is evident that this sample is not representative of all Asian immigrant women in the United States. Although every effort was taken to minimize the potential bias on the selection of the sample, the final sample included the more outgoing women rather than the more homebound.

3. Data were solely dependent upon the memories of these women, and data were retrospective in nature. One might suppose that errors of memory had occurred. Therefore, it is possible that a woman's feelings of vulnerability or simply the tendency to block out memories of her experience could have influenced the findings.

4. In most research with non-Western subjects, an immediate obstacle to overcome is the language barrier. All respondents in this study had difficulty with the English language. Difficulties involved in translation are well known, although cautionary translation was undertaken to ensure the most possible equivalent word.[11]

The final sample consisted of 6 nondepressed and 34 depressed postpartum women (13 with minor depression and 21 with moderate to major depression). Depressed and nondepressed women did not differ significantly on age (Ms = 27.7 vs. 26.9) or years of education (Ms = 15.2 vs. 16.3). However, the group differed on the sex of the infant of the total women interviewed: 67 percent of the nondepressed women, compared to 41 percent of the depressed women, had sons.

THE PSYCHOLOGICAL STATE OF THE NEW MOTHER

In this section, the complex psychological situation that childbir. creates for women will be discussed. I defined postpartum depression as any psychological disturbance occurring up to six months postpartum to which women referred as a condition, feeling, anxiety, or state characterized by disruptive behaviors or symptoms.

The existing research concerning the psychological state of new mothers varies in regard to definitions and methodology, and findings are often contradictory.[12] However, most researchers agree with a delineation of three different levels of postpartum depression.[13]

In level one, most of the study participants (95 percent) anticipated that they would have a pleasurable experience raising a baby. After a week or so, 85 percent began to have postpartum depression symptoms. They felt themselves to be less than competent, and when they found themselves not full of love twenty-four hours a day and occasionally angry at the baby or at themselves, they perceived that they were not good mothers (N = 32). Most of the women (N = 34) experienced an emotional letdown, known as the "baby blues" becoming sensitive and tearful and experiencing crying spells and confusion. These symptoms usually disappeared within a couple of weeks, except in two cases that lasted for four weeks.

Additionally, some postpartum women experienced a brief transitory depression known as "maternity blues." A wide spectrum of symptoms has been identified: crying spells, anxiety, depressed mood, fatigue, headaches, restlessness, irritability, feelings of unreality and confusion, feelings of guilt and self-dislike, and negative feelings toward the husband and baby.

In level two, approximately one half of the sample of 40 women (N = 21) noted feelings of clinical depression. In addition to moderate depression, lasting for six weeks or longer, they experienced mercurial mood swings, lost their appetites or went sleepless for nights. Most depressed women reported an inability to concentrate, and many reported a plunge in self-esteem. Over half (N = 25) noted physical symptoms such as headaches, constipation, tremors, episodes of palpitations, sweating, and diminished sexual response.

Symptoms similar to those of other depressive states included feelings of inadequacy and inability to cope, constant tearfulness, apathy, self-derogatory feelings, indecisiveness, inability to concentrate, and multiple somatic complaints. However, in most cases these symptoms were not severe enough to interfere with the women's functioning. Many women in this category showed anxiety concerning the infant's well-being.

In level three, approximately 25 percent of the women (N = 9) felt somewhat disabled by their depression and said it interrupted their nor-

behavior routines. Some were plagued by thoughts of suicide (N = extreme agitation (N = 3), and serious confusion and rapid mood vings (N = 4). On one occasion when the researcher contacted a potential subject for this study, the husband reported the death by suicide of his wife at three weeks postpartum (not included in the data). Others . reported an inability to eat (N = 3) and dramatic changes in sleep patterns (N = 4) other than fatigue or interrupted sleep. These included constant insomnia or constant sleeping. Some also experienced lack of interest in the world and other people (N = 4).

THE SOCIAL DIMENSION: STRESS FACTORS AND CHANGES IN SOCIAL SUPPORT

This section focuses on the mothers' social experience and the impact these changes made in this sphere. The arrival of a baby places a host of demands on the parents. They must hold, feed, and bathe the child, cope with crying and illness, and deal with major changes in their family system. Along with the joys, a new baby brings stress into the home, particularly for the mother.

The actual and perceived losses associated with childbirth are considerable. Important factors are the loss of time and often the loss of social contacts. The gaining of a child and the rewards of motherhood may not be immediately felt as adequate compensation for these losses.

A number of investigators hold that disruption caused by new demands during the postpartum period increases the woman's vulnerability to emotional disturbance.[14] In fact, the greater the disturbance in functioning, the greater the likelihood of serious depression.[15] This creates a type of feedback loop whereby the more serious the depression, the more likely the reduction in functioning. Recently, several investigators have begun to examine the role of stressful life events and social support in the development of depression.[16] Social support has been found to prevent or reduce depressive reactions even when circumstances are adverse.[17]

Focusing on the findings of the present study, it was found that of those women who experienced high stress factors (such as marital problems, difficult infant temperament, and lack of social support), 61 percent developed emotional problems following the birth of their babies. Of those who had not indicated stress factors, only 12 percent developed difficulties.

The dominant theme among subjects was lack of support. Repeatedly, respondents confessed that they don't have a support structure to relieve them of the added pressure especially if the infant is "temperamentally difficult." They found caring for the newborn extremely demanding both physically and emotionally. One-third of the depressed women believed that raising a difficult infant leads to greater exhaustion depression. Women who have difficulty comforting their babies or feel less competent as mothers. They develop ambivalent feelings toward their babies and subsequently experience guilt for feeling this way. This ambivalence further lowers their sense of self-esteem.

Professional women in this study confessed that they were used to being able to control everything, and that became impossible with a new baby in the house. Of the professional women, 67 percent felt that they have a harder time with postpartum depression due to the double demands of their home and career.

Two of the most common complaints reported by subjects were constant feelings of fatigue and of being tied down. Seventy-nine percent of the mothers reported that physical fatigue bothered them somewhat or very much. More than two-thirds reported feeling that mothering was more stressful than they had expected, largely because they felt burdened and tied down by the unrelieved responsibility of being at home alone for long periods of time with the baby. Sixty-eight percent of the women confessed lack of support from their husbands. Many of these women (75 percent) reported that they have no close relatives residing in the area. Others, who did have close relatives living near by, reported that these relatives were not available for help due to conflicts such as work schedules or transportation problems. In fact, of the mothers who did have adequate support provided both by family members (usually the grandmother) and by others, only 11 percent developed depression.

DISCUSSION

The findings of this study suggest that Asian immigrant women are extremely vulnerable to experiencing postpartum depression. These women's subordinate societal status is a major factor leading to the fragility of their self-esteem and renders them sensitive to stress at each turning point in their lives, particularly childbirth. For women, entry into womanhood carries a significant risk of becoming depressed. Many women seemed terrified of this emotional confrontation with motherhood. They felt alienated from their husbands, family, and friends.

Cutrona reviewed six studies, revealing that 50 to 70 percent of women experienced at least transitory symptoms of depression in the week following childbirth.[18] It thus seems that the degree and length of the experiences reported by women in the present study were problems unique to Asian immigrant women.

Essentially, postpartum depression is a disorder; however, it differs from other forms of depression. The physiological symptoms reported here, such as severe insomnia, confusion, and constipation, are not usu-

present in depression. To a startling degree these depressed women . "up" one day and "down" the next. Regular depression does not include such striking alterations of mood.[19]

Postpartum depression experienced by Asian immigrant women is unique in another regard. One striking finding of the study was that almost 70 percent of the nondepressed women had sons. This apparent favoritism may be a clear indication that the concept of male dominance still strongly prevails in Asian immigrant families. In Asian countries, sons have traditionally been favored over daughters because only sons can carry on the official family line and were parents' only source of support in old age. As such, sons were more highly prized, as were the women who gave birth to sons. The high proportion (85 percent) of depressed women in this study indicates that cultural differences may be a factor in determining postpartum depression.

This study also revealed a consistent empirical trend supporting the hypothesis that social and spousal support reduces vulnerability to postpartum depression. The vast majority of these women do not have relatives living nearby. Moreover, the majority of depressed women indicated a lack of support from their husbands. The lack of support from the husband arises where there is a clear-cut distinction in the roles that wives and husbands play. The role of babysitter or shopper is rarely performed by the husband in Asian culture. This places the burden for these tasks on the wife, who is expected to carry out the many responsibilities herself. Help is no longer available from female relatives as was the case in an extended Oriental family structure.

Under these circumstances, it is important to seek friends and companions and to allow some time for outside activities to diminish the sense of isolation that is commonly experienced by a new mother. Isolation can have a devastating effect on both mothers and babies. Women who reported high levels of support from spouses, parents, or friends felt less depressed during the postpartum period. This is because social contacts can help a person maintain a sense of self-worth in times of stress. A woman, then, can help fend off postpartum depression by cultivating supportive people. Too often, though, the problem goes undetected. Husbands frequently fail to appreciate the gravity of the depression, or, in extreme cases, may become hostile to their wives for not conforming to the idealized female role, resulting in an even more negative experience for the women.

As other studies such as Song's have shown, women tend to take responsibility for any negative experience incurred within the family, including abusive behavior by their husbands, which they feel they have "caused."[20] Women in the present study very strongly felt that they were to blame for their own experience of depression following childbirth. This experience may also be perceived as shameful in that the women

are apparently deviating from the conceptualized ideal of womanho
and there is a danger that, as in the case of wife abuse, this shame w
cause women to isolate themselves, thus perpetuating their isolation.[21]

CONCLUSION AND RECOMMENDATIONS

Women in this study were largely ignorant about postpartum depression, and very few women sought help when it occurred. This indicates
not only that the cultural pattern of Asian immigrant women rejects the
idea of professional help but also that there may be many untreated
cases of women suffering from postpartum depression.

These women need to know they are not alone. The most common
complaint of women suffering from postpartum depression is that no
one listens and no one believes them. This makes postpartum depression
much harder to overcome. If a woman is depressed and doesn't get help,
the likelihood of a recurrence of postpartum depression in subsequent
pregnancies is as high as 25 percent.[22]

In spite of the emotions and anxieties that the interview aroused,
however, many women said that they had felt talking about the experience had been greatly beneficial, especially those who had held it inside
without telling anybody. It was not unusual for a woman to say that she
had gained new insight and a better understanding of her situation. It
appeared that although actual counseling was not provided, the discussion of the situation in an accepting, nonjudgmental setting was indeed
therapeutic, as indicated in other researches.[23]

The findings and observations of the study pose a challenge to the
community to provide appropriate services for these women. These
women face language barriers, cultural differences, myths, and stereotypes. Thus they are in vulnerable situations and in more need of professional help. Improving the provision of services for Asian immigrant
women requires specifically focused programs on postpartum care in
general and specifically targeted programs for concentrated areas of
Asian populations.

Public education should be geared toward specific objectives. There
must be consciousness raising in the Asian immigrant community about
the extent and nature of postpartum depression. At the same time,
women themselves need to be reached through counseling agencies,
public services, and the media.

Future research may indicate a need for intervention as a technique
by concerned helping professionals. Postpartum depression is poorly
understood by Asian immigrant communities and poses a distinct challenge to provide adequate services for these women.

Isolation is a key factor; hence it is hoped that as more information
regarding postpartum depression is made available to Asian immigrant

...nen, they will begin to appreciate that their experience is neither ...re nor a cause for blame.

The postpartum period is a time of potential crisis. It is also a time of primary prevention for future hazardous events. The teaching of social service organization staff and helping professionals such as social workers, counselors, physicians, and nurses (who provide help during this time) is crucial in assisting the women to balance their needs and their babies' needs. These professionals are in a pivotal position to support women through this experience by being attentive to readiness to learn, by teaching what mothers need to know, and by providing necessary resources for the women.

This study concludes that the symptoms, severity, and length of postpartum depression in Asian immigrant families is culturally related to being a member of that community. In addition to the stresses of cultural adaptation and isolation from extended families in this community, childbirth is a key event rendering women, men, and children vulnerable to family crisis. As such, it must be treated as a subject worthy of the utmost respect.

NOTES

1. Lel Soo Zong, *The History of Korea* (Seoul: The Eul-Yoo Publishing Co., 1970), pp. 189–190.

2. Young Sook Harvey, *Six Korean Women* (St. Paul: West, 1979).

3. Dug-Soo Son, "The Status of Korean Women from the Perspective of the Women's Emancipation Movement," in Harold Hakwon Sunoo and Dong Soo Kim, eds., *Korean Women* (Memphis: Christian Scholars, 1978), pp. 257–282.

4. Soon Man Rhim, "The Status of Women in Traditional Korean Society," in Sunoo and Kim, *Korean Women*; J. Robert Moose, *Village Life in Korea* (Nashville: Publishing House of the M. E. Church, South, 1911).

5. Song, *Silent Victims*.

6. Richard Kalish and S. Yuen, "Americans of East Asian Ancestry: Aging and the Aged," *The Gerontologist* 11 (1971): 37.

7. Ann Oakley, *Women Confined: Toward a Sociology of Childbirth* (New York: Schocken Books, 1980).

8. Carolyn E. Cutrona, "Social Support and Stress in the Transition to Parenthood," *Journal of Abnormal Psychology* 93 (1984): 378–390; Michael W. O'Hara, Lynn, P. Rehm, and Susan B. Campbell, "Postpartum Depression: A Role for Social Network and Life Stress Variables," *Journal of Nervous and Mental Diseases* 171 (1983): 336–341; Joyce Hopkins, Marsha Marcus, and Susan B. Campbell, "Postpartum Depression: A Critical Review," *Psychological Bulletin* 95 (1984): 498–515.

9. Hopkins, Marcus, and Campbell, "Postpartum Depression."

10. Won Mu Hurh and Kwang Chung Kim, *The Korean Immigrant in America: A Structural Analysis of Ethnic Confinement and Adhesive Adaptation* (Cranberry, N.J.: Association of University Presses, 1984).

11. Won Mu Hurh and Kwang Chung Kim, *Korean Immigrants in America: Structural Analysis of Ethnic Confinement and Adhesive Adaptation* (Macomb, Ill: Western Illinois University Press, 1980).

12. Carolyn E. Cutrona, "Nonpsychotic Postpartum Depression: A Review of Recent Research," *Clinical Psychology Review* 2 (1982): 487–583.

13. G. W. Brown, "A Three-Factor Causal Model of Depression," in J. E. Barrett, ed., *Stress and Mental Disorder* (New York: Raven Press, 1979), pp. 111–120; E. S. Paykel et al., "Life Events and Social Support in Puerperal Depression," *British Journal of Psychiatry* 136 (1980): 339–346.

14. R. E. Gordon et al., "Factors in Postpartum Emotional Adjustment," *Obstetrics and Gynecology* 25 (1965): 158–166; Pauline M. Shereshefsy and Leon J. Yarrow, *Psychological Aspects of a First Pregnancy and Postnatal Adaption* (New York: Raven Press, 1973); I. Yalom et al., "Postpartum Blues Syndrome: A Description and Related Variables," *Archives of General Psychiatry* 18 (1968): 16–27.

15. Barbara Snell Dohrenwend and Bruce Philip Dohrenwend, *Stressful Life Events: Their Natures and Effects* (New York: Wiley, 1974); Cutrona, "Social Support"; Michael W. O'Hara, D. J. Neuhaber, and E. M. Zekoski, "Prospective Study of Postpartum Depression: Prevalence, Course, Predictive Factors," *Journal of Abnormal Psychology* 93 (1984): 158–181; J. L. Alpert et al., "Onset of Parenting and Stressful Events," *Journal of Primary Prevention* 3 (1983): 149–159.

16. O'Hara et al., "Postpartum Depression"; Paykel et al., "Life Events"; Scott M. Monroe and Stephen C. Steiner, "Social Support and Psychopathology: Interrelations with Preexisting Disorder Stress of Personality," *Journal of Abnormal Psychology* 95 (1986): 29–39.

17. O'Hara et al., "Postpartum Depression."

18. Cutrona, "Nonpsychotic Postpartum Depression."

19. James Hamilton, "Medics," *People* 26 (1986): 101.

20. Song, *Silent Victims*.

21. Lenore E. Walker, "Battered Women and Learned Helplessness," *Victimology: An International Journal* 3/4, 2 (1977): 525–534.

22. Lyn Delli Quadri and Kati Breckenridge, *Mother Care* (New York: J. P. Tarcher, 1978).

23. H. Hofeller, "Social, Psychological and Situational Factors in Wife Abuse," *The Gerontologist* 11 (1971): 34.

Afterword

Donna Gabaccia

Because the study of immigrant women has been undertaken to contribute to our understanding of many different phenomena from many
different perspectives, any summary of the state of the literature on this
topic must note simultaneously its great richness and its considerable
fragmentation. Readers of *Seeking Common Ground* will have gained insight into the rich diversity of female experience and consciousness while
recognizing the common themes and experiences that originate in foreign birth, mobility, gender ideologies, marginality, discrimination, and
cultural transformation. Careful readers, it is hoped, will also have been
struck by what is missing from these chapters. We know much of immigrant women of some backgrounds and some time periods, and at
least something of how gender functioned in migration, ethnic group
formation, and cultural change from generation to generation. Still, the
scholar formulating new research is faced with some very tough choices
when pondering what remains to be done. This afterword briefly addresses those choices.

Lacking basic information about the lives of women of many groups
and many time periods, it seems logical to call for more woman-centered
studies of the type presented in this volume. Such studies would provide
the foundation for future synthesis, surely a current desideratum in
immigration and ethnic studies. Filling the gaps, however, begs what is
currently a central issue in women's studies: troubling questions have
been raised about the biases and assumptions of any study that focuses
on women as a natural or homogeneous category.

If scholars instead prefer to make gender their analytical tool, they
will still face choices. Will they use gender in the social-historical fashion

Suzanne Sinke, or adopt the postmodernist approach of Betty Berg-
and? The use of gender as an analytical category has a long history in
anthropology, and is increasingly used in history's and sociology's contributions to immigration and ethnic studies as well—although most
often still in the social-historical sense. By contrast, the deconstructionist's
attention to language has become increasingly central in women's studies;
for the study of the foreign-born, it raises fascinating questions about
gender and bilingualism and language usage. The choice of social-
historical or postmodern stance will heavily influence whether research
on immigrant women reaches an audience in immigration and ethnic
studies or in women's studies. Although the basis for divergence between
these two fields continues to change, the divergence itself remains striking, and should not be ignored by those formulating new research.

Seeking Common Ground has argued for the benefits of comparison and
interdisciplinary communication and for viewing foreign birth as an
important dimension of human diversity in multicultural studies. Scholars formulating future research need to think hard about what is being
compared and why. Does it make more sense to compare immigrant
women to immigrant men of similar backgrounds or to compare them
to other immigrant women—tracing the impact of race, ethnicity, class,
nationality, language, and religion? Or, alternatively, are the logical comparisons to native-born women, whether of the white middle classes or
the minorities of this country? In several chapters in this volume, comparisons to native-born and middle-class white American women have
been implicitly made in defining immigrant women's steps toward autonomy or emancipation, especially in the area of sexuality.

Scholars in both women's studies and immigration and ethnic studies
now hesitate to see cultural change as unidirectional or female emancipation as culturally transcendent, and this raises some interesting challenges for comparativists. In fact, for those who prefer social-historical
approaches, attention to the contacts and interaction of immigrant
women with others—male and female, inside or outside their own families and communities—might be a fruitful alternative to comparison.
Common sense tells us that the foreign-born adjust to life in the United
States while at the same time redefining notions of who is American and
what constitutes American womanhood. How that adjustment takes place
and how definitions of American womanhood change in response are
hinted at in most of the chapters in *Seeking Common Ground* but not
directly examined in most. A focus on points of intersection and interaction—hospitals, schools, workplaces, and neighborhoods, and so
forth—would shed light on the process of social and cultural change
without assuming that cultural change for women has inevitably meant
linear progress toward an ethnically neutral yet "modern" and "eman-
cipated" American womanhood.

While there may be hard choices for those studying the lives of the female and foreign-born, there are clearly many opportunities for exciting and innovative research. This volume has established that there are many common grounds to be found in scholarship and in American life. My hope is that the decade ahead will identify more, not fewer, of these.

Select Bibliography

Ahern, Susan, Dexter Bryan, and Reynaldo Baca. "Migration and La Mujer Fuerte." *Migration Today* 13, 1 (1985): 14–20.

Anker, Laura. "Family, Work and Community: Southern and Eastern European Immigrant Women Speak from the Connecticut Federal Writers' Project." In *Connected Domains*, ed. Susan Reverby and Dorothy Healy. Ithaca: Cornell University Press, forthcoming 1992.

———. "Women, Work and Family: Polish, Italian and Eastern European Immigrants in Industrial Connecticut, 1890–1940." *Polish American Studies* (Winter 1988): 23–49.

Antin, Mary. *The Promised Land*. Boston: Houghton Mifflin, 1912.

Baum, Charlotte, Paula Hyman, and Sonya Michel. *The Jewish Woman in America*. New York: Dial Press, 1976.

Beechey, Veronica. *Unequal Work*. London: Verso, 1987.

Bell, Sue E., and Michael B. Whiteford. "Tai Dam Health Care Practices: Asian Refugee Women in Iowa." *Social Science and Medicine* 24 (1987): 317–325.

Bergland, Betty. "Immigrant History and the Gendered Subject: A Review Essay." *Ethnic Forum* 8, 2 (1988): 24–39.

Bernard, Richard N. *The Melting Pot and the Altar*. Minneapolis: University of Minnesota Press, 1980.

Bloch, Harriet. "Changing Domestic Roles among Polish Women." *Anthropological Quarterly* 49 (1976): 3–10.

Boone, Margaret. "The Uses of Traditional Concepts in the Development of New Urban Roles: Cuban Women in the United States." In *A World of Women*, ed. Erika Bourguignon, 235–270. New York: Praeger, 1980.

Boyd, Monique. "At a Disadvantage: The Occupational Attainment of Foreign-Born Women in Canada." *International Migration Review* 18 (Winter 1984): 1091–1120.

Brettell, Caroline B. *Men who Migrate, Women who Wait: Population and History in a Portuguese Parish.* Princeton: Princeton University Press, 1986.

―――. *We Have Already Cried Many Tears: The Stories of Three Portuguese Migrant Women.* Cambridge, Mass.: Schenkman, 1982.

Brewer, Eileen. *Nuns and the Education of American Catholic Women, 1860–1920.* Chicago: Loyola University Press, 1987.

Caroli, Betty Boyd, Robert F. Harney, and Lydio F. Tomasi. *The Italian Immigrant Woman in North America.* Toronto: The Multicultural History Society of Ontario, 1978.

Chai, Alice Yun. "Adaptive Strategies of Recent Korean Immigrant Women in Hawaii." In *Beyond the Public/Domestic Dichotomy: Contemporary Perspectives on Women's Public Lives,* ed. Janet Sharistanian, 65–100. New York: Greenwood Press, 1987.

―――. "Freed from the Elders but Locked into Labor: Korean Immigrant Women in Hawaii." *Women's Studies* 13 (1987): 223–233.

―――. "Korean Women in Hawaii: 1903–1945." In *Women in New Worlds,* ed. Hilah F. Thomas and Rosemary Skinner Keller, 328–344. Nashville, Tenn.: Abingdon Press, 1981.

Chavez, Leo R. "Coresidence and Resistance: Strategies for Survival among Undocumented Mexicans and Central Americans in the United States." *Urban Anthropology* 19, 1 (1990): 31–61.

Chavez, Leo R., Wayne Cornelius, and Oliver William Jones. "Utilization of Health Services by Mexican Immigrant Women in San Diego." *Women and Health* 11, 2 (1986): 3–19.

Cohen, Lucy M. "The Female Factor in Resettlement." *Society* 14, 6 (1977): 27–30.

Cordasco, Francesco. *The Immigrant Woman in North America: An Annotated Bibliography of Selected References.* Metuchen and London: The Scarecrow Press, 1985.

Dearborn, Mary. "Anzia Yezierska and the Making of an Ethnic American Self." In *The Invention of Ethnicity,* ed. Werner Sollors, 105–123. New York: Oxford University Press, 1989.

―――. *Pochahontas's Daughters: Gender and Ethnicity in American Culture.* New York: Oxford University Press, 1986.

DeSantis, Lydia. "Health Care Orientations of Cuban and Haitian Immigrant Mothers: Implications for Health Care Professionals." *Medical Anthropology* 12 (1989): 69–89.

Deutsch, Sarah. *No Separate Refuge: Culture, Class, and Gender on an Anglo-Hispanic Frontier in the American Southwest, 1880–1940.* New York: Oxford University Press, 1987.

Di Leonardo, Micaela. *The Varieties of Ethnic Experience: Kinship, Class and Gender among California's Italian-Americans.* Ithaca: Cornell University Press, 1984.

Diner, Hasia. *Erin's Daughters in America: Irish Women in the Nineteenth Century.* Baltimore and London: The Johns Hopkins University Press, 1983.

Donato, Katharine. "Recent Trends in Female Migration from Mexico." Forthcoming.

Donato, Katharine, Douglas S. Massey, and Joyce Durand. "Stemming the Tide?

Assessing the Deterrent Effects of the Immigration Reform and Control Act." *Demography* (forthcoming, May 1992).

Donato, Katharine, and Andrea Tyree. "Family Reunification, Health Professionals, and the Sex Composition of Immigrants to the United States." *Sociology and Social Research* 70, 3 (April 1986): 226–230.

DuBois, Ellen Carol, and Vicki L. Ruiz. *Unequal Sisters, a Multi-Cultural Reader in U.S. Women's History*. New York: Routledge, 1990.

Engle, Patricia, Susan Scrimshaw, and Robert Smidt. "Sex Differences in Attitudes towards Newborn Infants among Women of Mexican Origin." *Medical Anthropology* 8 (1984): 133–144.

Ets, Maria Hall. *The Life of an Immigrant Woman*. Minneapolis: University of Minnesota Press, 1970.

Evans, Mariah. "Immigrant Women in Australia: Resources, Family and Work." *International Migration Review* 18 (Winter 1984): 1063–1091.

Ewen, Elizabeth. *Immigrant Women in the Land of Dollars, 1820–1929*. New York: Monthly Review Press, 1985.

Ewens, Mary. "The Leadership of Nuns in Immigrant Catholicism." In *Women and Religion in America*, ed. Rosemary Ruether and Rosemary Keller, 101–149. New York: Harper and Row, 1981.

———. *The Role of the Nun in Nineteenth-Century America: Variations on the International Theme*. New York: Arno Press, 1978.

Fernandez-Kelly, Maria Patricia. "Mexican Border Industrialization, Female Labor Force Participation and Migration," In *Women, Men and the International Division of Labor*, ed. June Nash and Patricia Fernandez-Kelly, 205–223. Albany: State University of New York Press, 1983.

Fernandez-Kelly, M. Patricia, and Anna M. Garcia. "The Making of an Underground Economy: Hispanic Women, Home Work and the Advanced Capitalist State." *Urban Anthropology* 14 (1985): 59–90.

———. "Power Surrendered, Power Restored: The Politics of Home and Work among Hispanic Women in Southern California and Southern Florida." *Women and Politics in America*, ed. Louise Tilly and Patricia Guerin, 130–149. New York: Russell Sage Foundation, 1989.

Fishman, Claudia, Robin Evans, and Eloise Jenks. "Warm Bodies, Cool Milk: Conflicts in Postpartum Food Choices for Indochinese Women in California." *Social Science and Medicine* 26 (1988): 1125–1132.

Ford, Kathleen. "The Diverse Fertility of Caribbean, Central and South American Immigrants to the United States." *Sociology and Social Research* 70 (1986): 281–283.

———. "The Fertility of Immigrant Women." *Sociology and Social Research* 70 (1985): 68–70.

Fox, Geoffrey E. "Honor, Shame and Women's Liberation in Cuba." In *Female and Male in Latin America*, ed. Anne Pescatello, 273–292. Pittsburgh: University of Pittsburgh Press, 1970.

Gabaccia, Donna R. *From Sicily to Elizabeth Street: Housing and Social Change among Italian Immigrants, 1880–1930*. Albany: State University of New York Press, 1984.

———. "Immigrant Women: Nowhere at Home?" *Journal of American Ethnic History* 10, 4 (Summer 1991): 61–87.

————. *Immigrant Women in the United States, a Selectively Annotated Multidisciplinary Bibliography*. Westport, Conn.: Greenwood Press, 1989.

————. *"The Transplanted*: Women and Family in Immigrant America." *Social Science History* 12, 3 (Fall 1988): 243–252.

Gee, Emma. "Issei: The First Women." In *Asian Women*, ed. Lily Chang et al., 8–15. Berkeley: Asian American Studies, University of California, 1971.

Glenn, Evelyn Nakano. "The Dialectics of Wage Work: Japanese-American Women and Domestic Service, 1905–1940." *Feminist Studies* 6,3 (Fall 1980): 432–471.

————. *Issei, Nisei, War Bride: Three Generations of Japanese-American Women in Domestic Service*. Philadelphia: Temple University Press, 1986.

Glenn, Susan A. *Daughters of the Shtetl*. Ithaca: Cornell University Press, 1990.

Goldman, Emma. *Living My Life*. 2 vols. New York: Knopf, 1931.

Gonzalez, Nancie. "Multiple Migratory Experiences of Dominican Women." *Anthropological Quarterly* 49 (1976): 36–44.

Gonzalez, Rosalinda M. "Chicanas and Mexican Immigrant Families, 1920–1940: Women's Subordination and Family Exploitation." In *Decades of Discontent*, ed. Lois Scharf and Joan Jensen, 59–84. Westport, Conn.: Greenwood Press, 1983.

Goody, Esther. "Introduction to Female Migrants and the Work Force: Domestic Repercussions." *Anthropologica* 26, 2 (1980): 123–134.

Guendelman, Sylvia, and Auristela Perez-Itriago. "Double Lives: The Changing Role of Women in Seasonal Migration." *Women's Studies* 13 (1987): 249–271.

Gutiérrez, Ramon. "Honor, Ideology, and Class Gender Domination in New Mexico, 1690–1846." *Latin American Perspectives* 12 (Winter 1985): 81–104.

Harbison, Sarah F., and Marjorie E. Weishaar. "Samoan Migrant Fertility: Adaptation and Selection." *Human Organization* 40, 3 (1981): 268–273.

Hareven, Tamara. *Family Time and Industrial Time: The Relationship between the Family and Work in a New England Industrial Community*. Cambridge and New York: Cambridge University Press, 1982.

Hareven, Tamara, and Randolph Langenbach. *Amoskeag: Life and Work in an American Factory City*. New York: Pantheon, 1978.

Hewitt, Nancy A. "Beyond the Search for Sisterhood: American Women's History in the 1980s." *Social History* 10 (October 1985): 299–321.

Hirata, Lucie Cheng. "Free, Indentured, Enslaved: Chinese Prostitutes in Nineteenth-Century America." *SIGNS* 5, 1 (Autumn 1979): 3–29.

Houstoun, Marion F., Roger G. Kramer, and Joan M. Barrett. "Female Predominance of Immigration to the United States Since 1930: A First Look." *International Migration Review* 18 (Winter 1984): 908–963.

Hyman, Paula. "Immigrant Women and Consumer Protest: The New York City Kosher Meat Boycott of 1902." *American Jewish History* 71 (September 1980): 91–105.

Ichioka, Yuji. "Amerika Nadeshiko: Japanese Immigrant Women in the United States, 1900–1924." *Pacific Historical Review* 48, 2 (May 1980): 339–357.

————. "Ameyuki-San: Japanese Prostitutes in Nineteenth-Century America." *Amerasia Journal* 4, 1 (1977): 1–21.

Kay, Margarita, and Carmen Portillo. "Nervios and Dysphoria in Mexican-American Widows." In *Gender, Health and Illness: The Case of Nervios*, ed. Dona L. Davis and Seth M. Low, 181–201. New York: Praeger, 1989.

Kendall, Laurel. "Cold Wombs in Balmy Honolulu: Ethnogynecology among Korean Immigrants." *Social Science and Medicine* 25, 4 (1987): 367–376.

King, Miriam, and Steven Ruggles. "American Immigration, Fertility, and Race Suicide at the Turn of the Century." *Journal of Interdisciplinary History* 22 (Winter 1990): 347–369.

Kingston, Maxine Hong. *Woman Warrior: Memoir of a Girlhood among Ghosts*. New York: Vintage Books, 1975.

Kirby, Diana G. "Immigrants, Stress and Prescription Drug Use among Cuban Women in South Florida." *Medical Anthropology* 10 (1989): 287–295.

Kleinberg, S. J. *The Shadow of the Mills: Working-Class Families in Pittsburgh, 1870–1907*. Pittsburgh: University of Pittsburgh Press, 1989.

Lamphere, Louise. "Bringing the Family to Work: Women's Culture on the Shop Floor." *Feminist Studies* 11 (1985): 519–555.

———. *From Working Daughters to Working Mothers: Immigrant Women in a New England Community*. Ithaca: Cornell University Press, 1987.

———. "From Working Daughters to Working Mothers: Production and Reproduction in an Industrial Community." *American Ethnologist* 13 (1986): 118–130.

Lay, Katharine. "Migrant Women: Is Migration a Blessing or a Handicap?" *International Migration* 19 (1981): 83–93.

Lewin, Ellen. "The Nobility of Suffering: Illness and Misfortune among Latin American Women." *Anthropological Quarterly* 52 (1979): 152–157.

Lind, Andrew. "The Changing Position of Domestic Service in Hawaii." *Social Process in Hawaii* 15 (1951): 70–87.

Loo, Chalsa, and Paul Ong. "Slaying Demons with a Sewing Needle: Feminist Issues for Chinatown's Women." *Berkeley Journal of Sociology* 27 (1982): 77–88.

Margolis, Maxine. "From Mistress to Servant: Downward Mobility among Brazilian Immigrants in New York City." *Urban Anthropology* 19 (1990): 215–231.

Massey, Douglas S. "Economic Development and International Migration in Comparative Perspective." *Population Development and Review* 14, 2 (1988): 383–413.

Massey, Douglas S., Rafael Alarcon, Jorge Durand, and Humberto Gonzalez. *Return to Aztlan: The Social Process of International Migration from Western Mexico*. Berkeley: University of California Press, 1987.

Matsumoto, Valerie. "Japanese-American Women during World War II." *Frontiers* 8, 1 (1984): 6–14.

Melville, Margarita B. *Mexicans at Work in the United States*. Houston: Mexican American Studies Program, University of Houston, 1988.

———. "Mexican Women Adapt to Migration." *International Migration Review* 12 (1978): 225–235.

———., ed. *Twice a Minority, Mexican-American Women*. St. Louis: C. V. Mosby, 1980.

Michaelson, Karen, ed. *Childbirth in America: Anthropological Perspectives.* South Hadley, Mass.: Bergin and Garvey, 1988.

Mirandé, Alfredo, and Evangelina Enriquez. *La Chicana, the Mexican-American Woman.* Chicago and London: The University of Chicago Press, 1979.

Miyaski, Gail Y. "Contributions of Japanese Women in Hawaii." In *Montage: An Ethnic History of Women in Hawaii,* ed. Nancy Foon Young and Judith R. Parris, 27–35. Honolulu: General Assistance Center for the Pacific, College of Education, University of Hawaii and the State Commission on the Status of Women, 1977.

Mora, Magdalena, and Adelaida Del Castillo. *Mexican Women in the United States: Struggles Past and Present.* Los Angeles: University of California, Chicano Studies Publications, 1980.

Morawska, Ewa. *For Bread with Butter: The Life-Worlds of East Central Europeans in Johnstown, Pennsylvania, 1890–1940.* New York: Cambridge University Press, 1985.

Mortimer, Delores, and Roy S. Bryce Laporte, eds. *Female Immigrants in the United States.* Washington, D.C.: Smithsonian, 1981.

Muir, Karen L. S. *The Strongest Part of the Family: A Study of Lao Refugee Women in Columbus, Ohio.* New York: AMS Press, 1988.

Nash, June, and Helen Safa, eds. *Women and Change in Latin America.* South Hadley, Mass.: Bergin and Garvey, 1986.

Nolan, Janet A. *Ourselves Alone, Women's Emigration from Ireland, 1885–1920.* Lexington: The University Press of Kentucky, 1989.

Nomura, Gail M. "Issei Working Women in Hawaii." In *Making Waves: Writings about Asian-American Women,* ed. Asian Women United of California, 328–344. Boston: Beacon Press, 1989.

O'Connor, Mary I. "Women's Networks and the Social Needs of Mexican Immigrants." *Urban Anthropology* 19, 1 (1990): 81–98.

Parrino, Maria. "Breaking the Silence: Autobiographies of Italian Immigrant Women." *Storia Nord Americana* 5, 1 (1988): 137–158.

Pedraza, Silvia. "Women and Migration: The Social Consequences of Gender." *Annual Review of Sociology* 17 (1991): 303–325.

Pedraza-Bailey, Silvia. "Immigration Research: A Conceptual Map." *Social Science History* 14, 1 (1990): 43–67.

Peiss, Kathy. *Cheap Amusements.* Philadelphia: Temple University Press, 1986.

Pessar, Patricia. "The Constraints on and Release of Female Labor Power: Dominican Migration to the United States." In *A Home Divided: Women and Income in the Third World,* ed. Daisy Dwyer and Judith Bruce, 195–215. Stanford: Stanford University Press, 1988.

———. "The Dominicans: Women in the Household and the Garment Industry." In *New Immigrants in New York,* ed. Nancy Foner, 103–129. New York: Columbia University Press, 1987.

———. "The Linkage between the Household and Workplace Experience of Dominican Immigrant Women in the United States." *International Migration Review* 18 (1984): 1188–1211.

Peterson, Susan, and Courtney Ann Vaughn-Robertson. *Women with Vision: The Presentation Sisters of South Dakota, 1880–1985.* Urbana: University of Illinois Press, 1988.

Pickle, Linda S. "Stereotypes and Reality: Nineteenth-Century German Women in Missouri." *Missouri Historical Review* 79 (April 1985): 191–212.

Polacheck, Hilda. *I Came a Stranger: The Story of a Hull House Girl.* Urbana: University of Illinois Press, 1989.

Prieto, Yolanda. "Cuban Women in the U.S. Labor Force." *Cuban Studies* 17 (1987):73–91.

Ross, Carl, and K. Marianne Wargelin Brown. *Women who Dared: The History of Finnish-American Women.* St. Paul, Minn.: Immigration History Research Center, 1986.

Ruiz, Vicki L. *Cannery Women, Cannery Lives.* Albuquerque: University of New Mexico Press, 1987.

Safa, Helen I. "Runaway Shops and Female Employment: The Search for Cheap Labor." *SIGNS* 7, 2 (1981): 418–433.

Saiki, Patsy Sumie. *Japanese Women in Hawaii: The First 100 Years.* Honolulu: Kisaku, 1985.

Sargent, Carolyn, John Marcucci, and Ellen Elliston. "Tiger Bones, Fire and Wine: Maternity Care in a Kampuchean Refugee Community." *Medical Anthropology* 7 (1983): 67–79.

Sassen-Koob, Saskia. "Notes on the Incorporation of Third World Women in Wage-Labor through Immigration and Off-Shore Production." *International Migration Review* 18 (Winter 1984): 1144–1167.

Schneider, Dorothee. " 'For Whom Are All the Good Things in Life? ' German-American Housewives Discuss their Budgets." In *German Workers in Industrial Chicago, 1850–1910*, ed. Hartmut Keil and John B. Jentz, 145–162. DeKalb: Northern Illinois University Press, 1983.

Seller, Maxine. "Beyond the Stereotype: A New Look at the Immigrant Woman, 1880–1924." *Journal of Ethnic Studies* 3 (Spring 1975): 59–68.

———. *Immigrant Women.* Philadelphia: Temple University Press, 1981.

Simon, Rita, and Caroline B. Brettell, eds. *International Migration: The Female Experience.* Totowa, N.J.: Rowman and Allanheld, 1986.

Simon, Rita, and Margo DeLey. "The Work Experience of Undocumented Mexican Women Migrants in Los Angeles." *International Migration Review* 18 (Winter 1984): 1212–1230.

Sinke, Suzanne. "A Historiography of Immigrant Women in the Nineteenth and Early Twentieth Centuries." *Ethnic Forum* 9, 1–2 (1989): 122–145.

———. "Home Is Where You Build It: Dutch Immigrant Women and Social Reproduction." In *The Dutch in North America: Their Immigration and Cultural Continuity*, ed. Rob Kroes and Henk-Otto Neuschäfer, 410–421. Amsterdam: VU University Press, 1991.

Smith, Judith E. *Family Connections: A History of Italian and Jewish Immigrant Lives in Providence, Rhode Island, 1890–1940.* Albany: State University of New York Press, 1985.

Smith, M. Estellie. "Networks and Migration Resettlement: Cherchez la Femme." *Anthropological Quarterly* 49 (January 1976): 20–27.

Song, Young I. *Silent Victims: Battered Women in Korean Families.* San Francisco: Oxford Press, 1987.

Stafford, Susan H. Buchanan. "Haitian Immigrant Women: A Cultural Perspective." *Anthropologica* 26, 2 (1984): 171–189.

Sullivan, Teresa. "The Occupational Prestige of Women Immigrants: A Comparison of Cubans and Mexicans." *International Migration Review* 18 (Winter 1984): 1021–1045.

Takaki, Ronald. *Strangers from a Different Shore: A History of Asian-Americans.* Boston: Little, Brown, 1989.

Taylor, Paul S. "Mexican Women in Los Angeles Industry in 1928." *Aztlan* 11 (Spring 1980): 99–131.

Tienda, Marta. "Familism and Structural Assimilation of Mexican Immigrants in the United States." *International Migration Review* 14, 3, (1980): 383–408.

Vega, William A. Bohdan Kolody, and Juan Ramon Valle. "Migration and Mental Health: An Empirical Test of Depression Risk Factors among Immigrant Mexican Women." *International Migration Review* 21 (Fall 1987): 512–529.

Vega, William A., Bohdan Kolody, and Juan Ramon Valle. "Relationship of Marital Status, Confidant Support and Depression among Mexican Immigrant Women." *Journal of Marriage and the Family* 48 (1986): 597–605.

Vega, William A., Bohdan Kolody, Juan Ramon Valle, and Richard Hough. "Depressive Symptoms and Their Correlates among Immigrant Mexican Women in the United States." *Social Science and Medicine* 22 (1986): 645–652.

Weinberg, Sydney Stahl. "Jewish Mothers and Immigrant Daughters: Positive and Negative Role Models." *Journal of American Ethnic History* 6 (Spring 1987): 39–55.

———. "Longing to Learn: The Education of Jewish Immigrant Women in New York, 1890–1930." *Journal of American Ethnic History* 8, 2 (Spring 1989): 108–126.

———. *The World of Our Mothers: The Lives of Jewish Immigrant Women.* Chapel Hill: University of North Carolina Press, 1988.

Westermeyer, Joseph, Mayka Bouafuely, and Tou Fu Vang. "Hmong Refugees in Minnesota: Sex Roles and Mental Health." *Medical Anthropology* 8 (1984): 229–245.

Wexler, Alice. *Emma Goldman in Exile: From the Russian Revolution to the Spanish Civil War.* Boston: Beacon Press, 1989.

Yanagisako, Sylvia. *Transforming the Past: Tradition and Kinship among Japanese-Americans.* Stanford: Stanford University Press, 1985.

Yans-McLaughlin, Virginia. *Family and Community: Italian Immigrants in Buffalo, 1880–1939.* Ithaca: Cornell University Press, 1977.

Yung, Judy. " 'A Bowlful of Tears': Chinese Women Immigrants on Angel Island." *Frontiers* 2, 2 (Summer 1977): 41–44.

———. *Chinese Women of America, a Pictorial History.* Seattle: University of Washington Press, 1986.

Zavella, Patricia. "Abnormal Intimacy: The Varying Work Networks of Chicana Cannery Workers." *Feminist Studies* 11 (1988): 541–557.

———. *Women's Work and Chicano Families: Cannery Workers of the Santa Clara Valley.* Ithaca: Cornell University Press, 1987.

Index

About the Editor and Contributors

BETTY BERGLAND has completed a dissertation at the University of Minnesota on immigrant women's autobiographies, drawing on post-modern theories, feminist studies, and immigration history. She has published articles addressing questions of gender, ethnicity, and autobiography and currently teaches in the history department at the University of Wisconsin, River Falls.

CAROLINE B. BRETTELL is the Director of Women's Studies and Associate Professor of Anthropology at Southern Methodist University. She is the author of *Men who Migrate, Women who Wait* and *We Have Already Cried Many Tears* and coeditor of *International Migration: The Female Experience.*

ALICE YUN CHAI, a native of South Korea, is Associate Professor of Women's Studies at the University of Hawaii at Manoa. She received her Ph.D. in anthropology from Ohio State University, and her research interests and publications are in Asian-American Women's Studies, Korean women, and Asian immigrant women in Hawaii.

PATRICIA A. DEBERJEOIS is an advanced graduate student in the Department of Anthropology at Southern Methodist University. She is interested in Amer-Asian immigrants in the United States.

KATHARINE M. DONATO is presently Assistant Professor of Sociology at Louisiana State University and a Research Associate of the National Opinion Research Center at the University of Chicago. Her research interests include the international migration of women and immigration policy.

DONNA GABACCIA is Charles H. Stone Professor of American History at the University of North Carolina, Charlotte. Major publications include *From Sicily to Elizabeth Street, Militants and Migrants* and "Immigrant Women: Nowhere at Home?" (*Journal of American Ethnic History*, Summer 1991). She is currently preparing a history of immigrant women in the United States.

STEPHEN GROSS is a doctoral student at the University of Minnesota.

DEIRDRE MAGEEAN is in the Department of Public Administration at the University of Maine, Orono. Her current research focuses on Irish immigrant women in Chicago in the nineteenth century.

YOLANDA PRIETO is Associate Professor of Sociology at Ramapo College of New Jersey. She is coeditor of "Sex, Gender, and Revolution" in *Cuban Studies*, and author of numerous articles on Cuban immigrant women and the Cuban migration to the United States. Her main research interests are women and work, gender relations, and migration.

VICKI L. RUIZ is Professor of history at the Claremont Graduate School. She has written *Cannery Women, Cannery Lives* and coedited *Unequal Sisters* (with Ellen DuBois), *Women on the U.S.-Mexico Border* (with Susan Tiano), and *Western Women* (with Lillian Schlissel and Janice Monk). She also directs an undergraduate minority mentorship program at the University of California, Davis.

RITA J. SIMON is University Professor in the School of Public Affairs and the Washington College of Law at American University. She is the author of *Continuity and Change: A Study of Two Ethnic Communities in Israel; Transracial Adoptees and Their Families; The Crimes Women Commit, the Punishments They Receive*; and *New Lives: The Adjustment of Soviet Jewish Immigrants in the United States and Israel* and coeditor of *International Migration: The Female Experience*. Her current research includes a study of women rabbis and ministers, transracial and intercountry adoptions, and the use of social science data by the appellate courts.

SUZANNE SINKE is a doctoral student at the University of Minnesota, where she is completing a dissertation on the migration of Dutch women to the United States. She is the coeditor (with Rudolph Vecoli) of *A Century of European Migrations, 1890–1930*, and is the author of several articles on Dutch and German women immigrants.

YOUNG I. SONG is Associate Professor in the Department of Sociology and Social Services at California State University, Hayward. She has carried out a variety of research and programs in Asian-American communities in the United States. She is former president of the National Asian-American Social Work Educators Association. She has written *Silent Victims* and *American Mosaic: Selected Readings on America's Multicultural Heritage*.

SYDNEY STAHL WEINBERG is the author of *The World of Our Mothers; The Lives of Jewish Immigrant Women* and many articles on the same topic. She is Professor of History at Ramapo College of New Jersey.